FIFTH AN...

RESOLVED

13 Resolutions for LIFE

ORRIN WOODWARD

FOREWORD BY CHRIS BRADY

FIFTH ANNIVERSARY EDITION

RESOLVED

13 Resolutions for LIFE

ORRIN WOODWARD

Copyright © 2011 by Life

All rights reserved. No part of this book may be reproduced or transmitted in any form or by any means, electronic or mechanical, including photocopying and recording, or by any information storage and retrieval system, without the written permission of Obstaclés Press. Inquiries should be sent to the publisher.

Obstaclés Press and the Obstaclés logo are trademarks of Life.

Third Edition, March 2017

Published by:
Obstaclés Press
200 Commonwealth Court
Cary NC 27511

OBSTACLÉS PRESS

orrinwoodward.com

ISBN: 978-0-9983070-6-0

Cover design and layout by
Norm Williams - nwa-inc.com

Printed in the United States of America

032117

To those who RESOLVE to change the world
through changing themselves.

*The ancients who wished to manifest their clear character
to the world would first bring order to their states.*

*Those who wished to bring order to their states
would first regulate their families.*

*Those who wished to regulate their families
would first cultivate their personal lives.*

*Those who wished to cultivate their personal
lives would first rectify their minds.*

*Those who wished to rectify their minds
would first make their wills sincere.*

*Those who wished to make their wills sincere
would first extend their knowledge.*

The extension of knowledge consists in the investigation of things.

When things are investigated, knowledge is extended.

When knowledge is extended, the will becomes sincere.

When the will is sincere, the mind is rectified.

When the mind is rectified, the personal life is cultivated.

When the personal life is cultivated, the family will be regulated.

When the family is regulated, the state will be in order.

*When the state is in order, there will be
peace throughout the world.*

*From the Son of Heaven down to the common people,
all must regard cultivation of the personal
life as the root or foundation.*

*There is never a case when the roots are in disorder
and yet the branches are in order*

Confucius—*The Great Learning*

What People Are Saying about *Resolved*

"I don't know what challenges you have been through, but in the past 3 years my whole life was turned upside down. One of the main reasons that I was able to remain sane was because of the principles that Orrin Woodward has lived, taught, and written about. The Resolved principles are all encompassing and will help you survive life's challenges and live a better life."
—Bill Lewis

"I too have read the Resolutions of George Washington, Ben Franklin, and Jonathon Edwards. Orrin Woodward provides a modern day version of a blueprint that if applied, will transform the reader's life. In ***Resolved: 13 Resolutions for LIFE***, Orrin describes the very principles that he's applied in his own life to achieve a level of success that most of us are striving for. This book is one of the most relevant books in the 21st Century. My life is better for having applied the information found within. I've also had the opportunity to witness countless other lives transformed when applying the principles of ***Resolved*** as a blueprint. I'm looking forward to making the 5th edition a staple of my book collection."
—George Guzzardo

"This book gave me principles that I can apply at any point in my life. These resolutions should be the foundational stones for anyone who is trying to reach a level of significance."
—Steve Morgan

"***Resolved*** has been one of the most impactful books I have ever read. I have personally seen this book discussed and watched lives change forever."
—Curtis Spolar

"After focusing on one **resolution** every week for over a year, Orrin Woodward's masterpiece has changed my life! The problem that you have is not the problem. How you think about that problem is the problem. Resolve to change your thinking, and you will change your life. **RESOLVED** is the game plan to do just that!!"
—Holger Spiewak

"Absolutely amazing!! A guidebook for a life well lived."
—Marc Militello

Acknowledgments

Winston Churchill once said, "Writing a book is an adventure. To begin with, it is a toy and an amusement; then it becomes a mistress, and then it becomes a master, and then a tyrant. The last phase is that just as you are about to be reconciled to your servitude, you kill the monster and fling him out to the public." Although I thoroughly enjoyed the writing process, I can relate to Churchill's comments. Thankfully, I am now ready to fling this "toy-to-monster" book out to the public.

Writing a book, however, is never a solo project. I am deeply indebted to many people whose expertise, wisdom, and encouragement kept me going long after the emotion of the moment was gone. My wife's and children's (Jordan, Christina, Lance, and Jeremy) encouragements and sacrifices made this book possible, and for that, I am forever thankful. On numerous occasions, in the middle of family time, ideas that would help improve this book occurred to me. Only a wife with the patience of Job could have patiently handled her husband's increasingly erratic behavior over my magnificent obsession. Laurie Woodward is this kind of wife, and she is an immeasurable blessing in my life.

Furthermore, Chris Brady's belief in the concepts shared in this book helped me endure the many setbacks and revisions needed to produce the completed work. Everyone needs a balcony person like Chris in his life to help him perform at his best. Additionally, many thanks goes to the Militellos (Kristine and Marc) for their endless hours of reading, editing, and insightful suggestions. Kristine's background as an English teacher was taxed to the limit by her patient editing of the math-rich and English-poor writings of a former engineer.

Last, but not least, I would like to thank the Life office and field leaders for providing real-life examples of leadership on the front lines. It is their example of servant-based leadership that inspired me to write the book in the first place. The entire staff of Obstaclés Press, particularly Bill Rousseau, Michelle Turner, Norm Williams, and Rob Hallstrand, worked around the clock to bring this book to fruition. I could not have asked for a better team to work with.

Finally, none of this would have been possible were it not for the saving grace of my precious Lord and Savior Jesus Christ. His patience in bringing a prodigal son back to Him surpasses all levels of comprehension. To Him be all the honor, glory, and praise.

Contents

Foreword 11
Introduction 13

Private Achievements

Chapter 1   Purpose
Resolved: To Discover My God-Given Purpose 29
John Wooden 43

Chapter 2   Character
Resolved: To Choose Character over Reputation
Any Time They Conflict 51
Ludwig von Mises: Indomitable Character........... 66

Chapter 3   Attitude
Resolved: To Have a Positive Attitude
in All Situations 75
Roger Bannister: Attitude and the Quest for the
Four-Minute Mile 88

Chapter 4   Vision
Resolved: To Align My Conscious (Ant)
with My Subconscious (Elephant) Mind
toward My Vision 95
Will Smith 109

Public Achievements

Chapter 5   Plan and Do
Resolved: To Develop and Implement a Game
Plan in Each Area of My Life 115
Lou Holtz: Planning and Doing............................ 131

Chapter 6   Scoreboard
Resolved: To Keep Score in the Game of Life 137
Sam Walton: Tracking the Scoreboard 151

RESOLVED

Chapter 7	Friendship Resolved: To Develop the Art and Science of Friendship .... 159 C. S. Lewis and J. R. R. Tolkien: Friendship 172

Chapter 8	Finance Resolved: To Develop Financial Intelligence ...... 179 Ben Franklin: Financial Management - Money and Time 192

Leadership Achievements

Chapter 9	Leadership Resolved: To Develop the Art and Science of Leadership .... 199 Sam Walton: Leadership Excellence 214

Chapter 10	Conflict Resolution Resolved: To Develop the Art and Science of Conflict Resolution .... 223 Lewis and Tolkien: Lost Friends 237

Chapter 11	Systems Resolved: To Develop Systems Thinking............. 245 Ray Kroc and McDonald's 259

Chapter 12	Adversity Quotient (AQ) Resolved: To Develop Adversity Quotient .... 267 Billy Durant: Adversity Quotient 280

Chapter 13	Legacy Resolved: To Reverse the Current of Decline in My Field of Mastery... 287 Colonial New England Fiat Money 300

Appendix A	George Washington's Rules of Civility and Decent Behavior in Company and Conversation 307

Appendix B	George Washington's Partial List of Maxims 315

Appendix C	Ben Franklin's Thirteen Virtues 319

Appendix D	Jonathan Edwards's Seventy Resolutions 321

Bibliography 329

Foreword

It has been said that everyone wants to change the world, but only a few feel the need to change themselves. Even just a basic study of history, however, would show that those who first focus on self-improvement usually end up doing the most good in the world. Why should this be so? Perhaps it stems from the fact that excellence doesn't occur by accident, but rather, from intentional effort correctly applied over time. Subsequently, a person's example of excellence increases his ability to influence others. The much-touted "ripple effect" then takes hold, and change resonates outward in ever-widening circles from the genesis of a lone individual who cares to change his or her own life first.

I have been in a unique position to observe for nearly two decades a real-life example of the above-mentioned type of person. At age eighteen, I struck up an acquaintance with a young man roughly my age as we were entering an engineering co-op program together with a handful of other equally bright but naïve students. Orrin Woodward came from humble origins, having a sometimes-stressful home life, extremely tight finances, and no connections whatsoever. With nothing but hope and ambition, he worked his way through college until he landed in an engineering position, where he thrived and was quickly recognized as a dedicated worker and a creative problem solver. He soon won several accolades and promotions, including four US patents and a National Technical Benchmarking Award. Then he decided to try his hand at being an entrepreneur, and our paths once again crossed. I had heard of his corporate success and had seen his achievements from a distance, and when he chose to invite me into his business endeavors, I at once got a front-row seat to witness what would become a true Horatio Alger story.

Orrin Woodward began his business journey by immediately working on himself. A voracious reader, he devoured books on people skills, sales techniques, relationship building, success, leadership, and attitude. Over time, his self-directed education went deeper, from the surface-level genres of skills to the heart-level categories of principles. He also broadened his education, studying economics, history, theology, literature, philosophy, and even art. As he applied his aggressive learning to his entrepreneurial activities, his business began to thrive. Today, Orrin Woodward is

11

widely recognized as one of the top leaders in America in several business categories and is a sought-after expert on leadership. His success (which, in addition to his professional achievements, includes a healthy and productive family life, a marriage of twenty years, a worshipful faith, and a worldwide network of friends and supporters) and lifestyle are diametrically opposite to his beginnings. A larger contrast between origins and accomplishments would be hard to imagine.

The kind of success obtained by Orrin Woodward is admirable and desirable—worthy of study and emulation. It is for this reason that I have been encouraging him to endure the hardships and hard work of crafting this book. Although we collaborated on a number of books before—and Orrin already enjoys bestseller status—this project is different. It is his answer to the question: "How did you do it?" It is, therefore, extremely personal (although he doesn't wish it to be about himself) and laborious. It is full of historical research and illuminating examples, which required much study and fact checking. And, quite frankly, with the depth of its content and the width of its application, it is stunning. Anyone who reads this book will be immediately struck by the scholarship of its author. It is so much more than a well-researched tome, however; it is a road map. In a world full of formulas for success and quick fixes, *RESOLVED: 13 Resolutions for LIFE* goes all the way to the core. It reaches into the heart, stimulates the mind, and motivates the will.

In my book *Rascal: Making a Difference by Becoming an Original Character*, I attempted to depict the type of person who musters the courage to go against the grain and boldly pursue a God-given direction, regardless of who follows or fights against such a move. If, indeed, that book succeeded in showing how to step out of the crowd, this book shows what to do after having done so. Through thirteen profound resolutions, readily applicable to daily life, Orrin Woodward gives us a window to the reasons undergirding his monumental success and a very specific ladder of success for us to climb for our own success. More importantly, he shows us how we can maximize our potentials and, yes, perhaps even change the world by first working to become the best that we can be. In these pages, it becomes clear that success is no accident and significance is ever more the result of strenuous intentionality. I believe the overall effect of this book on the reader will be a life transformed, and that, I surmise, would be Orrin's greatest wish.

Chris Brady
Apex, North Carolina
September 2011

Introduction

In the early eighteenth century, three young Colonial Americans resolved to build lives of virtue by studying and applying daily resolutions. Each of them made his life count, creating a legacy of selfless thoughts, words, and deeds. The first, through tireless sacrificial leadership and against indescribable odds, defeated the mighty British Empire with his ragtag group of colonial volunteers. The second—through his growing international fame, sterling character, and endless tact—became America's leading diplomat, forming international alliances that secured war funding, without which the Colonials' cause would have been doomed. The third, through his striking intellectual and spiritual gifts, became Colonial America's greatest minister, who, by preaching and writing, fanned the flames of the colonies' Great Awakening, leading to the later political and economic freedoms after the American Revolution. These men—George Washington, Benjamin Franklin, and Jonathan Edwards—transformed themselves by the diligent study and application of their resolutions, creating an enduring legacy, not just through what they did but more importantly through what they were. Washington transformed into a man of character whose love of principles surpassed his love of power; Franklin transformed into a man of tact whose desire for influence surpassed his need for recognition; and Edwards transformed into a spiritual giant whose humility surpassed his need for career advancement. All three developed wisdom by overcoming "self." Paradoxically, by developing, studying, and consistently applying their resolutions, these men changed the world by focusing on changing themselves.

Strangely, although three of the greatest Americans utilized resolutions to develop wisdom and virtue, this practice is little known and almost a forgotten art. Nonetheless, the author believes nothing would change the course of education more than the resolutions being taught in every family, school, and church around the world.

Stephen Covey suggested a possible answer for the paradox: "As my study took me back through 200 years of writing about success, I noticed a startling pattern emerging in the content of literature.... I began to feel more and more that much of the successful literature of the past 50 years was superficial. It was filled with social image consciousness, techniques, and quick fixes—with

INTRODUCTION

social band-aids and aspirin that addressed acute problems and sometimes appeared to solve them temporarily, but left the underlying chronic problems untouched to fester and resurface time and again." Society, it seems, values image over integrity, commercialism over character, and fame over foundations—and what a high price has been paid for these errors.

Philosopher/historian José Ortega y Gasset describes this dichotomy: "The most radical division that is possible to make of humanity is that which splits it into two classes of creatures: those who make great demands on themselves, piling up difficulties and duties; and those who demand nothing special of themselves, but for whom to live is to be every moment what they already are, without imposing upon themselves any effort towards perfection—mere buoys that float on the waves."

Washington, Franklin, and Edwards achieved lasting greatness not by floating as buoys but by swimming against the current. Resolved to be different, they nurtured themselves on principle-ethics instead of personality-ethics, seeking the true greatness of character, not the false friendship of fame. Author Jim Black wrote, "For most of our history, Americans placed greater stock in a man's character than in his possessions. The American Dream held that, by hard work and self-discipline, we could achieve success. And success was not measured in material possessions alone.... The common wisdom of the day taught that greed, luxury, and self-indulgence were the passions of weak character. And the frugal nature of the pioneers taught that the treasures to be valued most were the virtues of honesty, good character, and moral strength." Covey, again, noted similarly, describing America's founding success literature: "The first 150 years or so focused on what could be called the Character Ethic as the foundation of success—things like integrity, humility, fidelity, temperance, courage, justice, patience, industry, simplicity, modesty, and the Golden Rule." Without character, in other words, one can never be truly successful because the foundation of all long-term successes isn't a person's property but rather who he is. Regretfully, society seems to have forgotten this commonsense principle, probably because common sense isn't so common today.

A Natural Nobility

Life's timeless principles have fallen victim to today's microwave age thinking. Practically everyone wants to be successful, but most settle for "personality ethic" tomatoes when true success requires "character ethic" oak trees. Indeed, it's time to get out of

INTRODUCTION

the tomato patch and return to the foundation forest of character development, the forest that fed mighty oaks like Washington, Franklin, and Edwards. True character-based leadership requires endless hours of self-examination, a process of comparing one's actions to stated resolutions, and making the necessary adjustments to grow character. After all, people who take shortcuts in character development only end up shortening themselves. Economist William Roepke described this process:

> *Only a few from every stratum of society can ascend into this thin layer of natural nobility. The way to it is an exemplary and slowly maturing life of dedicated endeavor on behalf of all, unimpeachable integrity, constant restraint of our common greed, proved soundness of judgment, a spotless private life, indomitable courage in standing up for truth and law, and generally the highest example. This is how the few, carried upward by the trust of the people, gradually attain to a position above the classes, interests, passions, wickedness, and foolishness of men and finally become the nation's conscience. To belong to this group of moral aristocrats should be the highest and most desirable aim, next to which all the other triumphs of life are pale and insipid.... The continued existence of our free world will ultimately depend on whether our age can produce a sufficient number of such aristocrats of public spirit.*

The best way to become a moral aristocrat is to build trust in others by building trust in oneself. Following one's own deeply held principles by using resolutions, therefore, is the path to building both personal and public trusts. Simply put, a person who does not follow through on his own commitments should not be shocked when others do not trust his commitments either. For a person who lies to himself will certainly lie to others also. Trust, however, isn't the work of a day, a week, a month, or even a year. Instead, it's built over a lifetime as character is molded into a person's core-being through consistent study and application of his principles (resolutions) into his life. Dismally, a person could ask a thousand people and, probably not find one who has developed, written, studied, and applied specific resolutions in his life.

INTRODUCTION

In the modern world, character development and written resolutions are a lost art; predictably, this loss is followed by the subsequent losses in life's significance, meaning, and morality. The West, in a word, is fatally wounded, suicidally stabbing at its own heart.

Resolved—Definitions

Resolutions are written resolves that are studied daily to help guide a person's behavior while he is forming his fundamental character. Dictionary.com has several definitions of the term *resolve*, some of which are relevant when discussing life resolutions:

1. To come to a definite or earnest decision about; determine (to do something): I have resolved that I shall live to the full.
2. To deal with (a question, a matter of uncertainty, etc.) conclusively; settle; solve: to resolve the question before the board.
3. *Music.* (a voice part or the harmony as a whole) to progress from a dissonance to a consonance.

The purpose of this book is to teach how to apply resolutions into one's life, and then see all three of these definitions fulfilled. Written resolutions should encompass the whole person; they are a written plan to develop a person's character and thinking, from who he is today to who he desires to be tomorrow. When a person writes and studies his resolutions, he resolves to live internally what he proclaims externally. Above all, a person cannot influence others until he has influenced himself. As Mahatma Gandhi stated, "Be the change you want to see in the world." By beginning with himself, forging the resolutions into his being, he becomes a living model of his principles and a change agent for others by modeling what he is messaging.

George Washington—Resolved to Develop Character

When he was young, Washington had a fiery temper, but he developed an iron-willed discipline in order to check its excesses. Richard Norton Smith, in his book *Patriarch*, said, "The adolescent Washington examined Seneca's dialogues and laboriously copied from a London magazine one hundred and ten 'rules of civility' intended to buff a rude country boy into at least the first draft of a gentleman." The French Jesuits had developed these 110 rules as principles to live by, and Washington's methodical writing process helped him adopt many of these maxims as his resolutions in life.

16

INTRODUCTION

As Richard Brookhiser, author of *Founding Father*, wrote, "His manner and his morals kept his temperament under control. His commitment to ideas gave him guidance. Washington's relation to ideas has been underestimated by almost everyone who wrote of him or knew him, and modern education has encouraged this neglect…. His attention to courtesy and correct behavior anticipated his political philosophy. He was influenced by Roman notions of nobility, but he was even more deeply influenced by a list of table manners and rules for conversation by Jesuits." Character and self-mastery were his goals, which he endeavored to reach by living his guiding ideals of fortitude, justice, moderation, and dignity inherent in every human being.

Life became a series of resolutions, which he wrote and studied many times over his life, to live by. Here are two his maxims as examples (see appendix for more):

1. With me it has always been a maxim rather to let my designs appear from my works rather than by my expressions.
2. Happiness and moral duty are inseparably connected.

Washington studied and practiced his maxims consistently, becoming convinced of the correctness of the maxims, teaching virtue over happiness and duty over rights and resolving to live based on the principles implied in them. In the book *George Washington's Character*, Katherine Kersten asked:

What would Washington have accomplished if happiness, rather than integrity and service, had been his life-goal? Instead of suffering with his men through the snows of Valley Forge, he might have followed the example of Benedict Arnold, another Revolutionary War general. Though brave and talented, Arnold valued his own well-being and prosperity above all else. Out of self-interest, he plotted to betray West Point to the British, and died a traitor to his nation. What can we learn from Washington and his contemporaries about character-building? They teach us, most importantly, that "the soul can be schooled." Exercising reason and will, we can mold ourselves into beings far nobler than nature made us.

The end of Kersten's quotation summarizes character-based training beautifully: "the soul can be schooled." Washington attended soul school daily, developing the nobility of character

17

INTRODUCTION

needed to unite the American colonies. General Henry Knox spoke truth when he explained that it was the strength of Washington's character—not the laws of the new Constitution—that held the young republic together. In a tribute to his friend, Congressman Henry "Light-Horse Harry" Lee eulogized Washington: "First in war, first in peace, and first in the hearts of his countrymen, he was second to none in humble and enduring scenes of private life. Pious, just, humane, temperate, and sincere; uniform, dignified, and commanding; his example was as edifying to all around him as were the effects of that example lasting....Correct throughout, vice shuddered in his presence and virtue always felt his fostering hand. The purity of his private character gave effulgence to his public virtues.... Such was the man for whom our nation mourns." Lee's tribute testified to Washington's faithful application of his resolutions into his life, living his maxims both privately and publicly.

Ben Franklin—Resolved to Develop Wisdom

When he was young, Ben Franklin didn't always behave in a sensible manner. In reality, he offended many of the leading citizens of Philadelphia with his self-assumed air of importance. In our book *Launching a Leadership Revolution*, Chris Brady and I shared a story about young Franklin: "A confidant took him aside one day and was both bold and kind enough to share the truth with Franklin that people didn't like him. Although amazingly brilliant, nobody cared. They couldn't stand to be around him. He was too argumentative and opinionated. His informer even told him that people would see Franklin approaching on the street and cross the road so as to avoid any contact with him. Naturally, Franklin was devastated, but his reaction to the cold, hard brutal facts was one of the main reasons for his subsequent success and rise to fame.

At twenty years of age, Franklin transformed himself launching a self-improvement project he called "moral perfection." Initially, he started with four resolutions: "He resolved to become more frugal so that he could save enough money to repay what he owed to others. He decided that he would be very honest and sincere 'in every word and action.' He promised himself to be industrious 'to whatever business [he took] in hand.' Lastly he vowed 'to speak ill of no man whatever, not even in a manner of truth' and to 'speak all the good I know of everybody.'"

Beginning with these four resolutions, he eventually created his world-renowned list of thirteen virtues (see appendix for com-

INTRODUCTION

plete list) and developed a plan to study one virtue every week of the fifty-two weeks in a year. Here are two of his virtues:

1. *Silence.* Speak not but what may benefit others or yourself; avoid trifling conversation.
2. *Justice.* Wrong none by doing injuries, or omitting the benefits that are your duty.

Franklin's methodical approach to developing character and wisdom, rotating through 13 resolutions in 13 weeks, caused each virtue to be studied four weeks per year. Moreover, he evaluated his performance each week against his standard of moral perfection. Of course, he never reached perfection but he did improve every year. In Franklin's autobiography, he discussed his plan to check his results against his resolution, "I made a little book, in which I allotted a page for each of the virtues...I might mark, by a little black spot, every fault I found upon examination to have been committed respecting that virtue upon that day." With time and effort, Franklin's personal improvement plan helped him become one of the most respected citizens of Philadelphia, routinely requested to serve in the numerous volunteer organizations of the city. Writer Walter Isaacson described how Franklin's improved personal leadership led to his public leadership and service to humanity:

That led him to make the link between private virtue and civic virtue and to suspect, based on the meager evidence he could muster about God's will, that these earthly virtues were linked to heavenly ones as well. As he put it in the motto for the library he founded, "To pour forth benefits for the common good is divine." It is useful for us to engage anew with Franklin, for in doing so we are grappling with a fundamental issue: How does one live a life that is useful, virtuous, worthy, moral, and spiritually meaningful?

By studying a different virtue every week, Franklin made great gains throughout the course of his long life. Franklin's people skills and tact were world-renowned and his commonsense wisdom helped him become one of the world's most influential diplomats. Indeed, many historians believed he (even more than Washington) was the indispensable man of the 1787 Constitutional Convention, tempering the rhetoric from both the Federalists and the anti-Federalists. Historian William MacDonald noted, "Franklin's voice was always in favor of the more generous provision, the ampler liberty; was always earnestly opposed to whatever might tend

INTRODUCTION

to make governmental oppression at some future time possible.... Some of his finest utterances were in maintenance of that plea; and it is a symptom of the noble feeling with which Franklin was regarded by the noblest men, that Hamilton would give his support to Franklin's recommendations, though they were essentially moral criticisms of the policy which he himself thought best for the country." Franklin's principle-centered diplomacy, as a result, influenced people not only of the same turn of mind but also his political opponents—a true testament to his character and honor.

Jonathan Edwards—Resolved to Serve with Humility

Jonathan Edwards was a preacher, a theologian, and a missionary to Native Americans. Shortly before his death, he assumed the presidency at the College of New Jersey (Princeton University today). He is acknowledged by many to be America's most important and original philosophical theologian. His mind ranged over the field of knowledge with a depth and clarity rarely matched in any age. Author George Marsden concurs, "Edwards was extraordinary. By many estimates, he was the most acute early American philosopher and the most brilliant of all American theologians. At least three of his many works—*Religious Affections, Freedom of the Will*, and *The Nature of True Virtue*—stand as masterpieces in the larger history of Christian literature."

Edwards began his ministry with little advance billing. His first pastoral position at nineteen years of age in 1722 in New York City, then a thriving metropolis of ten thousand people, was far away from his Connecticut hometown. Dr. Stephen Nichols, author of *The Resolutions of Jonathan Edwards*, wrote of the young pastor, "Amidst all of this uncertainty and flux, this young man Jonathan Edwards needed both a place to stand and a compass for some direction. So he took to writing. He kept a diary and he penned some guidelines, which he came to call his 'Resolutions.' These resolutions would supply both that place for him to stand and a compass to guide him as he made his way." Historian A. C. McGiffert described Edwards's method of resolutions: "Deliberately he set about to temper his character into steel." Tempering is a process that "toughens". In a similar fashion, written resolutions temper a person's character, "toughening" the internal person through study and course corrections. This tempering process takes time, but the internal fortitude and self-mastery gained by living one's convictions, not one's preferences, are worth paying any price.

Jonathan Edwards dutifully wrote 70 resolutions (see appendix) between 1722 and 1723. He committed to read these 70 reso-

20

INTRODUCTION

lutions once every week for the rest of his life. Needless to say, he fulfilled his commitment, reading the resolutions more than one thousand eight hundred times over the next thirty-five years. Here are two of his resolutions:

1. Resolved, that I will do whatsoever I think to be most to God's glory, and my own good, profit and pleasure, in the whole of my duration, without any consideration of the time, whether now, or never so many myriads of ages hence. Resolved to do whatever I think to be my duty and most for the good and advantage of mankind in general. Resolved to do this, whatever difficulties I meet with, how many and how great so ever.

31. Resolved, never to say anything at all against anybody, but when it is perfectly agreeable to the highest degree of Christian honor, and of love to mankind, agreeable to the lowest humility, and sense of my own faults and failings, and agreeable to the golden rule; often, when I have said anything against anyone, to bring it to, and try it strictly by the test of this resolution.

Be that as it may, Edwards viewed his dismissal as God's will and vowed to redeem the time by writing down the thoughts he had developed over his years of pastoring a church. Not surprisingly, Edwards was, as author Randall Stewart observed,, "not only the greatest of all American theologians and philosophers but the greatest of our pre-19th century writers as well." His gracious attitude and humble spirit allowed him to focus on what God had planned for him next, rather than bewailing his unfair treatment. Indeed, he didn't fight for his rights; instead, he accepted the congregation's ruling as God's plan. He took a position as missionary to the frontier Indians because he knew this assignment would give him more time to write. Interestingly, his consistent grace-filled spirit of forgiveness to his detractors led several of them to apologize for their participation in the spread of misinformation. Can anyone imagine the historical infamy of being one of the members of the congregation who dismissed one of the best theologians and philosophers in American history?

Edwards, in his final years, never missed a beat, writing several Christian classics of literature and leaving a powerful example of how character-based resolutions can transform a person from

INTRODUCTION

the inside out. He faithfully lived his principles externally because it was who he was internally. In other words, he didn't just give lip service to his resolutions; he actually lived them.

Mind, Heart, and Will

Still, if success was as simple as writing a few resolutions and studying them daily, wouldn't more people apply this method to become successful? Perhaps Dr. Martyn Lloyd-Jones description of man explains why so few achieve lasting success: "Man is a wonderful creature; he is mind, he is heart, and he is will. Those are the three main constituents of man. God has given him a mind; He has given him a heart; He has given him a will whereby he can act." Transforming one's life, in consequence, requires the whole person to be involved—his mind, his heart, and his will—to truly change. Transformation isn't just a mental (mind) assent, isn't just an emotional (heart) experience, and it isn't just a regimented (will) learning. Instead, all three must work together to drive real change. This is where most people miss out. For some will read the resolutions and make a mental nod of approval but won't involve the heart or will. Even though they claim to have knowledge on how to succeed in life, they never seem to achieve anything. To know and not to do is to not really know since if one knew how satisfying authentic success would be, he would strive for it. Resolutions must engage the mind, but also go beyond it, tapping into the heart and will to produce lasting change.

Without uniting the mind, the heart, and the will together, people will not achieve their desired results. For example, many who attend a seminar have their hearts touched by the seminar's message but don't seem to comprehend mentally (mind) or follow through physically (will) with a plan for success. These people jump from one success fad to the next and gain emotional (heart) releases but accomplish little of real substance. Life has been hard on them, so they attend another seminar, seeking not real change but rather a cathartic release of tension. Other people study their resolutions and attempt to transform themselves through sheer willpower, but unless their minds and hearts are engaged, their efforts will not last. For they attempt to take up the resolutions rather than be taken up by them. The will can withstand motions; but without the heart and the mind (the passion and the understanding) the process of transformation lacks zeal. As the old saying goes, "A man convinced against his will is of the same opinion

INTRODUCTION

still." A methodical, passionless, robot like study of the resolutions will not get the job done.

Needless to say, it's only with a mind that understands, a heart that generates passion, and a disciplined will to follow through that change true inside change occurs. Unfortunately, most success seekers' journeys end in disappointment after they have made the common mistake of compartmentalizing the parts of personhood rather than allowing them to work together. The good news, though, is that anyone can develop this ability, namely, to work on the mind, heart, and will simultaneously. The process is simple, but certainly not easy, and requires immense discipline to marry the three constituent parts together in the pursuit of excellence in any area that a person has resolved to change. By seriously thinking about where to focus, writing clear resolutions, resolving to read, and applying them on a consistent basis, anybody can—like Washington, Franklin, and Edwards—resolve to change. After all, only when a person truly changes himself, can he begins the process that truly transforms the world.

Living the 13 Resolutions

Throughout my life, I have studied the greatest men and women in history. Learning from their examples, I developed and applied the 13 resolutions, the 13 principles necessary for long-term success, to move from "purpose detected" to "vision fulfilled." Peter Senge shared that purpose, vision, and core principles (resolutions) are the three key concepts: "These governing ideas answer three critical questions: 'What?' 'Why?' and 'How?'... Taken as a unit, all three governing ideas answer the question, 'What do we believe in?'" A person who believes in his life's mission, in turn, should know the resolutions are the "how", the purpose is the "why", and the vision is the "what". When he knows why he is living, what he is supposed to do, and how he plans to achieve his purpose, his date with destiny is set. First, he detects his purpose; second, he studies and applies the 13 resolutions with his mind, heart, and will; and third, he journeys toward his God-given personal vision. Lamentably, only a few get all three parts correctly. And just as it takes three legs to stabilize a stool, it takes all three "governing ideas" to fulfill a person's destiny because destiny is fulfilling the what, why, and how of life.

23

INTRODUCTION

Vision is tomorrow's reality expressed as an idea today. The ladder that connects a person's vision with his purpose is his resolutions. The 13 resolutions are the ladder's rungs that help a person climb from where he is to where he desires to be. Philosopher Ortega y Gasset wrote, "Destiny does not consist in what we feel we should like to do; rather it is recognized in its clear features in the consciousness that we must do what we do not feel like doing." In the same way, climbing the resolution ladder of success isn't easy, but when a person knows why he started, what he desires to accomplish, and how he plans on getting there, his personal preference pales in comparison to his destiny's fulfillment. Sure, the 13 resolutions will demand endless hours of effort in "schooling the soul" to climb the ladder rungs up to his vision, but what could possibly be a better time investment? Thousands of years ago, philosopher Heraclitus conveyed a message for the ages when he proclaimed, "Character is destiny." A noble character, in a word, must precede a noble destiny. Living the 13 resolutions develops character, transforming a person from the inside out, helping him climb the ladder from "purpose detected" to "vision fulfilled". Only then can a person complete his God-given destiny.

The following are the 13 resolutions placed in the weekly order in which they should be studied. By focusing on one resolution per week and applying the principles, a person will complete each resolution four times per year. The resolutions are broken into three sections—private achievements, public achievements, and leadership achievements. The order that the resolutions and sections are discussed represent the natural progression from private victories to public victories and finally to leadership victories. The private and public achievements combined create the character and the competence needed to produce leadership influence. After all, leaders must have followers, for according to John Maxwell, "if you call yourself a leader but no one is following you, then you are only out for a walk." The 13 resolutions walk you through the entire process, from private to public to leadership achievements. The goal, naturally, is to develop wisdom, applying the right principles at the right time. Indeed, this is the ultimate goal of learning and applying the 13 resolutions, developing wisdom for life.

INTRODUCTION

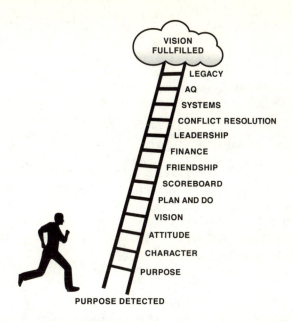

Private Achievements

1. *Resolved: To Discover My God-Given Purpose.* I know that when my potential, passions, and profits intersect, my purpose is revealed.
2. *Resolved: To Choose Character over Reputation Any Time They Conflict.* I know that my character is who I am, and my reputation is only what others say that I am.
3. *Resolved: To Have a Positive Attitude in All Situations.* I know that by listening to my *positive voice* and turning down my *negative voice*, I will own a positive attitude.
4. *Resolved: To Align My Conscious (Ant) with My Subconscious (Elephant) Mind toward My Vision.* I know that ending the civil war between the two is crucial for all achievements.

Public Achievements

5. *Resolved: To Develop and Implement a Game Plan in Each Area of My Life.* I know that planning and doing are essential parts of the success process.
6. *Resolved: To Keep Score in the Game of Life.* I know that the scoreboard forces me to check and confront the results and make the needed adjustments in order to win.

INTRODUCTION

7. *Resolved: To Develop the Art and Science of Friendship.* I know that everyone needs a true friend to lighten the load when life gets heavy.
8. *Resolved: To Develop Financial Intelligence.* I know that over time, my wealth is compounded when income is higher than expenses.

Leadership Achievements

9. *Resolved: To Develop the Art and Science of Leadership.* I know that everything rises and falls based on the leadership culture created in my community.
10. *Resolved: To Develop the Art and Science of Conflict Resolution.* I know that relationship bombs and unresolved conflicts destroy a community's unity and growth.
11. *Resolved: To Develop Systems Thinking.* I know that by viewing life as interconnected patterns rather than isolated events, I improve my leverage.
12. *Resolved: To Develop Adversity Quotient.* I know that AQ leads to perseverance in overcoming obstacles and setbacks.
13. *Resolved: To Reverse the Current of Decline in My Field of Mastery.* I know that a true legacy leaves the world a better place than I found it.

Imagine each of these resolutions as an instrument in an orchestra. Each plays beautiful music by itself, but when they work together, they produce an orchestral masterpiece, a living symphony of success. This book provides the instruments for life's symphonic masterpiece. Personally, once I learned and implemented the 13 resolutions into my life, I found answers to the challenges every life faces. No, the 13 resolutions will not make life perfect, but it does provide the wisdom necessary to navigate through the storms of life. Strangely, with all this said, most will only browse through this book; some will actually read it; but only a few will read, study, and apply the resolutions into their lives. This book was written for the few—the few who yearn to be champions, the few who search for purpose, the few who desire to reach their potentials, and lastly, the few who hunger to fulfill their destinies.

On a bishop's tomb in Westminster Abbey is written:

When I was young and free and my imagination had no limits, I dreamed of changing the world. As I grew older

INTRODUCTION

and wiser, I discovered the world would not change, so I shortened my sights somewhat and decided to change only my country. But it, too, seemed immovable. As I grew into my twilight years, in one last desperate attempt, I settled for changing only my family, those closest to me, but alas, they would have none of it. And now as I lie on my deathbed, I suddenly realize: If I had only changed myself first, then by example I would have changed my family. From their inspiration and encouragement, I would then have been able to better my country and, who knows, I may have even changed the world.

Resolve to master the principles of this book, to apply the 13 resolutions into your life, and to climb the ladder from "purpose detected" to "vision fulfilled." Resolve to be transformed by the wisdom gained from your journey. Resolve through your journey to first transform yourself and then transform your community. Finally, through your transformed community, you will be provided the means to change the world. These are bold words, but they are, nevertheless, true. Opportunity is knocking. Don't knock it. Don't fear it. Instead, seize the day by opening the door and fulfilling your destiny.

CHAPTER 1

PURPOSE
Resolved: To Discover My God-Given Purpose

*I know that when my potential, passions, and profits
intersect, my purpose is revealed.*
—Orrin Woodward

Living on Purpose

Viktor Frankl, a Nazi camp survivor, learned the importance of having a purpose during his struggle to survive the brutal treatment inflicted on him by his captors. In the process, he developed a philosophy of life called "logotherapy." Stephen Covey's described Frankl's theory: "Many so-called mental and emotional illnesses are really symptoms of an underlying sense of meaninglessness or emptiness. Logotherapy eliminates that emptiness by helping the individual to detect his unique meaning, his mission in life." A life worth living, in other words, is a life with meaning. Author Charles Perkhurst noted similarly when he wrote, "Purpose is what gives a life meaning." Sadly, many people live their entire lives without detecting their purpose. In effect, they passively float downriver and accept whatever destination comes rather than swim against the current to achieve the desired destination.

A purposeless life is similar to a hoopless basketball game—one can hurriedly dribble up and down the court, but nothing of any consequence is accomplished. Doesn't this describe the majority of people? Running to and fro with no particular plan, having no purpose, meaning, or significance. In contrast, when hoops are placed on life's backboards, the objective of the game becomes clear. The game now has meaning for the people running up and down the court—to put the ball through the hoop and to score points.

RESOLVED

What previously seemed like a waste of energy now has a specific intent. This is what a purpose does for one's life: gives it meaning by having a worthwhile goal. Dr. Myles Monroe wrote, "The poor man, the rich man, the black man, the white man—every person has a dream in his heart. Your vision may already be clear to you, or it may still be buried somewhere deep in your heart, waiting to be discovered. Fulfilling this dream is what gives purpose and meaning to life.... When you die, you're meant to leave this earth not on a pension but on a purpose." Purpose provides direction to a person's life, filling every task, even seemingly mundane ones, with significance. Disastrously, modern man is suffering the effects of his self-imposed denial of purpose and meaning in life. For instance, when Friedrich Nietzsche wrote, "God is dead. God remains dead. And we have killed him," he understood that by rejecting God, he had also killed meaning and purpose. Bertrand Russell, a highly celebrated atheistic philosopher, elaborated on the meaning of Nietzsche's proclamation, "Unless you assume a God, the question of life's purpose is meaningless." Russell drove this point home when he confronted what the "death of God" worldview meant for hope and purpose in an atheistic philosophy:

> *That man is the product of causes which had no prevision of the end they were achieving; that his origin, his growth, his hopes and fears, his loves and his beliefs, are but the outcome of accidental collocations of atoms; that no fire, no heroism, no intensity of thought and feeling, can preserve an individual life beyond the grave; that all the labors of the ages, all the devotion, all the inspiration, all the noonday brightness of human genius, are destined to extinction in the vast death of the solar system, and that the whole temple of Man's achievement must inevitably be buried beneath the debris of a universe in ruins—all these things, if not quite beyond dispute, are yet so nearly certain, that no philosophy which rejects them can hope to stand. Only within the scaffolding of these truths, only on the firm foundation of unyielding despair, can the soul's habitation henceforth be safely built.*

Russell's philosophy is depressing to say the least. No wonder depression medication and drug use are at an all-time high! Nonetheless, this philosophy has infected millions of people, leaving them without purpose (hoops) in the game of life. Comic Woody Allen reflected, "More than any other time in history, mankind faces a crossroad: One path leads to despair and hopelessness, and the other to total extinction. Let us pray we have the wisdom to choose

PURPOSE

correctly." Needless to say, the legacy of this acidic belief, poured directly on the roots of purpose, destroyed the fruits of hope, meaning, and significance, leaving only the bitter fruits of paralysis and cynicism to fill the void. Thankfully, one doesn't have to drink the modern man's toxic brew of beliefs. In fact, many are rejecting the fatalistic views of these godless philosophers and returning to a purpose-centered life filled with meaning, significance, and destiny.

For example, Pastor Rick Warren's *The Purpose Driven Life* has sold over thirty million copies since 2002 – one of the top-selling books of the modern era. Warren's book is reaching many people with a message of purpose and meaning, who have been lost in a sea of despair. Warren wrote, "You cannot arrive at your life's purpose by starting with a focus on yourself. You must begin with God, your Creator. You exist only because God wills that you exist. You were made by God and for God—and until you understand that, life will never make sense. It is only in God that we discover our origin, our identity, our meaning, our purpose, our significance, and our destiny. Every other path leads to a dead end."

People have a purpose, Warren states, because God is purposeful. Hence, one of the keys to life is to determine what our purpose is. As author Carl Townsend said, "They say there are two important days in your life: the day you were born and the day you find out why you were born." No one chose the day he was born, but everyone can learn why he was born.

> **No one chose the day he was born, but everyone can learn why he was born.**

Why are people created? What is the purpose of one's life? Author Daniel Pink identifies three elements that are included in a purposeful life:

1. Autonomy: the urge to direct our own lives
2. Mastery: the desire to get better at something that matters
3. Purpose: the yearning to do what we do in the service of something larger than ourselves

To achieve one's purpose, autonomy, mastery, and character must combine together. For without autonomy, a person isn't directing his life and, therefore, isn't accomplishing his purpose but someone else's. Furthermore, without mastery, he is not improving in something that matters; and if what he is doing doesn't matter, then it certainly isn't his purpose. Lastly, only a person of character desires to serve something larger than himself, contributing to others and making a difference, leaving his mark in the world by transcending selfish motives and actions. In order to fulfill his purpose, then, a person must have or build all three prerequisites. He must build personal character, hunger for autonomy, and develop mastery in his profession to live a life of excellence.

Purpose Hedgehog

In his book *Good to Great*, Jim Collins discussed the Hedgehog Concept as a way to understand how a company or an individual becomes exceptional. Interestingly, once a person understands Collins's Hedgehog circles, he will notice that these circles also help define his purpose. Collins explained, "More precisely, a Hedgehog Concept is a simple, crystalline concept that flows from deep understanding about the intersection of the following three circles:

1. What can you be the best in the world at (and, equally important, what *can't* you be the best in the world at)?
2. What drives your economic engine?
3. What are you deeply passionate about?"

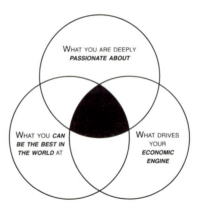

Collins further explained the Hedgehog Concept through an example:

> To quickly grasp the three circles, consider the following personal analogy. Suppose you were able to construct a work life that meets the following three tests. First, you are doing work for which you have a genetic or God-given talent. ("I feel that I was just born to be doing this.") Second, you are well paid for what you do. ("I get paid to do this?

PURPOSE

Am I dreaming?") Third, you are doing work you are passionate about and absolutely love to do, enjoying the actual process for its own sake. ("I look forward to getting up and throwing myself into my daily work, and I really believe in what I'm doing.") The intersection of these three circles is the Hedgehog Concept.

Collins explained that it's essential to have all three circles intersecting to determine a person's Hedgehog Concept. For example, if a person makes a copious amount of money but cannot be the best in his field, then he is only good, not great. Similarly, if he becomes the best at something but isn't passionate about it, then he will not maintain his greatness, as others who are more committed will surpass him. Finally, a person can be as passionate as anyone can be about something, but if he isn't the best at it or it is not economically viable, then he has a fun hobby, not a productive business enterprise. Collins's book teaches that only when all three circles intersect can a company unlock its potential and move from good to great.

In a similar fashion, what would happen if, using the Hedgehog Concept as a model, a person developed the three circles for his Hedgehog Purpose? By slightly changing the three circles, we can create the Purpose Hedgehog.

1. Passion
2. Potential
3. Profits

Purpose, in consequence, is the intersection of a person's passion (motivation), potential (God-given talents), and profits (economic engine). Furthermore, it's only when a person intersects all three circles that he will fulfill his destiny by living a purposeful life.

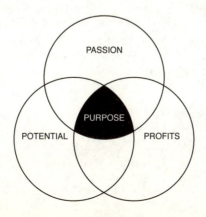

Passion

Passion, the first attribute of purpose, is a mixture of what a person loves and what he hates. This generates his motivation to change his current reality more towards what he loves and away from what he hates. What would a person do with his life if he could do anything? Sometimes it's love that fuels the passion to change the world, at other times, in contrast, it's anger or rejection that fuels the passion to change. In either event, all great achievements are driven by passion; otherwise, criticisms, setbacks, and pressures drain the would-be achiever of his drive. In a word, no passion equals no purpose. Author Jay Elliot described how Steve Jobs, when told someone wanted to be an entrepreneur, would ask, "What's your idea?" Typically the potential entrepreneur would answer, "I don't know yet." Jobs would respond, "I think you should go get a job as a bus-boy or something until you find something you're really passionate about."

> **All great achievements are driven by passion.**

Jobs understood the difference between successful entrepreneurs and unsuccessful ones is a combination of passion and perseverance (which is part of adversity quotient discussed in Resolution 12). He said, "You put so much of your life into this thing. There are such rough moments that I think most people give up.... You have to be burning with an idea, or a problem, or a wrong that you want to right." Without passion, the inspiration will not last when the going gets tough. Passion is non-negotiable because it keeps one going in the face of overwhelming odds, refusing to quit until the purpose is completed.

Potential

The second key to purpose is discovering a person's potential: What are his unique gifts and skills? Everyone is born an original, but sadly most die a copy. What abilities can a person bring to the table that can benefit the world? Author Marianne Williamson magnified the nearly unlimited potential inside of people when she wrote:

> *Our deepest fear is not that we are inadequate. Our deepest fear is that we are powerful beyond measure. It is our light, not our darkness that most frightens us. We ask ourselves, "Who am I to be brilliant, gorgeous, talented and fabulous?" Actually, who are you NOT to be? You are a child*

PURPOSE

of God. Your playing small does NOT serve the world. There is nothing enlightened about shrinking so that other people won't feel insecure around you. We were born to manifest the glory that is within us. And as we let our light shine we unconsciously give other people permission to do the same. As we are liberated from our own fear, our presence automatically liberates others.

Regretfully, the greatest buried treasures are found in cemeteries across the world. For in these cemeteries lie the buried potential of billions who played it small, believing it to be the "safe" plan. Why is everyone playing it "safe" in life when no one makes it out alive anyway? Life isn't safe, but it is a great adventure to be experienced! Why not dream a big dream? The worst thing that can happen in a small dream is it comes true. After all, playing small and "safe" only ensures a person doesn't reach his potential and thus never fulfills his unique purpose.

Profits

The third aspect of purpose is profits—converting one's potential and passion into a fruitful calling. At first blush, many object to profits being included in a person's purpose, but without a viable economic engine, one simply does not have the time or funds to complete his calling. Little details like eating, drinking, and housing keep interfering with his purpose. In a free society, people compensate others financially when they are satisfied with the products or services offered. By pursuing passion and potential to satisfy customers, a person fulfills his purpose and thrives. Indeed, the corporate cradle-to-grave jobs are passing away, but serving a customer's needs will never go out of style. If anything, serving customers has never been more important since today's competition comes from all over the globe in this flat world. Shoddy products and services will simply not be tolerated, making it imperative to apply passion and potential with profits to fulfill one's purpose.

Wally Amos, an Air Force veteran who worked as a talent agent with the William Morris Agency, loved chocolate chip cookies. His aunt Della raised him and taught him a tasty cookie recipe when he was a child. He would give home-baked chocolate chip cookies to celebrities, enticing them to meet with him in an effort to have William Morris Company represent them (it was effective as Amos inked entertainers Simon & Garfunkel, among others, using this method). Although he was a good agent, his passion was his cookies. Finally, Amos's passion won out and on March 10, 1975,

Amos opened his first cookie store in Los Angeles, California, calling it Famous Amos. In his first year, he sold over $300,000 of cookies, and in the second year, he brought in more than $1,000,000 in sales. His company grew meteorically from there and when he sold his company, he became a multimillionaire. Today, his brand is still one of the most recognized names in the field of cookies. Amos's passion is what drove him to leave a successful career and to pursue his dream. Above all, he succeeded by aligning his passion, potential, and profits towards his purpose, making Famous Amos cookies a worldwide phenomenon.

What, Why, and How

Whatever a person is doing, he should do it with all his might, because this is how doors open to reveal his purpose. And, when a person discovers his purpose, all his actions are based upon fulfilling the vision (to be discussed in Resolution 4) that he sees in his mind when the purpose is completed. However, in order to turn this vision into reality, he must become a living embodiment of the principles needed to accomplish it. Senge described these principles by asking a question: "How do we act, consistent with our mission along the path toward achieving our vision?...[This will] describe how the company [or individual] wants life to be on a day-to-day basis, while pursuing the vision."

> **Whatever a person is doing, he should do it with all his might, because this is how doors open to reveal his purpose.**

The 13 resolutions, accordingly, are the principles by which a person lives in order to achieve his vision and fulfill his purpose. Regardless of the specific field in which people apply these principles, they will find every one of the 13 resolutions vital to achieve their purpose and vision. Since the resolutions are based upon human nature and the laws of life, they are applicable in any field, at any time, and under all circumstances. With the resolutions in his tool belt, all a person has to do is determine his purpose, clear the fog from his vision, and form a team of people to help turn the vision into a reality.

All businesses were first created metaphysically (as visions in the entrepreneur's mind) and then created physically in the material world. Not surprisingly, this aligns with Ralph Waldo Emerson's statement: "An institution is the lengthened shadow of one man." Still, this isn't quite right, for when a person detects his mission, he surrounds himself with others not only to compete with

PURPOSE

but also to improve the mission. Moreover, when the team buys into the vision, they add their own unique gifts and talents to make the vision even better than when it started. Together Everyone Achieves More is the true definition of a team. Senge described this phenomena when he wrote, "They now have partners, 'co-creators'; the vision no longer rests on their shoulders alone. Early on, when they are nurturing an individual vision, people may say it is 'my vision.' But as the shared vision develops, it becomes both 'my vision' and 'our vision.'" As a result, when the purpose, vision, and principles align, a disciplined culture develops and it is this culture that propels businesses forward.

Steve Jobs—Hedgehog Purpose

Steve Jobs, founder and CEO of Apple, displayed how living one's purpose personally and professionally can produce huge results in the world. Chris Brady, co-author of *Launching a Leadership Revolution*, defined Apple's Hedgehog Concept this way: "To deliver incredibly creative and 'cool' technology that is intuitively useful and reliable for any class of user—particularly the user who doesn't care to know about the intricacies of a hammer in order to make productive use of one. (In other words, to make the technology invisible and the usability and dependability dominant.)" Jobs wanted not only an intuitive product but also one that created an experience of satisfaction so good that a customer would feel emotionally attached to the product and share his experience with others. Jobs may have had the firmest grasp on consumer preferences of any CEO. He intuitively understood that customers love simplicity, elegance of design, and the "cool" factor. Furthermore, his obsession, according to Elliot, was "a passion for the product...a passion for product perfection." Jobs's personal Purpose Hedgehog and Apple's Purpose Hedgehog closely resembled each other since both emerged from the intersection of Jobs's passions, potential, and profits. In other words, the personal resolutions that the leader lives his life by become the foundation of the company's culture. To improve upon Emerson's statement, then, it would read, "Great company cultures are the shadows of the great personal principles lived by its leaders." This is why the 13 Resolutions are essential for cultural influence in the world.

With Jobs's passion aligning wonderfully with his potential, the last piece of the puzzle was to make it profitable. Apple, although not the top seller of computers, was and is the most profitable. Apple's offerings of unique products, like iPod, iPad, and iPhone, in a market of Windows software clones, have revolutionized the high-tech field. Jobs, through both Apple and Pixar, aligned his passion and his potential to create profits, thus fulfilling his purpose.

Because of Jobs's powerful vision, he created a culture around his passion that attracted, as Senge said, "co-creators." Jobs's purpose was the driving force, helping attract many talented people to Apple's culture. The assembled team of these talented people could then fulfill the company's purpose by living its principles and completing its vision. Mac engineer Trip Hawkins described Jobs as having "a power of vision that [was] almost frightening. When Steve [believed] in something, the power of that vision [could] literally sweep aside any objections, problems or whatever. They just [ceased] to exist." Elliot agreed, writing, "The Mac and every product since then are more than 'just products.' They are a representation of Steve Jobs's intense commitment. Visionaries are able to create great art or great products because their work isn't nine-to-five. What Steve was doing represented him; it was intuitive but inspired."

Purposeful people like Jobs infect their entire community, bringing a community's passion, potential, and profits to the forefront. Purpose unites everyone with an organization's culture to make achieving the team's goals even more important than their personal goals. This unity creates loyalty as Elliot explained. "When you believe in your product and people as totally as Steve [did], your people stick with you. Apple has one of the highest retention rates in Silicon Valley." This is mainly because Jobs's purpose, vision, and principles united the Apple community with a highly effective culture. Jobs, speaking at the Stanford commencement ceremonies, shared the importance of purpose: "Again, you can't connect the dots looking forward; you can only connect them looking backwards. So you have to trust that the dots will somehow connect in your future. You have to trust in something—your gut, destiny, life, karma, whatever. This approach has never let me down, and it has made all the difference in my life."

Big Rocks First

One more thought on living a life of purpose is to learn to focus one's time on actions that fulfill the purpose. Don't just be busy—be productive. Time is the stuff that life is made of which is why time management directed towards one's purpose is crucial. Indeed, effective time management without directing it toward one's purpose is to efficiently waste one's life. For even with good time management, the majority of a person's time will be dribbled away on unimportant activities. Only when time-management is orga-

38

PURPOSE

nized and prioritized around purpose and vision is it effective. Author Hyrum Smith, wrote, "Time is just like money. When you decide to spend one hour watching TV, you have also decided not to spend the time on what? Everything else. You would be very upset if someone gained access to your bank account and stole all your money. Most people, though, don't blink an eye when all sorts of culprits sneak into their lives and steal their time."

For instance, practically every executive would agree that reading is important to grow as a leader, but only a few read as much as they should. Smith asked a group of executives, if reading was so important, why do so few actually read? After an uncomfortably long silence, someone in the back row finally offered, "Because books don't ring." What a profound response! Books don't hop up and say, "Hey, I'm a really good book. Why don't you read me?" Instead, they passively wait for hungry leaders to devour them. Reading is important and helps fulfill purpose without being so blatantly in one's face. Regretfully, for many people, the urgent crowds out the important and they are busy doing nothing significant. Covey explained the importance of prioritization:

> *In the middle of the lecture the presenter pulled out a wide-mouth jar and placed it on the table, next to some fist-sized rocks. After filling the jar to the top with rocks, he asked, "Is the jar full?" People could see that no more rocks would fit, so they replied, "Yes!"*
>
> *"Not so fast," he cautioned. He then got some gravel from under the table and added it to the jar, filling the spaces between the rocks. Again, he asked, "Is the jar full?"*
>
> *This time the students replied, "Probably not."*
>
> *The presenter then reached for a bucket of sand below the table, and dumped it on the jar, filling the spaces between the rocks and the gravel. Once again he asked, "Is the jar full?"*
>
> *"No!" the students shouted. Finally, he grabbed a pitcher of water and filled the jar completely, asking the public what they could learn from that illustration.*
>
> *One of the participants answered, "If you work at it, you can always fit more into your life."*
>
> *"No," said the presenter. "The point is, if you don't put the big rocks in first...would you never have gotten any of them in?"*

The person living a life of purpose makes the big rocks the most important because these are the activities that move him closer to fulfilling his purpose and vision. He must learn to say no to the good so he has time to say yes to the great. When a person says that he doesn't have time, this really isn't true. The truth is that he doesn't prioritize his time for the specific activity. For both the wealthiest and poorest person both have twenty-four hours in a day, but what they do with them makes all the difference. Mastery of any activity, according to Malcolm Gladwell, requires ten thousand hours—meaning, a person can master nearly any field by focusing on it. Nonetheless, he cannot master all fields because there aren't enough ten-thousand-hour time segments to go around. Hence, laser-like focus—the ability to narrow options to the essential few—is crucial for all successful people. Covey described his thoughts on the difference between urgent and important:

> *Urgent matters are usually visible. They press on us; they insist on action. They're often popular with others. They're usually right in front of us. And often they are pleasant, easy and fun to do. But so often unimportant! Importance, on the other hand, has to do with results. If something is important, it contributes to your mission, your values, and your high priority goals.*

Urgent and important matters should be addressed right away, but many high-priority items, although important, are not urgent. These require disciplined planning to schedule and invest the time. Failure to do this is the root cause of most failures. Learn to delegate any task that others can do nearly as well, leaving only the things only the leader can do on his plate. Remember, busyness is not the goal—productivity is. If someone in the community can perform a task nearly as well or even better, why not delegate it? Delegating the tasks and inspecting the results is an essential skill for every purpose-centered productive leader. Leaders must invest their time in the activities only they can do for the organization to achieve its purpose and delegate the rest.

Purpose-Oriented Time Management

With this said, time management doesn't have to be overly complicated. In fact, in the early twentieth century, Ivy Lee, one of America's first public relations stars, discussed a simple but effective time management technique with Charles Schwab, a leader in Andrew Carnegie's steel company:

> *One day a management consultant, Ivy Lee, called on Schwab of the Bethlehem Steel Company. Lee briefly out-*

PURPOSE

lined his firm's services, ending with the statement: "With our service, you'll know how to manage better."

The indignant Schwab said, "I'm not managing as well now as I know how. What we need around here is not more 'knowing' but more doing; not 'knowledge', but action; if you can give us something to pep us up to do the things we AL-READY KNOW we ought to do, I'll gladly listen to you and pay you anything you ask."

"Fine," said Lee. "I can give you something in twenty minutes that will step up your action and doing at least 50%."

"Okay," said Schwab. "I have just about that much time before I must leave to catch a train. What's your idea?"

Lee pulled a blank 3 x 5 note sheet out of his pocket, handed it to Schwab and said: "Write on this sheet the five most important tasks you have to do tomorrow." That took about three minutes.

"Now," said Lee, "Number them in the order of their importance." Five more minutes passed.

"Now," said Lee, "Put this sheet in your pocket and the first thing tomorrow morning, look at item one and start working on it. Pull the sheet out of your pocket every fifteen minutes and look at item one until it is finished. Then tackle item two in the same way, then item three. Do this until quitting time. Don't be concerned if you only finished two or three, or even if you only finish one item. You'll be working on the important ones. The others can wait. If you can't finish them all by this method, you couldn't with another method either, and without some system you'd probably not even decide which are most important."

He went on, "Spend the last five minutes of every working day making out a 'must do' list for the next day's tasks. After you've convinced yourself of the worth of this system, have your people try it. Try it out as long as you wish and then send me a check for what YOU think it's worth."

The whole interview lasted about twenty-five minutes. In two weeks, Schwab sent Lee a check for $25,000—$1,000 a minute. He added a note saying the lesson was the most profitable he had ever learned. Did it work? In five years, it turned the unknown Bethlehem Steel Company into the biggest independent steel producer in the world and made Schwab a hundred-million-dollar fortune and made him the best known steel man alive at that time.

RESOLVED

Time management is one of the most powerful results multipliers known to mankind. Place the big purpose rocks first by prioritizing the task. Then, perform the work in the order of priorities to ensure the most important work to complete the purpose and vision is not neglected. The productivity of an entire leadership team will multiply as the important replaces the urgent in people's schedules, aligning everyone toward the purpose and vision of the company. Pointedly, if a person cannot manage his time, then he cannot lead his life.

Remember, if a person cannot manage his time, then he cannot lead his life.

The crucial lesson to learn is people cannot manage time correctly until they know their purpose—what they are called to do, why they are doing it, and finally, how they are going to accomplish it. Only then will he ensure every action he takes moves him closer to fulfilling his life's purpose. Living a life on purpose isn't easy, but neither is living a life of chaos. Plus, fulfilling one's purpose satisfies a person at a much deeper level than comfort or convenience. As author E. N. Gray noted, "The successful person has the habit of doing the things failures don't like to do. They don't like doing them either necessarily. But their dislike is subordinated to the strength of their purpose."

In summary, people follow people who know where they are going and why they are going there. These private achievements must be won before the public achievements will be and public achievements must be won before the leadership achievements will be. For a person must model his message before his message will spread. This is why a person must move up the ladder from private to public to leadership achievements before he will ever leave a legacy. Purpose, in turn, is the cornerstone of all true successes, for without it, people will not resolve to climb the ladder. Purpose must come first.

PURPOSE

John Wooden

On October 14, 1910, in Hall, Indiana, John Robert Wooden was born to a Dutch-Irish family. The farmhouse where young John grew up did not have many of today's modern conveniences, but what it did have was something much more valuable, namely, love and encouragement. His parents instilled in John that with hard work and dedication, a person could achieve his purpose. Needless to say, Wooden fulfilled his purpose, winning more NCAA basketball championships than any other coach by aligning his passion, potential, and profits to achieve mastery.

Wooden thought of himself as a teacher and his purpose to teach the principles he learned to his team. As he explained: "What occurred in the practices is what gave me joy and satisfaction—teaching others how to bring forth the best of which they are capable. Ultimately, I believe that's what leadership is about: helping others to achieve their own greatness by helping the organization to succeed." Of course, Wooden didn't win every contest, but even when he lost, he still fulfilled his purpose, to teach young men how to overcome setbacks and win in the game of life. Indeed, his legendary sense of purpose was one of the cornerstones of his success, driving a farm boy from the fields of Indiana to capture ten NCAA titles in his last 12 years of coaching at UCLA, including a record seven in a row. While there are many qualities a person can learn from John Wooden, one of his central tenets is that everything in life happens for a purpose.

For instance, Wooden was not blessed with a Michael Jordan physical frame, but this is what led to his superhuman work ethic. He made up for his lack of size with added intensity. After all, at a height of only 5'10" and a weight of only 175 pounds, he knew he better outhustle everyone if he was to make it as a basketball player. It was this determination that led Wooden's college coach, Piggy Lambert, to speak of young Johnny as the best-conditioned athlete he ever coached in any sport. Author Steve Jamison interviewed Wooden and captured the secret to his superhuman work ethic:

My dad, Joshua, had great influence on my own personal definition of success.... One of the things that he

43

tried to get across to me was that I should never try to be better than someone else. Then he always added, "But Johnny, never cease trying to be the best you can be. That is under your control. The other isn't...."The concept that success is mine when I work my hardest to become my best, and that I alone determine whether I do so, became central to my life and affected me in a most profound manner.

Purpose, in a word, is about a person being the best he can be, not comparing himself to others. Wooden's legendary purpose led Purdue to the 1932 Helms Foundation unofficial national championship; further, it catapulted him into the College Sports Hall of Fame. Not surprisingly, to Wooden, the joy of winning was always secondary to the inner peace he received from knowing he had done his personal best. He defined success as "the peace of mind that is a direct result of self-satisfaction in knowing you did your best to become the best you are capable of becoming." A person may lose the contest but still be a champion, because he did his personal best. On the other hand, a person may win and yet still not be a winner because he didn't do his personal best. This philosophy, saturated into all of his teams, created an unquenchable drive for excellence to fulfill their purpose by becoming winners in the game of basketball and life. Wooden, as a result, believed the external scoreboard merely reflected the internal scoreboard. Players competed against their personal best selves more than they did against the other teams to reach their potential. Wooden explained: "Championships were never the cake; they were the icing. Doing our best was the cake."

Wooden, however, didn't set the coaching world on fire right away. In fact, after his playing days, he toiled in anonymity for eleven years as a high school basketball coach. Only someone who knew his purpose was to grow young men and serve where he was, would maintain the impressive drive to improve that this young high school coach displayed. Eventually, he moved on to the NCAA, accepting the head coaching position at Indiana State University. This time, it only took two years for Wooden to be noticed as he coached his team to the NAIB finals. This led to an offer to coach the

PURPOSE

UCLA Bruins, who promised to build a state-of-the-art basketball facility soon after his arrival. In 1948, Wooden packed his bags and moved his family from the Midwest to the West Coast, accepting the UCLA offer. Wooden's coaching experience at UCLA tested his purpose resolution. To begin with, the promise to start construction of the new basketball complex was delayed for nearly seventeen years! This forced the basketball team to practice under less than ideal conditions, to put it mildly. To be sure, many high schools today have better training facilities than Wooden's UCLA teams did. The squad practiced basketball on the third floor of the old Men's Gymnasium, the same floor the gymnastic and wrestling programs used for practices—sometimes forced to practice at the same time. The facility infamously received the nickname "the B.O. Barn" because of its lack of ventilation and the predictable smells emanating from its hardworking athletes. Wooden recalled:

> *For sixteen years, I helped our managers sweep and mop the floor every day before practice because of the dust stirred up from the other activities. These were hardship conditions, not only for the basketball team.... you could have written a long list of excuses why UCLA shouldn't have been able to develop a good basketball team there. Nevertheless, the B.O. Barn was where we built teams that won national championships in 1964 and 1965. You must take what is available and make the very most of it.*

The recurring theme in Wooden's life seems to be - no matter what the current situation is, so long as a person remembers his purpose, he can endure and overcome. Instead of waiting for conditions to improve, Wooden's purpose drove continuous improvement in the one thing he could control, the performance of his team. This eventually led to UCLA following through on its promise made over a decade and a half before.

Even with a driven purpose, however, Wooden still didn't break through right away at UCLA. In fact, it took sixteen years (his 1964 UCLA team) for Wooden to win his first NCAA title. Imagine, eleven years as a high school coach, then, even

45

when on the right track, it takes another sixteen years to win the his first championship! How many people would have endured this at all, let alone persisted with Wooden's drive? Unfortunately, most people are too impatient with the success process and change too quickly thus they never invest the ten thousand hours (see Chapter Five) to develop mastery. Success cannot be dickered with; this is why focusing on one's purpose is so vital. Indeed, the eleven years of high school coaching (toiling in anonymity) and the additional sixteen years of UCLA coaching (without a title) was Wooden's testing ground, determining whether his stated purpose was important enough to him to continue on despite the setbacks. Only a few people, the few who know their purpose, can maintain their attitude and work ethic through the ups and downs of the success journey. Wooden was one of the few who believed in his teams before anyone else did. The titles merely confirmed on the outside what Wooden instilled in his teams on the inside. Wooden described his philosophy:

> *There is a standard higher than merely winning the race: Effort is the ultimate measure of success.... When it's over, I want your heads up. And there's only one way your heads can be up—that's to give it your best out there, everything you have.... To my way of thinking, when you give your total effort—everything you have—the score can never make you a loser. And when you do less, it can't somehow magically turn you into a winner.*

For most champions, it's that extra effort, when everyone else has run out of gas, that turns defeat into victory. Without fail, one discovers a purpose-centered life mixes superhuman effort with Providential blessings. For instance, look at the events that led Lew Alcindor (Kareem Abdul-Jabbar), one of the most recruited collegiate athletes ever, to choose UCLA. Because Wooden instilled pride and superior work ethic in his teams, regardless of how bad the practice conditions at the B.O. barn, his teams won two consecutive NCAA titles. The finals were aired on national TV and a young Lew Alcindor happened to be one of the fans watching the game. Naturally, Lew became intrigued with Wooden's coaching philosophy,

PURPOSE

proven success, and disciplined teams. This led to UCLA's athletic director (J. D. Morgan) to finally commit to the new Pauley Pavilion basketball facility, if Lew Alcindor would commit to UCLA. Wooden wasn't lucky, but rather blessed with one of many Serendipities of Success that results from a person persistently pursuing his purpose. Besides, LUCK is just "laboring under correct knowledge" anyway. The Alcindor years launched UCLA's dynasty and Wooden's fame. Alcindor, and later Bill Walton, played center for Wooden's teams which produced winning streaks that may never be surpassed. Wooden's UCLA teams won a record seven consecutive championships and an unbelievable eighty-eight games in a row!

Nonetheless, it's important to remember that UCLA's competitive greatness was formed much earlier. UCLA's winning ways began sixteen years earlier when a young coach created a purposeful culture founded on a simple concept: hard work applied to fulfilling one's purpose. Wooden created a leadership based upon a superior work ethic and learning daily, which overcame the subpar practice facilities and helped the team win against teams with better funding, talent, and fan base than UCLA had. Wooden's purpose and life became the shadow to form UCLA's culture of excellence. Their finest moments were the endless hours invested in the B.O. Barn, developing mastery in the game of basketball, but more importantly, in the game of life. After all, it's the superhuman commitment when no one is watching that leads to the championship teams when everyone is watching. Former heavyweight boxing champion Joe Frazier believed similarly when he highlighted the importance of running early morning miles to build his endurance: "If I cheat when the lights are out, I will be found out under the big lights." Wooden's teams never cheated the success process and, with time, success revealed its secrets to them. And, in the process, they achieved something infinitely more important than championships, namely, the self-respect one earns by giving one's personal best to fulfill one's purpose. This is the "mirror test" which asks, win or lose, did I give it my personal best? When answered affirmatively, the competitive greatness will carry one forward. However, if answered nega-

47

tively, then no amount of trophies, recognitions, or awards can hide the fact that one failed the "mirror test" and cheated himself out of self-respect. Passing the "mirror test" daily is what made Wooden who he was. Sure, to the sports world, UCLA seems to have appeared out of nowhere, lighting up the NCAA tournament regularly after 1964. But to the few in the know, those who know the rest of the story, his last twelve years of public achievements were simply the fruits of his first twenty-seven years of private achievements. Champions discover their purpose, invest untold hours developing mastery in anonymity, and then splash onto the world scene to be called the next "overnight" success. Perhaps poet Henry Wadsworth Longfellow captured it best when he wrote: "The heights by great men reached and kept / Were not attained by sudden flight, / But they, while their companions slept, / Were toiling upward in the night."

Unfortunately, many athletes and coaches today do not understand the true purpose behind sports and coaching. They are so focused on getting wins that they shortcut the success process, skipping right past private achievements to achieve public ones. Not surprisingly, however, because they avoid the private achievement foundations, the shortcuts they choose (performance enhancing drugs, recreational drugs, and publicity gimmicks), lead to their fall even faster than their rise. Wooden, in contrast, would merely counsel them to understand that winning is an internal event before it's an external one. Anytime a person cuts an internal win for an external one, they have cheated themselves internally (and eternally) for a fleeting external "victory." Dave Meyers, the captain of Wooden's last championship team, pointed to the difference between society's definition of success and Wooden's when he noted:

> *As a pro, absolutely nothing else mattered but winning. If you missed a shot or made a mistake, you were made to feel so bad about it because all eyes were on the scoreboard. Winning was all that mattered and all anybody talked about: "We've gotta win this game," or "We shoulda won that game," or "How can we win the next game?" Win. Win. Win.*

PURPOSE

Coach Wooden didn't talk about winning—ever. His message was to give the game the best you've got. "That's the goal," he would tell us. "Do that and you should be happy. If enough of you do it, our team will be a success." He teaches this, he believes it, and he taught me to believe it.

Wooden taught the players he coached the importance of purpose in winning and losing in life, for if one handles the inner scoreboard, the outer scoreboard takes care of itself. Imagine the impact on society if this philosophy were adopted by the top leaders in every field. Leaders, instead of just emphasizing the outer scoreboard of life, would teach people to achieve their purpose by succeeding in the inner scoreboard by passing the "mirror test." After all, when enough people in a community pass the "mirror test," the external scoreboard is practically assured. True champions understand the internal scoreboard is more important than the external one, because only when a person achieves victory in the first can they truly achieve victory in the second. Moreover, because one can always grow internally, the motivation to improve perseveres regardless of how many victories and outside recognitions one has racked up.

John Robert Wooden passed away on June 4, 2010, after completing ninety-nine years of purposeful living. His life modeled his message and is summed up nicely in Grantland Rice's words: "For when the One Great Scorer comes to mark against your name, He writes— not that you won or lost—but how you played the game." Wooden knew how to play the game of life, modeling character, passion, and hard work to all who knew him. He leaves a powerful legacy by passing the baton of excellence to the next generation of leaders.

Shortly before his death, Wooden wrote these poignant words: "I am ready to meet Him [the Lord] and I am eager to see my wife, Nellie." Wooden is with his Lord and wife today, having fulfilled his life's purpose by hearing the words, "Well done, thou good and faithful servant."

CHAPTER 2

CHARACTER
Resolved: To Choose Character over Reputation Any Time They Conflict

*I know that my character is who I am, and my reputation
is only what others say that I am.*
—Orrin Woodward

*To sin by silence when they should protest makes
cowards of men.*
—Abraham Lincoln

In a person's life, he will have many opportunities to choose between character and reputation. To consistently make character-based choices, however, he must understand the separate aspects that combine together to make sterling character.

Integrity

Integrity is essential for leadership, because without it, people will not follow the leader for long. They will tire of the leader's words not matching up with his actions. Of course, even when leaders have integrity, they still receive criticism from others without integrity. Nevertheless, leaders of integrity expect to be believed, and when they are not, they let time prove them right. Author Mark Sanborn explained the importance of integrity to leadership: "When integrity ceases to be a leader's top priority, when a compromise of ethics is rationalized away as necessary for the 'greater good,' when achieving results becomes more important than the means to their achievement—that is the moment when a leader steps onto the slippery slope of failure. It is imperative to your leadership that you constantly subject your life and work to the highest scrutiny." Words like honorable, honest, trustworthy, dutiful, and faithful describe a person with integrity.

History is filled with examples of men and women who developed integrity based upon moral precepts. In America, for instance, at the turn of the twentieth century, one could pass through nearly every Midwest town (known as the Bible Belt) and discover a community nurtured on moral absolutes. In one such small town, Joshua Wooden, a farmer, taught his young son John the meaning of integrity. Here were the three principles that John Wooden carried with him every day for the rest of his life.

John Wooden's Three Principles

1. Never lie.
2. Never cheat.
3. Never steal.

Imagine how simple life would be if everyone followed these principles, for these are essential to becoming a person of integrity and building the trust necessary for leadership. Everyone must compare his actions to these three absolute principles. These three rules help a person determine if he is playing the game of life straight. As C. S. Lewis once remarked, "A man does not call a line crooked unless he has some idea of a straight line." Needless to say, no one will freely follow a leader who violates these three principles since people will only follow leaders as far as they trust them. No trust, no leadership.

Never Lie

The first principle (Never lie) indicates a person's worth is his word. This demands the person speaks the truth, which over time leads to trust. When a person states the facts as they are, rather than as he wishes them to be, he is being truthful. Unfortunately, many people fall into the habit of lying because they want to impress others with their "amazing" stories and accomplishments. While the truth may not be as impressive, it is the truth and that is what should be shared. Nonetheless, many people, through being more concerned with their reputation than their integrity, choose to exaggerate and manufacture lies rather than tell the truth, evidently

> **The first principle (Never lie) indicates a person's worth is his word.**

CHARACTER

choosing to appear impressive rather than be impressive. What an odd perspective of what is truly important!

Author Jack Canfield observed, "In reality, lying is the product of low self-esteem—the belief that you and your abilities are not good enough to get what you want…the false belief that you cannot handle the consequences of people knowing the truth about you—which is simply another way of saying, 'I am not good enough.'" Lies warp a person's character over time, making it difficult to discern fact from fiction in the liar's mind. The biblical belief system teaches that lying comes from the author of all lies—Satan. Thus, the more a person lies, the more his conscience becomes hardened and the more difficult it is to tell the truth the next time. Outside of God's grace, the hardened liar would be trapped in his own web of deceit and mass of fabrications. As Walter Scott noted many years ago, Change this sentence to - "Oh! What a tangled web we weave, when first we practice to deceive!" Tell the truth, the whole truth, and nothing but the truth when speaking to others and self. In fact, the exception to this rule is when the truth will hurt a person more than help them, at which point the tactful thing is to say nothing rather than a hurtful truth. Gossip is another exception; just because a person has truth does not mean he should kill another person's reputation, usually in an effort to make his own look better. In this example, unless a person is sharing truth with someone in a position to resolve a conflict, it's best not to share anything, protecting another's reputation by maintaining silence. Not sharing hurtful truths is not lying but instead loving others by practicing tact.

People of integrity protect others' reputations while examining their own hearts for hypocrisy. Doesn't it make sense that in order to speak truthfully to others, one must start by speaking truthfully to oneself? This is tougher than it sounds because our minds constantly want to make ourselves look better compared to others. Martin Luther, the great Reformer, once wrote, "Unless a man is always humble, distrustful of himself, always fearing his own understanding and passions, he will be unable to stand for long without offense. Truth will pass him by." A person must be on guard, always remaining vigilant, because he will not speak truth to others if he is lying to himself. C. S. Lewis observed the principle, writing, "When a man is getting better he understands more clearly the evil that is still left in him…. A moderately bad man knows he is not very good; a thoroughly bad man thinks he is all right." Do not be deceived; internal lies always lead to external ones.

Never Cheat

The second principle (Never cheat) ensures a person maintains integrity by never harming others to benefit self. Cheating destroys the trust of others, for who would trust someone who cheated them? Ironically, because cheating ruins the trust necessary for leadership, the person who cheats ends up cheating himself the most. Think about it; if a person is bragging about how he cheated someone, isn't he most likely to cheat others if given the opportunity? Either a person is trustworthy or he isn't and this all begins with personal integrity. There is no honor among thieves and associating with liars, cheaters, and stealers can only damage your integrity. Like the old saying states, "You become what you associate with."

Cheating may appear to be a shortcut to success, but in reality, it's a dead end. Don't be fooled by people who seem to get away with cheating because the chickens always come home to roost. Dishonest leaders cannot maintain trust, which forces them to do more work for less results because they are always replacing their community of followers. Integrity many seem old-fashioned, but it's foundational for all true success. Great movements are built by people of principle who follow through on their word and fulfilling their commitments, without needing legal coercion to force them to do the right thing. Socrates taught, "If it were necessary to do or to suffer injustice, I would choose rather to suffer than to do injustice." Whereas suffering injustice may hurt temporarily, performing an injustice hurts permanently, damaging the soul. A person cheats himself when he cheats, even if he can get away with it; the damage done internally is incalculable.

Tennis professional Andy Roddick modeled integrity and honor in a 2005 Italia Masters tournament in Rome. It was match point, and he needed only one more point to win the match. Fernando Verdasco's second serve was called "out" by the line judge, which would have given Roddick the match. But, in a move as rare as it is honorable, Roddick refused to accept the point. Instead, he patiently explained to the line judge that the serve was actually "in," pointing to a faint indentation on the clay court directly on the white line. Verdasco, having already conceded defeat, had moved to the net, believing the match was over. Roddick, however, refused to accept a victory he knew he hadn't earned, because he believed his integrity was worth more than a fake victory. The line judge, impressed by Roddick's honesty, overruled his call, and the match continued. Verdasco made a surprising comeback and eventually

CHARACTER

won the tennis match. Nevertheless, Roddick won a bigger victory, namely, victory over self. Roddick's display of personal integrity is now part of ethics classes around the world. In fact, Stephen M. R. Covey has defined "Roddick's choice" as the ability to demonstrate integrity even when it's costly to do so. The line judge might have called the serve "out," but Roddick knew the truth and refused to accept the erroneous call because he knew he would have cheated Verdasco and the fans to benefit himself. Roddick believed his integrity and self-respect were more important than maintaining his win-loss percentage, a standard of ethics worthy of emulation.

Never Steal

The third principle (Never steal) is another essential for building leadership trust. If a person steals from others, he forfeits the trust of that person and the rest of the team who is aware of the lack of integrity. Strikingly, one of the biggest reasons for the decline in economic productivity is the stealing epidemic that exists in society today. For example, Robert Half Personnel staffing agency has estimated that time theft alone is costing the American economy approximately $70 billion a year; this is equivalent to the annual revenues of conglomerates the size of Boeing, Walgreens, and Apple, to name just a few. Time theft, the deliberate misuse of time by employees while one the company clock, causes permanent damage to production and profitability.

Curiously, many who wouldn't dare steal directly from their employers' wallets or purses have no qualms indirectly stealing time and their hourly wage from them. What exactly is the difference? Perhaps one is easier to get away with, but it is stealing regardless. Some may argue that physically stealing would end in job termination where time stealing would only be a warning. However, if his only reason for not stealing is the fear of getting caught, then one's integrity is already in need of work. After all, integrity is not concerned with the outside consequences but rather the inside ones.

These three principles certainly improve economic production, but they are worth much more than improved output, for the foundation of a person's character is personal integrity. When this aspect is considered, the value of these three principles is priceless. Sure, a person who steals from others may gain materially in the short-term, but only by robbing himself of his character, a

> **Commit now to never lie, never cheat, and never steal.**

55

much more costly long-term eternal loss. This isn't a good exchange on any terms.

Commit now to never lie, never cheat, and never steal. No matter how many people sell out their personal integrity, do not stoop to this level. Two wrongs, or more, can never make anything right. Author Chuck Colson challenged Harvard Business School situational ethics, claiming that its commitment to philosophical relativism has ruined the foundation necessary for ethics in the real world. Colson spoke to Harvard MBAs, titling his talk "Why Harvard Can't Teach Ethics," and later described the event:

> *I expected a riot after my 45-minute talk in a packed lecture hall. But the students were docile; I didn't hear a single good question. Were the students so unfamiliar with moral philosophy they didn't know enough to challenge me?*
>
> *I left Harvard worried. What would happen to these students when they became leaders of American business? One of the students at Harvard during that period was Jeffrey Skilling, the now-discredited former Enron CEO.*
>
> *Enron's collapse exposes the glaring failure of the academy. Ethics historically rests on absolute truth, which these institutions have systematically assaulted for four decades.*

Fortunately, Wooden's three principles are absolute principles, not relativistic recommendations, and have been the foundation for ethics since man's creation.

Character

Personal integrity is crucial to a leader's success, but it is not sufficient by itself to ensure unimpeachable character. To move from integrity to character, one must combine courage with integrity. Courage, the strength to follow one's convictions even when it hurts, is a rare trait today. Whereas integrity is not doing the wrong thing, character goes further and does the right thing. For example, suppose John, an older boy, bullied young Billy at school. Tom watched the incident happen but didn't participate. Tom displayed integrity, by not joining the bully, but he did not display character. Tom, to display character, should have moved beyond personal integrity (not doing wrong) and mustered his courage to confront the bullying injustice by defending young Billy. Character, in other words, applies both integrity to determine what is right and the courage to address situations that aren't right. Integrity doesn't participate in wrong, but character displays the courage

CHARACTER

of one's convictions to participate in righting the wrong. People of character risk personal peace, affluence, and safety for the sake of justice. Integrity (refusing to do wrong) is good, but character (the courage to do right) is even better. When Tom confronts John and ends the bullying of Billy, he has moved from integrity to character.

This is easier said than done because addressing wrongs can create enemies. Hence, many choose the easier path of not doing wrong with the comfort of non-involvement rather than the discomfort of tactful confrontation. A person, regretfully, who fears conflict more than hypocrisy usually ends up surrendering his principles for peace. This is the beginning of the end for character, for inevitably, every loss in character begins when convictions are compromised for convenience. Leaders know that character comes at a price, especially when moral stands must be made, moral stands that upset those who choose comfort; but character-based leaders cannot do otherwise, for one's reputation is not as important as one's character. Wooden said it best, "Be more concerned with your character than your reputation, because your character is what you really are, while your reputation is merely what others think you are."

Character is that special quality inside a person that enhances all his other virtues, making him appear larger than life. In truth, without character, none of the other resolutions matter since character is the mortar that strengthens all the other resolutions. All the resolutions without character are like building a house of cards on top of quicksand. After all, character is more than what a person says or even what he does; it's simply who he is.

Developing Character

Still, even after acknowledging that character is more important than reputation, how exactly does one develop character? The simple, but not easy, answer is contained in the formula: character = integrity × courage. This formula indicates the relationship between each of the attributes. Author C. S. Lewis highlighted the importance of courage when he wrote, "Courage is not simply one of the virtues, but the form of every virtue at the testing point." Therefore, a person of integrity who is without courage fails the test and lacks the character to stand his ground when his highest principles are challenged. It's only at the testing point, as a matter of fact, when his integrity and courage are stretched to the limit that a person's character is determined.

Character demands courage and this is the virtue most lacking in today's culture. Most people would rather enjoy peace and afflu-

57

ence, minding their own business, than standing against injustice, especially if the injustice is not directed towards them. People of character, however, respond differently, knowing that by refusing to check injustice, they are tacitly supporting it. Reverend Martin Niemoeller, a Nazi prison camp survivor, explained, "First they arrested the Communists—but I was not a Communist, so I did nothing. Then they came for the Social Democrats—but I was not a Social Democrat, so I did nothing. Then they arrested the trade unionists—and I did nothing because I was not one. And then they came for the Jews and then the Catholics, but I was neither a Jew nor a Catholic and I did nothing. At last they came and arrested me—and there was no one left to do anything about it." So many times, injustice spreads, not because everyone approves, but rather because too few people have the courage to disapprove, and instead of shining light into darkness, they hide in the dark themselves. Character acts, even when it's uncomfortable, to end injustice.

Perhaps just as puzzling a question for a person with courage in today's relativistic age is determining what principles are worth sacrificing for. For without moral absolutes, a compass to discern right from wrong, anything is permissible. Who says stealing is wrong? What if 51% of the people voted in favor of stealing, does that really make it right? Moral absolutes then are not based on votes but on the moral order inherent in the world. Biblical principles were foundational to building modern civilization, even when they weren't practiced consistently; at least we had a standard to call out hypocrites. Without a standard, there are no hypocrites because no absolutes are claimed. This moral foundation produces freedom with order, wealth with morality, and charity with love, which makes progress possible in the various fields of civilization. Although these principles have never been applied perfectly, and with notable moments of hypocrisy, Western civilization has advanced the cause of truth in the physical, mental, and spiritual realms greatly. Dismally, however, for the past one hundred years, the moral order is decaying, rotting at its roots. Naturally, this rot has led to a subsequent decline in freedom, order, wealth, morality, charity, and love. Is mankind truly secure when it consists of technological giants and moral midgets? To restore character, then, leaders must restore their courage, which is fed from having convictions worth sacrificing for.

Courage Isn't Pragmatism

Courage is a person's choice to get involved in defending his highest principles, even when his own personal interest isn't at

CHARACTER

stake. Courage isn't pragmatism, a determination to get involved only if it enhances one's position, power, or wealth; rather, as author Gus Lee explained, "Courage doesn't depend on practical outcomes, risk versus gains analysis, or collateral impact on others—that's pragmatism. Pragmatism is the application of practicality, utility and consequences to decision making." Courage is principle-based, causing leaders with courage to sacrifice personal benefits to defend what is right. Winston Churchill boasted, "Courage is rightly esteemed the first of human qualities…because it is the quality which guarantees all others." Perhaps the reason we have so few people with courage is because we have lost any convictions worth sacrificing for. Why, in other words, would anyone display courage if he doesn't think the ideal is worth sacrificing for? Lee observed, "Courage is addressing wrongs in the face of fear, regardless of consequences, of risk to self, or of potential practical gains. That's why everyone practices pragmatism and risk balancing…. Courageous leadership is about utilizing all of our brains, character and spirit to advocate principles regardless of the odds, heedless of fear, apart from collateral impact, and independent of personal career needs." Leaders of this quality are a dying breed today. Les Csorba described the debilitating effects of pragmatism on character-centered leadership: "When we follow leaders without a moral compass interested in only results, get ready for the ditch. The ditch into which modern leadership has fallen is the pit of pragmatism." Many confuse compromise and pragmatism, but Yale law professor Stephen L. Carter, pinpointed the difference: "Compromises that advance high principles are acceptable; those that do not advance high principles are not."

Pragmatism, then, is compromising one's highest principles for short-term personal advancements. Courage, on the other hand, accepts only noble compromises, willingly sacrificing personal gains to advance one's highest principles. Robert Morrisette explained, "I have heard it said that courage is not the absence of fear, but the perception that there is something far more important at stake. Having such a 'something' gives us the ability to resist giving in to fear and to eventually rise above it. It is only in the presence of fear that true courage can be exercised, but without this 'something,' how can we see beyond those things we're afraid of?" If a leader's objectives aren't important enough for him to face his fears, then he isn't going to experience much success in leadership. Imagine, if David hadn't had the courage to face Goliath, he would have simply compromised his faith for a false peace. Furthermore, he would have remained an unknown shepherd boy instead of becom-

59

ing the king of Israel. In the same way, people without the courage to confront their Goliaths will not achieve leadership mastery because they refuse to confront and learn from challenges. Courage, in today's pragmatic world, is a lost virtue that must be rebirthed in order for character-based leadership to thrive again.

Professor Howard Hendricks said, "The greatest crisis in America is a crisis of leadership, and the greatest crisis of leadership is a crisis of character." Leadership is character in motion; without character, there cannot be leadership. Above all, one cannot develop character just by reading, thinking, and speaking (although these help). Instead, character is forged on the front lines under intense pressure with many around the leader appealing for him to compromise. Interestingly, character isn't a binary switch; it doesn't divide people into two groups, one with character and the other without. Instead, think of character less like an on/off switch and more like a dimmer switch. A few people have no character at all, a few have sterling character that cannot be purchased, and the masses fall into the dial range, where they move from little to a lot of character but have some price at which point they sell out. Perhaps, the prices at which a person would sell out others to benefit personally are the best measure of a person's character. Some sell out others for the most marginal of gains whereas a person of character will not sell out others for any price. A leader will not know for sure where he stands until his day of testing and every leader will have his test. The threatened loss of money is usually where character is revealed the quickest. The question is: Would the leader sell out others to protect himself? If he would, then his character is lacking.

> **The greatest crisis in America is a crisis of leadership, and the greatest crisis of leadership is a crisis of character.**
> **—Howard Hendricks**

Exploiters versus Producers

There are only two distinct paths a person can take in life. He can either choose to produce results through performance or search for ways to exploit other people's production. The question is: At what price does he switch from being a producer to being an exploiter? This is the price at which one sells out his character. People of character refuse to sell out at any price, but people without character pragmatically look for opportunities to sell to the highest bidder, sacrificing character for personal profits. Producers create value by serving other people's needs, while exploiters

CHARACTER

plunder from producers to serve their own needs. If producers do not satisfy their customers, either directly in the service industries or indirectly by creating products that are desired, they will fail in business. Since producers do not look for handouts, only hand-ups, they must have character in order to build trust with their customers. For without character, the customers' trust will be broken, driving customers to competitors who have been proven trustworthy. Producers focus on building long-term relationships through character, serving customers in a win-win fashion and developing repeat business.

Exploiters, on the other hand, produce nothing or next to nothing. They rely on privileged positions gained through their political maneuverings and are rewarded by other people's labors. Lord Acton said, "Power corrupts; absolute power corrupts absolutely." In reality, absolute power doesn't corrupt; it just reveals a person's character. His willingness to exploit is always present, lying dormant until his increased power places him in a position to reveal his lack of character by exploiting others. Exploiters love to live parasitically off producers, fattening themselves from fruits produced in others' gardens. Exploiters flock to professions where performance is difficult to measure; positions in government, bureaucratic corporations, and even large religious or charitable organizations all fit the bill. These fields are ripe for exploiters because here, they can more easily hide from the real customers and advance through office politics, not customer service. Any field protected from market-place realities will see exploiters increase and producers decrease. The higher a person's character is, the harder it is to buy him, for he resists all offers or threats intended to bend his character to an exploiter's will. However, most people do have a price, selling out their character for the rewards offered and surrendering their alleged principles for their pocketbooks or peace.

> **Producers create value by serving other people's needs, while exploiters plunder from producers to serve their own needs.**

Exploitation and Plunder

Frédéric Bastiat, a great nineteenth century French economist and statesman, wrote:

> *Now since man is naturally inclined to avoid pain—and since labor is pain in itself—it follows that men will resort to plunder whenever plunder is easier than work. History shows this quite clearly. And under these conditions, neither*

religion nor morality can stop it. When, then, does plunder stop? It stops when it becomes more painful and more dangerous than labor. It is evident, then, that the proper purpose of law is to use the power of its collective force to stop this fatal tendency to plunder instead of to work. All the measures of the law should protect property and punish plunder.

Absolute power opens an avenue for plunder, creating opportunities for exploitation and allowing the few to make money without serving the many. Since there aren't any free lunches in life, this "something for nothing" (SFN) is paid for by others in society who get "nothing for something". Indeed, when a person exploits another through coercion, he has stolen another individual's time, effort, and just reward. Just because someone has the power to exploit does not means it's right to do so. As writer Horace Greeley explained, "The darkest hour in any man's life is when he sits down to plan how to get money without earning it."

It takes people with impeccable personal character to withstand the temptation to exploit, choosing principles over profits by refusing to personally gain at the expense of others. In the annals of history, there are only a few recorded instances of people, like Cincinnatus or George Washington, willingly surrendering power for the sake of justice.

Self-Betrayal and Character

Perhaps the fatal flaw to success, a flaw so personal and painful that most people avoid its truth at all costs, an avoidance that derails more dreams than all other obstacles combined, is self-betrayal. Self-betrayal is part of personal character. After all, as stated previously, leadership is character in motion and how can someone have character if he betrays himself?

Self-betrayal begins the moment a person does not follow through on his personal commitments. This type of betrayal is so difficult to detect because it's so subtle. For instance, maybe the reader set a goal to get up early and study or exercise before work, but when the alarm went off, you quickly shut it off and rationalized you needed sleep more than following through on your commitment to yourself. Of course, this "little" lie fuels further compromises and before long, lying to oneself has become a habit. In fact, any time you make a commitment to yourself, and do not follow through, you have taught yourself that lying is acceptable. This is where most people fail—personal character to one's self. I know. I know. No one likes to be called a liar, but how many times have you committed to do something and didn't follow through?

CHARACTER

I'm not talking about commitments to others, but rather personal commitments.

I still remember the day, reading underneath a huge maple tree at lunch, when Stephen Covey kicked me below the belt. He said, "Many times success begins with mind over mattress!" Ugh! That one hurt, because I had made hundreds of excuses for why I just couldn't be more disciplined in Bible studies, believing I had too much work to do. Covey's statement changed my perspective, helping me realize that my self-betrayal had already progressed into self-deception, and I had convinced myself that lying was ok if it was only to myself. In reality, however, if one cannot tell the truth to himself, he stands no chance of telling the truth to others. Internal character, in a word, always precedes external character.

Today's age doesn't like self-analysis much, probably because these matters hit too close to home for most people and if thought upon for long, they would have to address some of the personal issues. Nevertheless, I believe self-deception is the biggest killer of dreams in the world! People deceive themselves to avoid changing, but the price for this avoidance is their own success. The self-betrayal blooms into self-denial and then people become offended if others dare to question their impeccable character. Most people react defensively, thinking, "How dare anyone question my character when I have spent years rationalizing it to myself?"

In all seriousness, I have never given a talk, nor written anything, without the guns first being directed at myself. I, along with every other human being, cannot live my ideals 100% of the time. I am in need of the grace just as much, if not more, than the reader. Still, why get offended by the truth? How is this going to help anyone change? Indeed, when a person gets offended at unpalatable facts, it's a sure sign that self-betrayal is already leading to self-deception. Truth has been sacrificed on the altar of personal ego.

Thankfully, there is a remedy for self-betrayal. The Bible states, "those who are faithful in the little things will be faithful in the bigger things." Did you catch that? Character begins by being faithful in the little things that if avoided, no one would know but you. Many believe this is ok, since you didn't let anyone else down, but this is a lie from the depths of Hell. For a person who would have no qualms about lying to himself, a self he typically loves more than any other human being alive, will not be a truth-teller to others. Internal lies lead to external ones. If anything, compromises in personal character lead to greater compromises in one's relationships with others.

Consequently, true character begins with character to self. Once the war for personal character is accomplished, the authentic individual is now ready to treat others with the same level of character. Not surprisingly, in today's age of self-betrayal and self-deception, it's pretty much a given that leaders with character will suffer attacks from those who have self-betrayed themselves. Since leaders with character grow big communities, simply by the law of averages, they will have people who perpetually lie to themselves join their community. Naturally, albeit ironically, the people who have cheated and lied to themselves the most are the ones who shout the loudest that others have lied and cheated them. Playing the victim, evidently, is their key strategy for not having to address the lies keeping them from success.

The simple, but painful, truth is no matter how much a leader wants to help others, he truly can't help them until they are ready to help themselves. Self-liars must confront reality and admit it's their own lies keeping them in bondage. For when people resist truth they are also fighting the change that would set them free. Nonetheless, when people have spent a lifetime betraying themselves, giving up for the umpteenth time in life, their self-deception quickly identifies the reason for the failure and they play the victim card once again. Self-deception has so entrapped them in a web of lies that the truth can no longer set them free. Thus, they are sentenced to a life of victimhood unless God's graces pierce the veil and wakes them up to this eternal truth, namely, as Shakespeare said, "The fault, dear Brutus, is not in our stars, but in ourselves, that we are underlings."

Heraclitus once said, "Character is fate" and I concur. Character is an inside job and only those who develop character will ever see long-term success. Start today! What is a personal commitment the reader can make to himself, his family, or his community? Make the commitment and keep it! Quit betraying yourself and your dreams! Quit playing the blame game! This is your mind over mattress, or to add others, life over lies, and purpose over Pokémon moment!

Character Plus Competence Equals Trust

Even if a person has the character to not join the SFN club, and not betray himself, he still must do more, adding competence to character to produce trust. Stephen M. R. Covey wrote, "Trust is a function of two things: character and competence. Character includes integrity, your motive, and your intent with people. Competence includes your capabilities, your skills, your results, and your track record. Both are vital." It takes a competent character-based leader, therefore, to propose plans that move his company forward. Covey described how trust creates speed in an organization by peo-

CHARACTER

ple not needing every 'i' dotted and every 't' crossed. Since the followers trust the leader, they know that details will be worked out properly, creating business at the speed of trust. When enough people with character and competence join together, they create trusting communities that change the world, one person and one team at a time. In order to create a team that creates change, one must build or find leaders who influence their teams with the principles found in the 13 resolutions. Edmund Burke called those low-profile leaders members of the 'little platoons.' Chuck Colson, creator of a little platoon that grew into a large group of small platoons (Prison Fellowship), believes little platoons led by common people with uncommon character can rejuvenate society. History records many examples of a brave minority, who, tired of the state of decline in their society, built leadership platoons of change through the trust formed by the convergence of character and competence, creating a tipping point for change and altering the course of history. Without jumping too far ahead in the resolutions, it's safe to say that positive change cannot happen without a moral foundation of character. A person of character, standing on his principles, influences more people than a thousand who have surrendered to the SFN club. Be a producer in life by refusing to fall into self-betrayal. Refuse to make decisions based on conveniences; instead, make decisions based upon character.

Be a producer in life.

J. R. R. Tolkien, in his novel *The Lord of the Rings: The Two Towers*, provided a powerful example of courageous leadership against all odds:

> **Frodo**. *I can't do this, Sam.*
>
> **Sam**. *I know. It's all wrong. By rights we shouldn't even be here. But we are. It's like in the great stories, Mr. Frodo. The ones that really mattered. Full of darkness and danger they were. And sometimes you didn't want to know the end. Because how could the end be happy?...But I think, Mr. Frodo, I do understand. I know now. Folk in those stories had lots of chances of turning back, only they didn't because they were holding on to something.*
>
> **Frodo**. *What were they holding on to, Sam?*
>
> **Sam**. *That there's some good in this world, Mr. Frodo, and it's worth fighting for.*

RESOLVED

Ludwig von Mises: Indomitable Character

The twentieth century Austrian economist, Ludwig von Mises, stood for economics truth against the many economic falsehoods of his day. In particular, he defended free enterprise and classical liberalism when nearly everyone was moving in the Statist direction. Mises taught how economic liberty promotes liberty in general:

In the market economy the consumers are supreme. Consumers determine, by their buying or abstention from buying, what should be produced, by whom and how, of what quality and in what quantity. The entrepreneurs, capitalists, and landowners who fail to satisfy in the best possible and cheapest way the most urgent of the not yet satisfied wishes of the consumers are forced to go out of business and forfeit their preferred position. . . . The fundamental principle of capitalism is mass production to supply the masses. It is the patronage of the masses that makes enterprises grow into bigness. The common man is supreme in the market economy. He is the customer "who is always right."

Whereas most economists jostled for the perks and preferment offered to those who would share Statist's doctrines, like government intervention and economic controls, Mises refused to join the stampede. Even more disheartening to Mises, many of the economists recognized the Statist errors in the Keynesian framework and yet taught them anyway. These economists chose career advancement over character development, surrendering their convictions for their conveniences. Mises, in contrast, who viewed himself as an economic scientist, stated: "In science, compromise is a betrayal of truth." His character forbade him practice deceit, the deceit of teaching a doctrine filled with logical fallacies. Mises believed the Keynesian system supported economic theft and damaged private property. Thus, he concluded, "If history could teach us anything, it would be that private property is inextricably linked with civilization." Private property is not the public's property and no one, argued Mises, had the right

CHARACTER

to steal another person's property. In Mises' mind, this was a matter of character, not just economic theory, for who has the right to legalize stealing even if 51% of the people vote for it? Naturally, this wasn't a popular stand in the first half of the twentieth century and the Mises family barely made it out of Europe ahead of the Nazi takeover. Author Jörg Hülsmann, wrote:

> *Mises was two months shy of his fifty-ninth birthday. He was on the invaders' list of wanted men. Two years earlier, they had ransacked his Vienna apartment, confiscating his records and freezing his assets. Mises then hoped to be safe in Geneva. Now nowhere in Europe seemed safe. Not only was he a prominent intellectual of Jewish descent; he was widely known to be an arch-enemy of National Socialism and of every other form of socialism. Some called him "the last knight of liberalism."*
>
> *He had personally steered Austria away from Bolshevism, saved his country from the level of hyperinflation that destroyed inter-war Germany, and convinced a generation of young socialist intellectuals to embrace the market. Now he was a political refugee headed for a foreign continent.*
>
> *The couple arrived in the United States with barely any money and no prospects for income. Mises's former students and disciples had found prestigious positions in British and American universities (often with his help), but Mises himself was considered an anachronism. In an age of growing government and central planning, he was a defender of private property and an opponent of all government intervention in the economy. Perhaps worst of all, he was a proponent of verbal logic and realism in the beginning heyday of positivism and mathematical modeling. No university would have him. Margit began to train as a secretary.*

At a time when most people are planning retirement, Mises was forced to start over, rebuilding his professional career in an environment that was openly hostile to the free-market system he espoused. Thankfully, Mises's voice and pen of reason did not go unnoticed for long. Over the next decade, Mises made many friends in the pursuit of economic truth. Somehow, despite the challenges, Mises published his most important book, *Human Action*, one of the classics of economic literature, during this painful period. With courage and reason, Mises systematically pinpointed the errors of and logically destroyed the theories of Socialism and Fascism, strengthening the growing intellectual resistance to Statism. Needless to say, Mises was a man of character, a man without a price, who lived his life according to Virgil's Latin motto, "Tu ne cede malis sed contra audentior ito," which translates, "Do not give in to evil, but proceed ever more boldly against it." True to his motto, Mises did just that as the late dean of the Austrian School, Murray Rothbard described:

> Holding these views, and hewing to truth indomitably in the face of a century increasingly devoted to Statism and collectivism, Mises became famous for his "intransigence" in insisting on a non-inflationary gold standard and on laissez-faire. Effectively barred from any paid university post in Austria and later in the United States, Mises pursued his course gallantly. As the chief economic adviser to the Austrian government in the 1920s, Mises was single-handedly able to slow down Austrian inflation and he developed his own "private seminar" which attracted the outstanding young economists, social scientists, and philosophers throughout Europe. As the founder of the "Neo-Austrian School" of economics, Mises's business cycle theory, which blamed inflation and depressions on inflationary bank credit encouraged by Central Banks, was adopted by most younger economists in England in the early 1930s as the best explanation of the Great Depression.

In an age when practically every doctoral economist was moving towards Statism in the form of Nazism, Fascism, Socialism, Communism, and the Keynesian New Deal, Mises stood his ground on truth, knowing that time would prove him

CHARACTER

right. People of character refuse to go along with the crowd, especially when the crowd is wrong. Regardless of the personal and professional consequences, Mises refused to teach what he knew wasn't true. He simply could not be bought at any price. The consequences, admittedly, were high, for Mises was passed over for tenured positions while his students, who surrendered their convictions for conveniences, consistently received tenured posts. Perhaps nothing displays Mises's character any better than this, sacrificing his family's financial security to maintain intellectual honesty. Mises knew Keynesian thought was wrong and refused to benefit from it by helping destroy society's health. As Rothbard explained:

> *For Mises was able to demonstrate (a) that the expansion of free markets, the division of labor, and private capital investment is the only possible path to the prosperity and flourishing of the human race; (b) that socialism would be disastrous for a modern economy because the absence of private ownership of land and capital goods prevents any sort of rational pricing, or estimate of costs, and (c) that government intervention, in addition to hampering and crippling the market, would prove counter-productive and cumulative, leading inevitably to Socialism unless the entire tissue of interventions was repealed.*

Today, Mises sounds prophetic for having predicted so much that has come to pass including the Communist collapse and the boom/bust instability caused by the fraudulent banking system. In consequence, many economists are finally waking up to the fact that Mises was right all along. For example, nearly sixty years before Communism fell apart in the Soviet Union and the Eastern Bloc, Mises wrote, "Without calculation, economic activity is impossible. Since under Socialism economic calculation is impossible, under Socialism there can be no economic activity in our sense of the word ... All economic change, therefore, would involve operations, the value of which could neither be predicted beforehand nor ascertained after they had taken place. Everything would be a leap in the dark. Socialism is the renunciation of a rational economy." Time, in other words, had proven Mises right. Character, the intellectual honesty to speak truth no matter what the consequences, is who Mises was. Furthermore, few things reveal a person's character as quickly as how he responds when his income is threatened. Mises passed this test with flying colors also, because he refused to compromise when his character was on the line. In fact, popular Keynesian economist Robert Heilbroner, in a classy act of professionalism, acknowledged Mises's (and the Austrian schools') contributions. For after Communism's surprising worldwide collapse (at least surprising to the Keynesians), Heilbroner conceded the Keynesians' intellectual defeat and confessed:

> But what spokesman of the present generation has anticipated the demise of Socialism or the "triumph of Capitalism"? Not a single writer in the Marxian tradition! Are there any in the left centrist group? None I can think of, including myself. As for the center itself—the Samuelsons, Solows, Glazers, Lipsets, Bells, and so on—I believe that many have expected Capitalism to experience serious and mounting, if not fatal, problems and have anticipated some form of Socialism to be the organizing force of the twenty-first century
>
> Here is the part that's hard to swallow. It has been the Friedmans, Hayeks, von Miseses, e tutti quanti who have maintained that Capitalism would flourish and that Socialism would develop incurable ailments. Mises called Socialism "impossible" because it has no means of establishing a rational pricing system; Hayek added additional reasons of a sociological kind ("the worst rise on top"). All three have regarded Capitalism as the "natural" system of free men; all have maintained that left to its own devices Capitalism would achieve material growth more successfully than any other system.

Heilbroner confronted the facts surrounding Socialism's demise rather than making excuses. He studied the economists' works, reviewed the historical data, and realized that Mises and his followers were correct. They had accurately

CHARACTER

predicted the collapse of the Communists, Socialists, and the Keynesian mixed system decades before it actually occurred. Heilbroner discussed the "elephant in the room" avoided by today's Statist-oriented economists—the lack of results wherever Socialism is instituted. To use a Southern saying—that dog doesn't hunt. Whereas previously Mises was laughed at, now he was lauded. Mises may not have lived to witness it, but his economic ideas expounding that even powerful States cannot violate economic law was proven in practice. Government intervention, far from being an economic miracle, is a destroyer of society's health as Mises noted: "The worship of the State is the worship of force. There is no more dangerous menace to civilization than a government of incompetent, corrupt, or vile men. The worst evils which mankind ever had to endure were inflicted by bad governments. The State can be and has often been in the course of history the main source of mischief and disaster." The State is a false-god. Unfortunately, however, once economic errors make their way into the classrooms, it becomes difficult to eradicate. Without students who think and learn outside of the classrooms, economic errors can threaten society. As Mises emphasized, "Everyone carries a part of society on his shoulders; no one is relieved of his share of responsibility by others. And no one can find a safe way out for himself if society is sweeping toward destruction. Therefore, everyone, in his own interests, must thrust himself vigorously into the intellectual battle. None can stand aside with unconcern; the interest of everyone hangs on the result. Whether he chooses or not, every man is drawn into the great historical struggle, the decisive battle into which our epoch has plunged us."

Mises even explained why the power of the State and political leaders increased; namely, they used the banking system to fund the welfare/warfare state through increasing national debt. Needless to say, Mises recognized the same root cause that drove economists to support increased State powers and which also drove other groups to align with the State for perks and profits. After all, just as "Follow the Money" (FTM) was the motive behind the economists' support of Statism, so too did other groups support Statism to benefit themselves. The FTM and its brother SFN combined to seduce the political, Big Banks, and Big Corporate leadership to sup-

71

port the State for their benefit. Free markets and liberty, in a word, were doomed. No longer does the State have to increase taxes in order to increase its income; instead, it can simply borrow more money from the central bank system eagerly supported by the economists who benefit by doing so. Where are the men and women who will expose this system for what it is—a system to benefit the few at the expense of the many. What is lacking, above all, is people who are "sold outs" to truth and justice, rather than "sell outs" to profits and perks. Ludwig von Mises may have passed away, but because he was "sold out" to truth, his ideas live on. In fact, he is now acknowledged as one of the greatest economists of all time and the free market economists have banded together to form the Mises Institute in recognition of his massive contributions. Today's leaders would do well to study books from the Mises Institute. This would help drive systematic change so politicians could focus on long-term results (society's health) and not just on short-term results (money and power) to get re-elected. Today's political system lacks character, for it rewards self-serving behavior while punishing character-based leadership. Absurdly, when criticized for policies that damaged society in the long run, Keynes sniffed, "In the long run, we are all dead." A humorous quip, perhaps, but not addressing the issue that modern society now must face. Any system that allows current politicians to access future tax dollars to buy current votes is unjust on its face. After all, the parties bid for the election with other people's money, promising gifts to current constituents, but paid for by future taxpayers, most of whom are not even born yet! The politicians gain power and money while the people receive higher taxes and debt systematically. Indeed, the FTM process flows something like this: Private Central Banks print or digitize money, which is then loaned to governments, paper, stealing value through inflation from the people. Government then rewards the economic educators (doctrinaires), who write mighty tomes (propaganda) in support of said governments and said Central Banks. This is shameful. Leaders should focus on leaving the world a better place for the next generation, not submitting them to debt-slavery.

To those who desire to drive real change, a good place to start is character. Quit swallowing what the mainstream

CHARACTER

media says without further study. When the masses do this, the all-powerful State thrives, despite a history of nearly five thousand years of failures. Propaganda masters the likes of Hitler and Lenin would be proud of today's half-truths and outright lies spouted on mainstream media and by universities. Remember, it was Hitler who said, "Make the lie big, make it simple, keep saying it, and eventually, they will believe it," along with, "How fortunate for leaders that men do not think." Not to be outdone, Lenin boasted, "A lie told often enough becomes truth." Mises's life proves that propaganda cannot change economic law because law works on cold-hard truths, not sugar-coated lies. Therefore, society must kill the "something for nothing" SFN or SFN will kill society. So far, SFN has had the better of this fight. If economists are rewarded for following the company line, and the company (university) is funded by the government, then it doesn't take a grand conspiracy theory (merely an understanding of FTM and SFN) to see why our present economic policies support increased State power. What other reasonable hypothesis could account for the United States going from no national debt (during Andrew Jackson's administration), to the multi-trillion-dollar national debt today?

Lack of character, be that as it may, isn't just a political, corporate, or banking issue—it's an issue that affects everyone. Yes, it's difficult to make a character-based stand in the workplace, especially when the boss rewards bad behaviors while punishing good ones. This leaves people in a moral quandary, having to choose between money and morals. Millions of people, in reality, have succumbed to this temptation, but this only quenches their light and engulfs the world in further darkness. Nevertheless, when a person sets his soul on fire for truth, his light shines a path out of the darkness. This is exactly what Ludwig von Mises did: he lit a path in the darkness for others to follow. Where is the next generation of men and women willing to set their souls on fire for the truth? Where are the courageous citizens who cannot tolerate falsehoods any longer and who bravely choose to live Virgil's quote, "Do not give in to evil, but proceed ever more boldly against it"?

CHAPTER 3

ATTITUDE
Resolved: To Have a Positive Attitude in All Situations

I know that by listening to my positive voice and turning down my negative voice, I will own a positive attitude.
—Orrin Woodward

It's amazing how much a person can learn about another's attitude by listening. People who claim to have a positive attitude but think negatively reveal their true state once they start speaking. For example, when mentoring, I like to start with, "Tell me the good, the bad, and the ugly. The good we will celebrate, the bad we will make adjustments for, and the ugly we will pray about." This is sure to get people talking, helping me identify not just what happened but what people think about what happened. A person's thinking, in reality, is more important than the actual event since the event occurs once, but what he thinks about what occurred is recycled through his heart and mind hundreds of times and then is shared with others. Painful experiences are common to both achievers and non-achievers, but whether they empower them forward or disempower them backwards depends on the story the person creates from the experience. As a result, paradoxically, failure in life is less from the actual event that occurred on the outside as much as the inside story told about the event.

Positive and Negative Voice Tellers

Inside a person's mind are two opposite voices. The first, the positive voice, speaks all the good about each situation, seeing the world through a positive perspective. The second, the negative voice, speaks all the bad about each situation, seeing the world from a negative perspective. One cannot eliminate either voice entirely, but he can learn to turn them up or down. Winners con-

RESOLVED

sistently turn up the positive voice while turning down the negative one, leading to a positive attitude about life. On the other hand, those who struggle with their attitudes reverse the process, turning up the negative voice while turning down the positive one. Thus, the reason most people struggle with negative attitudes is because they naturally listen to the negative voice shouting at them, not the positive voice whispering to them. Zig Ziglar once compared the two voices inside a person to a bank with a positive and negative bank teller:

> *In your mind bank, there are two tellers—both of whom are obedient to your every command. One teller is positive and handles positive deposits and positive withdrawals. The other teller is negative and will accept all negative deposits and provide you with negative feedback.*
>
> *As the owner of your mind, you have complete control over all withdrawals and most deposits. The deposits represent your total experiences in life. The withdrawals determine your success and happiness. Obviously, you can't withdraw anything that hasn't been deposited. (That's true in the cash bank too, isn't it?)*
>
> *Each transaction involves a choice of which teller to use. Confront the negative teller with a problem, and he will remind you of how poorly you performed in the past. He will predict failure with your current problem. Confront your positive teller, and he will enthusiastically tell you how you successfully dealt with far more difficult problems in the past. He will give you examples of your skill and genius and assure you that you can easily solve this problem. Both tellers are right because: whether you think you can or you think you can't—you are right.*

The difference between a positive person and a negative person then isn't determined by his experiences, but instead by which bank teller he consistently visits. Here's a humorous example of a person consulting the wrong voice:

> *An avid positive-oriented duck hunter was in the market for a new bird dog. His search ended when he found a dog that could actually walk on water to retrieve a duck. Shocked by his find, he was sure that his negative-oriented friend would never believe him. He decided to try to break the news to his most pessimistic friend by inviting him on a duck hunt to witness his amazing dog firsthand. As they waited by the shore, a flock of ducks flew by. They fired, and a duck*

ATTITUDE

fell. The dog responded and jumped into the water. The dog, however, did not sink but instead walked across the water to retrieve the bird, never getting more than his paws wet. The friend saw everything but did not say a single word.

On the drive home, the hunter asked his friend, "Did you notice anything unusual about my new dog?"

"I sure did," responded his friend. "He can't swim."

Aren't some people just like this? No matter what information is presented to them, they can find something negative about it. Cynics know the price of everything, but the value of nothing. People who routinely consult their negative voice, eventually become cynical because they only hear from the negative voice. The two hunters both experienced the same thing and yet developed completely different stories, based on which voice they listened to. Winners and non-winners, likewise, both receive similar experiences, but because they consult opposite voices, they interpret and respond to them differently.

Reframing

But how does listening to a positive voice change the situation? The positive voice, to be sure, doesn't change the facts; however, it radically changes the person who must respond to the experience. Indeed, there are two ways to change how a person views a situation through what is called reframing. A person can change either the content or the context of a situation to reframe how he thinks about it. Author Stewart Robertson explained, "Content reframing is changing the meaning of a behavior to help you see the good side and appreciate the otherwise unlovely character. Context reframing is finding a way to make an event or behavior to be represented in such a way that it would have value no matter how negative you think it might be."

> **A person can change either the content or the context of a situation by reframing how he thinks about it.**

The positive voice reframes potential negative events into empowering positive viewpoints, while the negative voice frames everything into disempowering viewpoints. Author Mary Hunt shared an inspiring example of reframing:

Years ago, my husband and I decided not to replace my car once the lease was up. The plan was that because we work

77

RESOLVED

together, we would share his car until we could pay cash for a second car. We figured that would take six months or so.

I won't say this new arrangement was enjoyable. Actually, I hated it. I felt as if I'd lost my freedom. My wings were clipped; no more spontaneity for me. If I wasn't being "chaperoned" as a passenger in my husband's car, I was having to ask permission to borrow it. Let me just put it this way: I was not the most pleasant passenger.

We'd been commuting together for about three months when I realized that it wasn't the situation that was intolerable. It was me. I was making myself miserable, not recognizing that the nicest guy in the world was willing to take me anywhere I wanted to go, anytime I wanted to get there. I was ungrateful and horribly self-centered. I needed an attitude change, and I needed it quickly.

I decided I had to reframe my thinking because the situation wasn't going to change anytime soon. I decided that rather than a pathetic dependent child, I would see myself as a woman of privilege. I have a driver!

Every day, I am driven back and forth to work, during which time I am free to chat, read, write, think, knit, or nap. I never have to wash a car. I don't have to pump gas into it, insure it, register it, or have it "smogged" (a California thing)—all because my driver is also my maintenance man. Several times a year when I need to go in a different direction, I get a rental car, which allows me to try out some brand new fancy cars and get my fix behind the wheel. See? A different way of looking at the same situation.

When Hunt listened to her negative voice, she framed the events negatively in content ("I am a pathetic dependent child") and in context ("My husband is too cheap to give me my own car"). It was only after she disciplined her thinking, turning down the volume of the negative voice and turning up her positive voice, that she reframed the events positively in content ("I have my own personal driver") and context ("I get more time with my husband while saving time and money"). While it may be easier to listen to the negative voice, it's much harder to live with the results. It takes practice to habitually turn down the negative voice and seek instead the positive voice, but it's essential to developing a positive mind-set. Leaders are perpetual re-framers of events for themselves and their organizations. A person's life can be fundamentally changed by turning former miserable experiences into joyful ones through the power of reframing, simply because the joy or misery

ATTITUDE

experienced isn't in the event itself but in the mindset chosen to define the event. This is the key to the positive mindset.

Another great example of reframing occurred during the 1984 presidential campaign. Many were concerned about Ronald Reagan's age, fearful that a man in his mid-seventies would not be able to handle the pressures of the presidency. When concern about Reagan's age was mentioned by Mondale during one of their debates, Reagan said, "I will not make age an issue of this campaign. I am not going to exploit, for political purposes, my opponent's youth and inexperience." Even Mondale laughed at that one and, needless to say, Reagan's age wasn't discussed again in the campaign.

The secret is to consult the positive voice teller immediately, reframing any event through a positive perspective as close to real time as possible. Of course, there will be times when a person listens to his negative voice inadvertently and must learn how to root out the negative seeds planted into his thinking by the negative voice.

Pulling Negative Weeds

People who listen to either their own or another person's negative voice are like horticulturalists who give others permission to cast seed weeds in their gardens. Naturally, these seeds germinate in the garden just like negative seeds germinate in the mind. Weeds are negative viewpoints that stick in a person's thinking, taking up space and blocking good ideas from taking root. These negative thoughts sneak into a person's mental garden, and if not pulled immediately begin to take root. If permitted to grow, they become stronger, developing deep roots into a person's thinking patterns, making eradication more difficult. Unaddressed weeds create "stinking thinking," a series of negative thought and attitudes that lead to selfish behaviors. In turn, the more weeds in the mental garden, the less ground there is to grow mental fruit (positive thoughts). Don't provide fertile soil for weeds in the mind; don't allow seed weeds to grow in the heart; and finally, do not allow negative seeds to spread out of the mouth, becoming a carrier of negativity to further infect yourself and others. If weeds are always growing in a person's thinking, then it indicates the person has regularly tuned to his negative voice. To change this, a person must take responsibility and listen to his positive voice, for positive attitudes are a choice, just like a weed-free garden is a choice.

As stated previously, what happens to a person is not nearly as important as how he handles what happens to him. No one should be given permission to plant weeds in a person's garden. Regrettably, however, most people just accept whatever seeds fly into their garden rather than select only the fruit seeds. The typical person, before learning the importance of mental gardening, allows seeds to be scattered anywhere they like in his garden. From the radio, television, friends, coworkers, and family, he is being constantly bombarded with weed seeds that hinder the growth of positive fruit. Most people have no idea of the damage negative weeds (thoughts) have on positive attitudes. Unless a person has a specific intent on what is and isn't allowed into his brain, he has surrendered his destiny to the seeds surrounding him instead of selecting the seeds that empower him. Winners have a positive attitude by choice, not chance. Since attitudes in one's life determine the altitudes of it, one must assume responsibility to nurture his mental garden, pulling seed weeds daily while nurturing the fruit-producing attitudes. One of the strange aspects of human nature is it is easier to have "stinking thinking" than positive thinking just like it's easier to grow weeds than fruit in a garden. Winners cannot change the laws of human nature, but they can learn to work with them to produce results. For instance, winners focus on solving, not whining about challenges. Challenges (negative people call them problems) are a given, but solutions are a choice. Pull the weeds to clear one's mind and protect one's heart, for out of the abundance of the heart, the mouth speaks.

> **Winners don't make the rules in the game of life; nonetheless, they must learn to apply the rules in their favor in order to win.**

Long-Term versus Short-Term Perspectives

Once negativity seeps into a person's heart, it negatively colors all future events. Ironically, many times it's the negativity from an event that leads to further poor choices that sink success. Especially when one considers many of the things people get upset about never come to pass, but the bad attitude perseveres anyway. Winners, in contrast, have learned that many times the obstacles are simply blessings in disguise. Since human beings cannot know the beginning from the end, the proper course is to reframe life events, maintaining a positive attitude while seeing how things shake out. For much of what people spend countless hours fretting and worrying about never comes to pass at all. Nonetheless, worrying so much stole their joy just the same. Worrying is similar to dreaming except from a negative perspective instead of a positive one. Imagine how much more useful it would be for people to turn

ATTITUDE

every challenge into an opportunity to see the potential positives instead of the pitfalls. This fable exemplifies many of these lessons:

A farmer had only one horse. One day, his horse ran away. All the neighbors came by, saying, "I'm so sorry. This is such bad news. You must be so upset."

The man just said, "We'll see."

A few days later, his horse came back with twenty wild horses. The man and his son corralled all twenty-one horses. All the neighbors came by, saying, "Congratulations! This is such good news. You must be so happy!"

The man just said, "We'll see."

One of the wild horses kicked the man's only son, breaking both his legs. All the neighbors came by, saying, "I'm so sorry. This is such bad news. You must be so upset."

The man just said, "We'll see."

The country went to war, and every able-bodied young man was drafted to fight. The war was terrible and killed every young man, but the farmer's son was spared since his broken legs prevented him from being drafted.

All the neighbors came by, saying, "Congratulations! This is such good news. You must be so happy!"

The man just said, "We'll see."

Attitude helps a person maintain hope in his plan, even when events seem to be going against him. The tide usually turns, but if a person's positive attitude is lost, then he won't capitalize on the new circumstances as he is too busy bewailing his bad luck. Moreover, people who focus on their negative voice seem to attract other negative people because misery loves company. By contrast, positive voice people seem to attract other positive people. Association, in other words, will make or break a person. Indeed, this is why the events in a person's life are not as important as one's attitudes about them because the attitudes are what attract or repel people one associates with. Achievement-oriented people do not associate for long with negative voices, be it their own or others. This is one of the greatest secrets to success; turning down one's negative voice and turning up the positive one so that he stops attracting negative people and begins attracting other positive people into his life. Pastor Charles Swindoll said it best:

The longer I live, the more I realize the impact of attitude on life. Attitude, to me, is more important than facts. It is more important than the past, than education, than money,

81

than circumstances, than failures, than successes, than what other people think or say or do. It is more important than appearance, giftedness, or skill. It will make or break a company...a church...a home. The remarkable thing is we have a choice every day regarding the attitude we will embrace for that day. We cannot change our past. We cannot change the fact that people will act in a certain way. We cannot change the inevitable. The only thing we can do is play on the one string we have, and that is our attitude...I am convinced that life is 10% what happens to me, and 90% how I react to it. And so it is with you...we are in charge of our attitudes.

Wooden's Three on Attitudes

Former UCLA coach John Wooden taught his teams a second set of three principles which relate to attitude:

1. Never whine.
2. Never complain.
3. Never make excuses.

These three principles help a person evaluate whether he is listening to his positive or negative voice. As discussed, the negative voice scatters weeds in the mental garden, producing bad fruits like whining, complaining, and excuse making. In fact, these three principles can be thought of as levels of negativity as a person continues to consult his negative voice. The first symptom from listening to the negative voice is whining; whining soon moves to complaining as the roots of bitterness take root, and eventually the bitterness carries a person down into full-fledged victimhood, where he makes excuses to justify his negativity. These three principles help a person identify if, and how far the seed weeds have spread into a person's thinking from listening to his negative voice. Thankfully, there is a cure for "stinking thinking". The gardener can quit making excuses and assume responsibility for pulling the weeds in his mental garden, turning down the negative voice and turning up the positive one. Predictably, the longer a person has listened to the negative voice, the more work he has to do to clean up his mental garden. This is no different than the amount of work a gardener would have if he neglected his garden for a month compared to neglecting it for a year. Nonetheless, the key is to start today. Whining, complaining, and excuse making lead to losing and no winner can tolerate these weeds growing for long.

ATTITUDE

Never Whine

Winners don't whine and whiners don't win. When a person responds to any situation by whining, it is a sure sign his negative voice is in command. Whining, a high-pitched or nasal-sounding appeal for sympathy, may get a person temporary attention, but it is deadly to leadership. Whiners ask, "Why is this happening to me?" Naturally, when a person asks a bad question, they get a bad answer because both indicate the negative voice is in charge. Learn instead to ask, "What can I learn from this?" Thankfully, only the positive voice can answer that question. So much of attitude is in learning to ask better questions so that the positive voice is turned up and the negative voice is turned down. Leaders don't search for sympathy from the negative voice; rather, they search for solutions from the positive one. Sure, there are times when solutions aren't readily available, but even then, there is no reason to turn to the negative voice and whine like a spoiled child. Instead, winners strap the helmet on a little tighter and ask, answer, and act their way out of the challenge. When milk is spilled, whining about who spilled it is practically useless; instead clean it up the mess and discuss how to ensure it doesn't happen again.

A positive attitude simply isn't optional for leaders.

When the going gets tough, the tough get going, becoming winners rather than whiners. If a leader does get knocked down and temporarily hears his negative voice, he quickly rejects it, pulling the weed and asking a better question to turn on his positive voice. Leaders refuse to stay tuned in to the negative voice because they desire leadership, not victimhood. If the weed is extra difficult, he seeks out mentors who have more experience with all the stronger mental weeds. To be sure, if a person doesn't kill his own weeds, he will become a carrier of negativity, forfeiting his leadership and contaminating others with a poisonous mixture of weeds and whining. Since leadership is the ability to create confidence and trust in people, a person who routinely consults his negative voice cannot lead effectively. Great leadership is impossible without a great attitude.

I believe Wooden placed whining first on the list because it is the first noticeable symptom when someone is tapping into the wrong voice. Listening to the negative voice soon leads to verbalizing that fact by whining with the mouth as weeds growing in his mind and heart soon sprout out of the mouth.

Never Complain

The second principle (Never complain) involves a deeper mental infection. If whining is the common cold variety of negativity, then complaining is the pneumonia. A complainer points his finger at others and away from himself, saying, "Why did they do it this way and make it so hard for me?" By complaining about others, a person feels less responsible for fixing his problems. Negative attitudes eventually turn into false beliefs, similar to seeds eventually growing into large weeds that infect the mental garden. One example, of a negative thought turning into a false belief is when the negative thinking seed, "I am not talented enough," soon becomes the full-grown false belief tree: "Success is only for the talented few, so I am not going to put forth any effort, since I am not talented enough." Strangely, when people adopt limiting beliefs, they will fight to defend them. Author Richard Bach noted similarly, "Argue for your limitations, and sure enough, they are yours." By listening to the negative voice, failure becomes a self-fulfilling prophecy; the person spends his life complaining about his bad luck. In this case, he has wrongly concluded that, since he doesn't have extraordinary talent, he cannot be part of that special group of achievers. Of course, this is hogwash. As Thomas Edison said, "Success is 99% perspiration and 1% inspiration." Nevertheless, if the person believes it to be true, it will be true for them and they will fail by not even trying. People, fearing the pain of change (the pain of pulling their own weeds), begin to self-deceive themselves to protect their fragile egos. Subconsciously, they know if they admitted they had what it takes to win, then they also would be responsible to pull the weeds and start making the changes they should have made years ago. This is why all true change begins with changed perspective on one's life. It's a person's lack of attitude, not his lack of talent, that is the main cause of failure. If a person complains, it indicates he is consulting his negative voice, sliding down the slope of negativity from whining to complaining. He is sick with a poisonous attitude (whining) and now officially has become a carrier of negativity (complaining). Leaders address issues head-on, seeking to resolve, not ignore, the issue. They know complaining kills leadership. Think about it; has complaining about something ever produced real change? Henry Ford II once said, "Never complain, and never explain," highlighting the worthlessness

> **Leaders address issues head-on, seeking to resolve, not worsen, the matter.**

ATTITUDE

of complaining about circumstances or seeking to explain them away by making excuses. Complaining may give a person temporary mental release from feeling responsible, but by passing the buck, he has also passed on leadership, for the leader always accepts responsibility. Bitter or better, those are the two choices people have in life. Complaining leads to bitterness and resentment, while changing leads to joy and thankfulness. Everyone plays a part in resolving challenges, even if it's just encouraging others to sit down and resolve conflict without complaining. Perhaps the best way to identify and turn down and eventually ignore the negative voice is to start a regimen of reading books, listening to CDs, and associating with other winners. The more a person engages the positive voices, the less time he will have to listen to the negative ones.

Never Make Excuses

This leads us to the Wooden's third principle—never make excuses, for excuses are the death knell of all leadership. People who make excuses no longer ask questions; instead, they are fully self-deceived, making self-justified statements like, "It's not my fault; others are fully responsible for my failures." Potential leaders who fall prey to the worst negativity violate all three of Wooden's principles, drinking and selling an intoxicating brew of negativity, taking the full slide ride from whining to complaining to making excuses, fulfilling the negative trifecta. Leaders find reasons to win; others find excuses to lose. In business and in life, a person can either make a million dollars or a million excuses, but he cannot make both at the same time. Winners have an attitude that states, "they will until," accepting no excuses from themselves or others. What is it about human nature that makes it so easy for a person to make excuses for his lack of results? For one thing, excuses help a person justify why he is not changing. For another, it helps a person blame others for why he is losing. Still, winners will never participate in the blame game. Blaming others may provide temporary relief from the pain; however, it's the pain that creates the leverage to drive real change. Coping mechanisms like blaming, excuse making, and finger pointing avoid the pain of defeat but only by avoiding the responsibility to grow and change. Remember, winners hate losing enough to change while losers hate changing enough to lose.

Failure is an event, not a person.

People with a positive attitude know that temporary defeats are only lessons on the path to success. Thomas

85

Edison was once asked how it felt to fail hundreds of times on the way to developing the incandescent light bulb. He replied that he hadn't failed hundreds of times, but actually had successfully identified hundreds of ways the light bulb wouldn't work. Edison proved that failure isn't final for a person with a good attitude. Winners realize that setbacks are merely stepping-stones to life advancement. Failure is an event, not a person, but without a winner's thought processes, people label themselves failures instead of learning from failure.

Success and failure, as a result, have more to do with attitude than circumstances. As Winston Churchill once said, "Success is going from one failure to another with no loss in enthusiasm." Study any of the top performers in any field and one will find that they refused to make excuses. Instead, they literally seek ways to be responsible so they can make adjustments and changes. It's time to do a checkup from the neck up. Has the reader ever fallen prey to whining, complaining, or the deadliest one of all, making excuses? If one finds any of these three negative principles at work within, perhaps it's time to start pulling weeds, turning down the negative voice, and launching a reading, listening, and associating program to restore one's mental garden.

Develop a Thankful Spirit

Another key to restoring the mental garden is to focus on one's blessings. It's hard to have a negative attitude when a person views his life through the lens of thankfulness. Conversely, it's hard to have a positive attitude when a person views his life through the lens of bitterness. Remember the story of a man who was complaining because he had no shoes? He stopped complaining when he saw someone else with no feet. Thankfulness is reframing one's perspective, choosing to listen to the positive voice inside. At times, a person must deal with negativity, but he doesn't have to swim in it. Rather, he should handle it as though it is garbage: gather it up and throw it out. Whatever he does, he should never fall into bitterness and resentment. Find the blessings in life because they are always present, even in the darkest of times. Leaders must train themselves to always look for the light not the darkness.

This powerful story of the attitude, by an amazing ninety-two-year-old lady, explains these concepts better than anything:

She is fully dressed each morning by eight o'clock, with her hair fashionably coiffed and her makeup perfectly applied,

ATTITUDE

in spite of the fact that she is legally blind. Today, she has moved to a nursing home. Her husband of seventy years recently passed away, making this move necessary. After many hours of waiting patiently in the lobby of the nursing home, where I am employed, she smiled sweetly when told her room was ready. As she maneuvered her walker to the elevator, I provided a visual description of her tiny room, including the eyelet curtains that had been hung on her window. "I love it," she stated with the enthusiasm of an eight-year-old having just been presented with a new puppy. "Mrs. Jones, you haven't seen the room... just wait," I said. Then she spoke these words that I will never forget. "That does not have anything to do with it," she gently replied. "Happiness is something you decide on ahead of time. Whether I like the room or not does not depend on how the furniture is arranged. It is how I arrange my mind. I have already decided to love it. It is a decision I make every morning when I wake up. I have a choice. I can spend the day in bed recounting the difficulty I have with the parts of my body that no longer work, or I can get out of bed and be thankful for the ones that do work. Each day is a gift, and as long as my eyes open, I will focus on the new day and all of the happy memories I have stored away... just for this time in my life."

This story encapsulates everything on attitude: listening to the positive voice while turning down the negative voice; reframing both the content and the context of her situation; and having a thankful, joyful spirit. When a person chooses to have a thankful spirit, turning habitually to his positive voice, he draws upon a wellspring of options, helping him to overcome the challenges that he is sure to meet in life's journey. The voice one listens to determines the quality of one's life. Choose wisely. For a bad attitude is like a dirty diaper; life stinks until it's changed.

Roger Bannister: Attitude and the Quest for the Four-Minute Mile

For nearly three thousand years, since the beginning of the ancient Greek Olympics, human beings have dreamed of breaking the four-minute mile. The Greeks loved their athletic events and believed the contest could develop the competitive spirit of its people. Although the Greek city-states seemed to love war, they loved their sporting events even more, even calling temporary truces, if necessary, to ensure that warring cities could compete in the athletic competitions. The Greek cities encouraged the best athletes to represent their city in the various competitions, with the largest, most honored, granddaddy of them all being the Olympics held every four years.

The Greeks sought after an ideal called paideia, the perfection of action, in every area achievement. For instance, in the Olympic mile race, the paideia was thought to be running the race in four minutes flat, or the perfect sixty seconds per quarter mile. To achieve this, the Olympic runners developed impressive training regimens. The Athenian herald Pheidippides trained constantly and once ran 150 miles from Athens to Sparta in under two days time. This is a noteworthy feat even by today's ironman standards. Other interesting techniques to improve the performance of runners and break the four minute barrier included running naked, soaking oneself in olive oil, and most bizarre of all, unleashing lions to chase after the runners! Nonetheless, despite over a thousand years of training, the Greeks fell short of the mark, never achieving the mythical paideia. Dismally, the dream of the four-minute mile was conceived, but never achieved.

Near the start of the twentieth century, the worldwide urge to compete in sporting events was reawakened, culminating in the first modern Olympics in 1896. The best athletes from around the world now met at the Olympics every four years, and many world records were shattered in the process. The rebirth of the Olympics, not surprisingly, also rebirthed the original Greek quest to run the mythical four-minute mile. The drama built from one Olympic competition to the next as the world record time inched closer to the coveted paideia.

ATTITUDE

As of 1915, the mile record stood at 4:12.6, still over twelve seconds off the mark. For the next thirty years, runners continued to shave time off the world record. On July 17, 1945, Gunder "the Wonder" Hägg ran a mile in 4:01.3, so close to the mark that many top runners believed it within their sights. Yet, strangely, the barrier refused to be broken. It was like three thousand years of failed attempts weighed down the runners. Shockingly, Hägg's world record stood for nearly nine more years, the longest period of time any mile record stood in the twentieth century! In other words, for nearly nine more years, this negative mental weed, this limiting belief, held sway over runners from every nation. Sure, the athletes had the physical capabilities to break the record, but mentally, they were lacking, battling three millennia worth of failed attempts to achieve the elusive dream. Needless to say, the negative voice reigned supreme, while the runners' positive voices were silenced as they focused on so many years of failure.

Enter medical student Roger Bannister, an innovative runner, who believed the four-minute barrier could be broken. Bannister viewed the long-standing barrier as a personal challenge, having heard from so many that it was "impossible." Curiously, although most people get demoralized from hearing the negative voices of others, winners seem to get energized by it. Indeed, winners convert the crowds' negativity into motivation and personal positivity, accepting the challenge to prove the naysayers wrong. Bannister, needless to say, was a winner, and the world's negativity only strengthened his determination to break the record by listening to his positive voice. In fact, he decided to train alone in order to deliberately avoid the coaches and managers, because he believed they were inadvertently planting their limiting beliefs seeds into the athletes. By 1953, his personal training regimen and medical field experience had reduced his mile time to 4:03.6. While still short of the goal, he knew he was progressing and under the right conditions could breakthrough. He increased his training, both mental (visualization) and physical, slowing his heart rate to less than 50 beats per minute (BPM), significantly below the 72 BPM of the average man. The lower heart rate allowed him, under the intense strain of running, to maintain a larger oxygen reserve, which prolonged how long he could run under anaerobic conditions, making the four-minute mile physically possible. Bannister, however, did more than just train intently. He also analyzed his performance after every practice, focusing on areas to improve. Bannister noted, "Improvement in running depends on continuous self-discipline by the athlete himself, on acute observation of his reaction to races and training, and above all on judgment, which he must learn for himself." This belief, along with research on the latest running mechanics and scientific methods, convinced him he was ready to break the record, a record that would smash three thousand-years of failure.

Although Bannister may have trained alone, he certainly was not alone in his quest for the coveted four-minute mile. Two other runners, Wes Santee and John Landy, also had impressive credentials in the history making contest. In fact, both of them went on record saying they intended to break the record. The field for track-and-field immortality, in effect, had been narrowed to these three men.

Santee, the American, was perhaps the best natural athlete of the three. The son of a Kansas ranch hand, he amazed crowds with his natural athletic prowess and confident spirit. In fact, Santee was the first to publicly state he would break the four-minute barrier. John Landy, the Australian, in contrast, relied more on training than talent, working harder than anyone because he dreamed of winning this international honor for himself and his country. He ran everywhere— in the woods, in the sand dunes, and on the beaches—in his drive to achieve the goal. This led to a three man race against time. On the one hand was the quest to break the four-minute barrier itself, certainly pressure enough. On the other hand was the race against the calendar, knowing that on any day, the right conditions would catapult one of them into everlasting fame and the other two into also-rans.

Each runner believed under the right conditions, he could break the four-minute barrier. Interestingly, the "dream mile" had been scientifically plotted by sports physiologists and coaches for decades. They believed it would take ideal conditions to achieve the milestone. It was theorized that temperatures needed to be around sixty-eight degrees with no discernible wind and a track made of hard dry clay in or-

ATTITUDE

der to set the stage for the "dream mile." In addition, along with the perfect weather and track conditions, a planned sequence of quarters had to be run—the first quarter clocked the slowest, with each subsequent quarter becoming faster and closing with the fastest time in the final quarter. Nearly everyone believed that without perfect conditions and planning, the "dream mile" would remain just that—a dream.

The pressure upon each runner increased with every race as each runner prepared himself to make track-and-field history. Author Neal Bascomb described the growing hoopla and drama: "For weeks in advance of every race, the headlines heralded an impending break in the barrier: 'Landy Likely to Achieve Impossible!'; 'Bannister Gets Chance of Four-Minute Mile!'; 'Santee Admits Getting Closer to Phantom Mile.' Articles dissected track conditions and the weather forecasts while millions around the world followed every attempt. When each runner failed—and there were many failures—he was criticized for coming up short, for not having what it took to achieve the nearly impossible dream. Naturally, such episodes tempted the runners to doubt themselves, but in the end, it only motivated these three winners to try even harder." The buzz throughout the athletic world centered upon which of the runners would be the first to break through the seemingly unbreakable four-minute mile barrier.

The debate ended on a chilly evening in Oxford, England, on May 6, 1954. Bannister's date with destiny had arrived. Despite weather conditions that were far from ideal, forced to run against nearly every prevailing "dream mile" theory to achieve his quest, Bannister set today as the day. Rain had drenched the cinder track, making the surface slippery, while the wind blew at practically gale-like force most of the day, reducing the crowd to a mere 1,500 spectators. Thankfully, because of the late six o'clock start time, the rain had died down. The biting wind, however, still howled across the track. Nevertheless, Bannister believed he was running out of chances and he knew Santee or Landy could break the record at any time. As a result, Bannister reached deep inside himself, listening to his positive voice, despite the negative conditions, and revealed the internal champion to the external world.

RESOLVED

At six o'clock sharp, the runners were at the starting line. Bannister, with two of his teammates from the British Amateur Athletic Association (BAAA), lined up against three Oxford runners. In a methodical plan developed before the race, Chris Brasher, a teammate of Bannister's, played the jackrabbit—the pacesetter for Bannister. Brasher's first lap set a blistering pace, with Bannister running right behind him, timing in at 57.5 seconds. This was way too fast, an impossible pace to maintain for even two laps, not to mention four. Many, after seeing the split times, believed the record was safe, at least for another day. Brasher, however, regained his pace and completed his two laps before collapsing, exhausted, to the side of the track. Bannister's half-mile time was 1:58.2, within the range he had set beforehand. The goal was now within his reach! The question was whether he had enough energy left to finish it. Near the start of the third lap, Chris Chataway (the third BAAA runner), in accordance with the plan, sprinted to the front and allowed Bannister to draft behind him. Chataway gave it all he had and ran an impressive third lap before falling back. Bannister, thanks to his pacesetters, had completed the third lap in 3:00.7—a mere fraction of a second off the prized pace. The only question left was if Bannister had enough gas left, after three grueling laps, to complete his quest. The answer was not long in coming because with three hundred yards to go, he launched his final kick, tapping into a reservoir of energy known only to himself. He lengthened his stride, rolled his head back awkwardly, and gave it everything he had, literally collapsing as he broke the final tape. He even passed out momentarily from the extended physical and mental exertion. Pensively, the crowd awaited for the official announcement to confirm the coach's watch. Finally, the loudspeaker proclaimed: "A time which is a new meeting and track record, and which, subject to ratification, will be a new English native, a British national, a British all-comers, European, British Empire, and world record. The time was three minutes.... fifty-nine and four-tenths seconds." The audience erupted, and pandemonium ensued as people realized the magnitude of the event they had just witnessed. Bannister had run the fourth lap in a scintillating 58.7 seconds, smashing through the four-minute-mile barrier with a final time of 3:59.4! Af-

ATTITUDE

ter his superhuman effort, Bannister regained consciousness quickly, although he did suffer momentary color blindness from his physical exertions. For instance, his standard heart rate of 50 BPM had soared to over 155 BPM, not returning to normal for nearly three hours. He completed his 1954 dream season in style, winning the British and Empire championships in the mile run, along with the European title in the 1,500-meter event. After wrapping up his record-breaking season, Bannister announced his retirement from athletic competitions and pursued his medical career full-time.

In 1955, he wrote a book on his track-and-field exploits, titled, "The Four-Minute Mile". He earned his medical degree from Oxford and became a neurologist. In 1975, he received the honor of being knighted by Queen Elizabeth II, a fitting close to an extraordinary career. Bannister raised the bar on what was possible, refusing to feed his negative voice and the criticisms and doubts within. Instead, he ignored them and fed his positive voice. The most incredible part of this story isn't even Bannister's four-minute mile, but rather what happened to the other mile runners after Bannister accomplished the "impossible" milestone. For the Greek paideia, the under four-minute mile, had stood at slightly over four minutes for nearly nine years, was broken thirty-seven times in the next two years. How did this happen? No scientific explanation suffices because the physical conditioning, tracks surfaces, and running shoes had not changed. What did change, however, were the psychological conditions, the beliefs and attitudes about what was possible. Bannister's example permitted other runners to tune into the positive voice and break through what the negative voice had convinced them was impossible. Bannister's record-breaking performance helped many others break through, and this has become commonly referred to in sports psychology as The Bannister Effect."

Unbelievably, in the third year after Bannister's achievement, things really went crazy, for over three hundred runners broke the four-minute mile—all because of a belief window change which led to runners believing in their positive voice. What once was impossible had now become routine, simply because one man with better beliefs and a positive attitude did it. Guardian News, in an interview with Bannister fifty years after his historic accomplishment, reported:

RESOLVED

"Until then, there had been a widespread belief that it was physically impossible for a man to run the mile in less than four minutes. People claimed the human body would burst amid such a trial of speed and endurance." Bannister, slipping into his best Inspector Clouse-au–style accent, remembered: "A Frenchman once said to my wife, 'but 'ow did 'ee know 'ees heart would not burst?' Landy also spoke of a 'cement wall' protecting the four-minute mark. But I knew it could be done." Bannister believed and this made all the difference because the real barrier to breaking the four-minute mile wasn't a physical one, but a mental one. Bannister's breakthrough, in effect, pulled a three-thousand-year-old mental weed from humanity's belief system. By removing this mental roadblock, he allowed tens of thousands of others to achieve success through "The Bannister Effect."

CHAPTER 4

VISION
Resolved: To Align My Conscious (Ant) with My Subconscious (Elephant) Mind toward My Vision

*I know that ending the civil war between the two is
crucial for all achievements.*
—Orrin Woodward

The Ant and the Elephant

Achievers in every field visualize successful outcomes before they make them a reality. Top performers, from athletes, salespeople, entertainers, business owners, and many others, have learned the value of visualization to goal achievement. In fact, author Jack Canfield explained people only have control over three things in life: "the thoughts you think, the images you visualize, and the actions you take."

> The conscious mind thinks in words, while the subconscious mind thinks in images.

There are two parts of the mind—the conscious and subconscious. Whereas the conscious mind thinks in words, the subconscious mind thinks in images. Although few people, outside of high-achiever know this, the programming of the subconscious mind is one of the keys to success. For the images formed and focused upon in the subconscious mind drive a person towards his dominating vision. Sadly, most people allow outside influences to program their subconscious mind and thus drive towards someone else's vision of their future instead of their own. Indeed, to break out of the crowd, a person must take charge of feeding his subconscious mind the vision for the future he desires.

This isn't just a nice add-on feature for success, but an absolutely vital part that, if missed, will cause a person to fall short of his potential.

Olympian Vince Poscente described how the conscious (ant) mind, in one second of thinking, stimulates around two thousand neurons, while the subconscious (elephant) mind, in a second of imagining, stimulates over four billion neurons. That's four billion neurons to two thousand! In other words, more than two million times more neurons are stimulated in the subconscious mind than in the conscious mind in one second of mental activity. Since "neurons are the cells essential for brain activity," according to brain researcher Antonio Damasio, the subconscious (elephant) mind's four billion neurons make it the mental prime mover for achievers. Moreover, the subconscious mind stores millions of times more data than the conscious part as author Michael Gelb asserted, "Brain researchers estimate that your unconscious data base outweighs the conscious on an order exceeding ten million to one. This data base is the source of your hidden, natural genius. In other words, a part of you is much smarter than you are. The wise people regularly consult that smarter part." Simply stated, success cannot be achieved unless both parts of the mind (ant and elephant) are tapped into. Author Erik Calonius remarked, "Scientists are discovering that the brain is a visionary device—that its primary function is to create pictures in our minds that can be used as blueprints for things that don't exist. They are also learning that our brains can work subconsciously to solve problems that we cannot crack through conscious reasoning, and that the brain is a relentless pattern seeker, constantly reinventing the world." "The ant and the elephant" analogy reminds people of the importance of consciously programming the subconscious mind with positive thoughts and visions. Albert Einstein even weighed in on the subconscious mind when he declared, "Imagination is everything. It is the preview of life's coming attractions," and, "Imagination is more important than knowledge." To be sure, both the ant and the elephant minds are important, but research continues to indicate the power of a properly programmed and charging elephant mind to create world-changing results.

The Civil War

Dr. Maxwell Maltz noted, "The brain and nervous system constitute a marvelous and complex 'goal-striving mechanism,' a sort of built-in automatic guidance system which works for you as a 'success mechanism,' or against you as a 'failure mechanism,' de-

VISION

pending on how YOU, the operator, operate it and the goals you set for it." Sadly, most people operate the elephant as a "failure mechanism," continually feeding it fears and negativity, producing dismal results. Perhaps this is why Henry David Thoreau observed, "Most men lead lives of quiet desperation," because he recognized few ever accomplish their dreams; instead, they merely resign themselves to their fate.

In reality, the "quiet desperation" is the result of the civil war between the ant and the elephant minds. The battle starts when the two minds disagree on the path the individual should take, the conscious mind seeking to go one way and the subconscious another. If not resolved, the protracted civil war leads to frustration, indecision, and inaction. This civil war, more than environment, genetics, or talent, is the greatest hindrance to someone's success. French thinker Émile Coué termed it, "the Law of Reversed Effort," saying, "When the will and imagination are in conflict, the imagination invariably wins the day." Coué's law indicates that inside mental alignment is greater than outside physical circumstances in the success journey. The good news is that mental alignment can be improved and this leads to better physical circumstances.

The Power of Alignment

When a person assumes responsibility for feeding his ant and elephant, he changes the direction of his thoughts. The moment that happens, he changes the direction of his actions and destiny. Every winner feeds the ant mind positive thoughts and the elephant mind positive images, realizing that when the ant and elephant align, practically any dream is possible. Just as an actor trains his subconscious to play a certain role in a movie, a person can train his elephant to fulfill a certain role in real life. In both cases the subconscious is fulfilling the script given it. Hence, to move in the direction of his dreams, a person must train his ant to think in a positive manner to feed his elephant the proper scripting. This is why attitude was the previous resolution; for how can a negative fearful ant feed a positive image to the elephant? However, if the right attitude (ant) and vision (elephant) is mixed with hard work, success will happen, just as Olympian Peter Vidmar emphasized, "Visualization is not a substitute for hard work and dedication. But if you add it to your training regimen—whether in sports, business, or your per-

> **When a person assumes responsibility for what is fed to his ant and elephant, he changes his thoughts.**

sonal relationships—you will prepare your mind for success, which is the first step in achieving all your goals and dreams."

Outside of the character resolution, this is probably the single most neglected resolution, leading to lives of quiet desperation instead of public celebrations. In effect, a person becomes the script he feeds his elephant; therefore, by changing the elephant's food, he changes its script, and thus changing his destiny. Businessman Richard Brooke summed it up nicely: "Your mind doesn't care what you want—or what you are willing to work hard for. It only cares that you perform in accordance with what you expect of yourself."

Who Is Feeding the Elephant?

If a person gets what he expects and what he expects is fed to the elephant imagination then what his elephant expects is a good indicator of coming realities. Make no mistake, the elephant must feed on something. In consequence, the only question is: Who is feeding a person's elephant? Absurdly, most people allow TV marketers to be the number one feeder of their subconscious mind! Does anyone really think the marketers have the person's best interest in mind? The latest research reveals the average American watches over five hours of TV every day; that is a ton of commercials exposed to the elephant mind. Calonius explained the impact of repeated exposures on the elephant mind: "The researchers found that the subjects like the pictures they had already seen. Researchers call this the 'mere exposure effect.' That's why advertisers pound ads repeatedly down our throats. It's why chain restaurants (you get the same meal coast to coast) thrive." Needless to say, advertisers skip right past the ant mind, feeding images to the elephant brain instead. Practically every single advertisement feeds the elephant with images and a vision of grandeur if the person will use the product. When is the last time someone saw an ad invest its thirty seconds or minute to share detailed notes on the functions, features, and benefits of a product? For most people, probably never! Instead, advertisers share images intended to create feelings to create a hunger that can only be satisfied by purchasing the company's product. Over the years, advertisers have learned that giving a list of functions, features, and benefits to your ant doesn't produce results; however, the ads that feed the elephant images of success produce feelings that generate purchases. Marketers have learned to ignore the ant and feed the starving elephant, creating a perceived need to the consumer's elephant mind by constant repetition of seductive images. As such, people end up emotionally

VISION

buying things they don't really need and rationally explaining why they did. Psychologist Timothy Wilson explained, "The adaptive unconscious plays a major executive role in our mental lives. It gathers information, interprets and evaluates it, and sets goals in motion, quickly and efficiently." Advertisers, in other words, fill a person's imagination with images of their choosing to program the person into buying what, many times, they do not truly need.

To illustrate, think of the commercials one sees aired during sporting events. Further, think about how many kids watch sports on TV, viewing football, basketball, and baseball, etc., any time they can. Throughout the years of watching TV sports, the children end up viewing thousands of beer commercials. When I was a kid, the 1980s beer commercials repeated jingles like "Tonight, Tonight, Let It Be" and slogans like "Tastes great; less filling," to name just a few. The sound bites are still remembered decades after most people have actually seen the commercial. These products were sold through memorable images and catchy slogans and they're effective. Can anyone recall a beer ad that explained the ratio of carbonated water to barley and hops? Can a person imagine an ant-version beer ad explaining how alcohol blocks oxygen from reaching the brain, causing impaired thinking and motor skills? That's an ad not likely to be produced in our lifetime. Instead, ads implant images into elephant minds. Moreover, since the number one market for beer is single males, the ads target them specifically by playing images of guys popping open beers, while somehow beautiful bikini-clad women appear out of nowhere. Rationally, the young men understand this isn't likely to happen, but the elephant charges to pick up the beer anyway. Sure, this probably won't happen the first time someone sees the ad, but with repeated exposures, a continuous daily feeding of the elephant, the young men will eventually fulfill the elephant mind's vision and purchase the product.

Companies must understand the effectiveness of their advertisements; otherwise, ad executives would not pay big dollars for commercial slots during sporting events. While some men resist, or at least minimize, beer drinking in high school because they are training for athletics, after high school, this no longer constrains them. Indeed, no longer in training for competitive sports, these young men, after finishing a pickup sports game, head to the bar for some male bonding and a cold one, just as their elephant minds were trained to do over the years by the commercials. Few have any idea why they perform this ritual, but the marketing executives know perfectly well why: the desire has been implanted into

99

their elephant minds by repeated exposures over many years. In other words, marketers rely on the child's love of sports to program his elephant mind to join the beer-drinking club in the future. Make no mistake; the "free" programs are bought and paid for by the viewers through the programming their subconscious minds receive. For the elephant mind is always working. The question is, who is feeding it? And, what is it feeding on? Winners take charge of their mental programming, creating brighter futures by feeding the right images to their elephant minds, drawing them towards their goals and dreams.

Controlling the Inside Conditions

To start programming his elephant mind, a person must first determine what it has been fed up to now. Most likely, it's a cacophony of images and desires without any sense of direction or purpose. Thankfully, if a person is willing to go through the process, he can change his programming and change his life. For what the elephant mind is feeding upon eventually becomes what a person is. For example, Karl Wallenda, a world-renowned aerial acrobat who did death-defying feats for years, tragically displayed the power of programming. He set up an event in Puerto Rico where he sought to traverse a seventy-five-foot-high wire. This was not an out-of-the-ordinary stunt for this high-wire actor, but Karl seemed out of sorts. Helen, Karl's widow, recalled, "All Karl thought about for three straight months prior to it was falling. It was the first time he'd ever thought about that, and it seemed to me that he put all his energies into not falling rather than walking the tightrope." Karl was the best in his field, but even the best, when they consistently feed fears instead of faith to their elephant minds, will miss the mark. Helen shared that her husband, contrary to his normal behavior, personally supervised the installation of the tightrope and guide wires. He fed the wrong images to his elephant mind, dividing his attention between the conscious mind's goal (to cross the wire successfully) and his subconscious mind's fear (falling off the wire). This is the civil war that leads to failure. Instead of feeding his ant and elephant minds positive thoughts and images, he fed them negative thoughts and images. His ant mind focused on doing what he had always done, but the civil war created cognitive dissonance, a mental state in which one's thoughts and beliefs are not aligned. Unfortunately, in this example Karl plunged to his death because the elephant's image was stronger than the ant's willpower. The civil war must end to terminate the "failure mechanism" and launch the "success mechanism".

VISION

Imagination, strikingly, is neutral when it comes to success or failure, dependent upon what the programmer feeds the ant and elephant minds. French emperor Napoleon understood the importance of imagination when he proclaimed, "Imagination rules the world." The difference between success and failure hinges upon what is consistently fed to the elephant mind.

> **The difference between success and failure hinges upon what is consistently fed to the elephant.**

Feed the ant positive thoughts (as discussed in Resolution #3) and feed the elephant imagination positive images of one's future reality. Remember, a person cannot set himself on fire with his dream if he's wetting on himself with his dread. The highest achievers are not better than anyone else, but they are more disciplined, having learned the importance of instilling faith, not fears into the elephant mind. Dr. Maltz said, "We act, or fail to act, not because of the will, as is so commonly believed, but because of imagination. A human being always acts and feels and performs in accordance with what he imagines to be true about himself and his environment." What a person imagines consistently soon becomes his reality. If dreams are compelling visions of the future, then worries are fearful visions of the future. Just as a dream inspires the elephant into action, worry paralyzes the elephant into inaction, creating a civil war between what the conscious mind says it wants and the elephant minds programming.

Author Jack Canfield shared another tragic example of the civil war between the ant mind and the elephant mind in the story of Nick Sitzman, a young railroad yardman who was accidentally locked in a refrigerator boxcar after the rest of the crew had gone home:

> *He banged and shouted until his fists were bloody and his voice was hoarse, but no one heard him. With his knowledge of "the numbers and the facts," he predicted the temperature to be zero degrees. Nick's thought was, "If I can't get out, I'll freeze to death in here." Wanting to let his wife and family know exactly what had happened to him, Nick found a knife and began to etch words on the wooden floor. He wrote, "It's so cold, my body is getting numb. If I could just go to sleep. These may be my last words." The next morning, the crew slid open the heavy doors of the boxcar and found Nick dead. An autopsy revealed that every physical sign of his body indicated he had frozen to death. And yet the refrigeration unit of the car was inoperative, and the*

RESOLVED

temperature inside indicated 55 degrees Fahrenheit. Nick had killed himself by the power of his own thoughts.

Protect the thoughts sent to the subconscious mind, for what is fed to the elephant eventually becomes one's reality.

Uniting the Ant and the Elephant

Once a person understands how the mind processes attitudes and images, it's time to unite the ant and elephant minds towards his dream. For when the positive ant learns to feed positive images to the elephant, a person is poised for his breakout from the crowd. To be sure, many people discipline the ant to perform basic work—routine habits like driving to work, scheduling one's day, performing various tasks, all routinized by the daily ant habits. But imagine if people disciplined their elephants in the same way that they disciplined their ants. This would cause a worldwide productivity revolution! Some may argue that they don't have time or they are not disciplined enough to do this, but that's not really the case. Everyone is disciplined when they value the activity. For instance, even someone who is typically late for everything will get up early for his favorite hobby. Discipline, in a sense, is a given; the only question is: Is it going to be internal discipline or external discipline? Jobs provide external discipline to get results; in contrast, feeding the elephant requires internal discipline since no job or profession can force a person to feed positive images to his elephant mind. In other words, although vital for success, the discipline must come from within, not without.

A person who disciplines his ant mind to feed the elephant is aligning his mind and ending the civil war. This permits the rational ant to hop on the back of the imaginative elephant in the drive towards success. He feed the elephant images and the ant positive thoughts to unite both of them in a common purpose, making success not only predictable, but also enjoyable.

The goal is to feed the elephant images of an oasis (the dream) in the distance, inspiring the elephant to charge ahead while the ant hops on for the ride, helping to direct and encourage the elephant's charge to success. Please understand, this isn't a magical elixir, but rather a logical plan to utilize and unite the total brain for goal achievement. It will still take work, effort, and drive to achieve; but by aligning the ant and the elephant, the civil war inside one's mind is ended, creating the right conditions that lead to massive results. Author Claude Bristol instructed people on the importance of feeding the subconscious when he wrote, "This subtle

102

VISION

force of repeated suggestion overcomes our reason. It acts directly on our emotions and our feelings, and finally penetrates to the very depths of our subconscious minds. It's the repeated suggestion that makes you believe."

To truly succeed, one must quit willing success with the ant while ignoring the elephant. Instead, determine where one wants to go and inspire the elephant with the images of how that future looks. The united ant and elephant, driving forward to a common vision, can achieve so much. A united ant and elephant ends the tug of war between the two, a war the elephant always win. The success journey needs both the ant and elephant contributions to achieve the desired results. For ants have neither the size nor the power to create radical change, but they do make great team players, working with the elephant to ensure he is moving in the right direction and tracking the progress on the success journey.

For example, author Eugene Ferguson shared, "Pyramids, cathedrals, and rockets exist not because of geometry, theory of structures, or thermodynamics, but because they were first pictures—literally visions—in the (elephant) minds of those who first conceived them. Usually the significant governing decisions regarding an artisan's or an engineer's design have been before the artisan picks up (ant) tools or the engineer turns to his (ant) drawing board." This is the creativity unleashed when the elephant is programmed properly. Calonius concluded the subconscious responds the same to both actual and imagined events when he noted, "When we look at something...the same part of the brain lights up as when we imagine that something. This is called the 'mutual interference' between imagery and perception." Dr. Maltz concurred, "Experimental and clinical psychologists have proved beyond a shadow of doubt that the human nervous system cannot tell the difference between an actual experience and an experience imagined vividly and in detail." Philosopher Dan Dennett went even further when he declared the subconscious mind is the "president," while the conscious mind is its "press secretary." Regardless of where the line of demarcation falls between the ant and elephant minds, one thing is clear; that is, the alignment between the ant and the elephant is crucial for massive achievement.

Success Is a Picture in the Mind's Eye

Dr. Maltz explained the importance of imagination in achieving goals: "The goals that the Creative Mechanism seeks to achieve are MENTAL IMAGES or mental pictures, which we create by the use of IMAGINATION." Success is first pictured in the mind, then,

103

through the use of the mind's Creative Mechanism, it's created in the real world. Every achiever, in effect, learns to run a successful advertisement in his mind. The more the ad is visualized and experienced as real in the imagination, the more believable it becomes. The subconscious mind, through the power of imagination, experiences the commercials as real since it doesn't discern the difference between an actual and imagined event. Interestingly, this is what separates humans from other mammals—the mind's ability to imagine a better future. Animals, by contrast, simply live on their genetically coded instincts. This makes man a creator with a little "c" as opposed to Creator God with a capital "C". As Dr. Maltz explained, "Man, on the other hand, has something animals haven't—Creative Imagination. Thus, man of all creatures is more than a creature; he is also a creator. With his imagination, he can formulate a variety of goals. Man alone can direct his Success Mechanism by the use of imagination, or imaging ability."

Peter Vidmar shared how he used creative imagination at the end of his practices to win a gold medal:

> I'd say, "Okay, Tim, let's imagine it's the men's gymnastics finals of the Olympic Games. The United States team is on its last event of the night, which just happens to be the high bar. The last two guys up for the United States are Tim Daggett and Peter Vidmar. Our team is neck and neck with the People's Republic of China, the reigning world champions, and we have to perform our routines perfectly to win the Olympic team gold medal...."
>
> We'd close our eyes and, in this empty gym at the end of a long day, we'd visualize an Olympic arena with 13,000 people in the seats and another 200 million watching live on television. Then we'd practice our routines....
>
> Tim would shout out, "Green light," and I'd look at the superior judge, who was usually our coach Mako. I'd raise my hand, and he'd raise his right back. Then I'd turn, face the bar, grab hold, and begin my routine.
>
> Well, a funny thing happened on July 31, 1984. It was the Olympic Games' men's gymnastics team finals in Pauley Pavilion on the UCLA campus. The 13,000 seats were filled and a television audience in excess of 200 million around the world tuned in. The United States team was on its last event of the night, the high bar. The last two guys up for the United States just happened to be Tim Daggett and Peter Vidmar. And just as we visualized, our team was neck and

VISION

neck with the People's Republic of China. We had to perform our high bar routines perfectly to win the gold medal.

I looked at Coach Mako, my coach for the past 12 years. As focused as ever, he simply said, "Okay, Peter, let's go. You know what to do. You've done it a thousand times, just like every day back in the gym. Let's just do it one more time, and let's go home. You're prepared."

He was right. I had planned for this moment and visualized it hundreds of times. I was prepared to perform my routine. Rather than seeing myself actually standing in the Olympic arena with 13,000 people in the stands and 200 million watching on television, in my mind, I pictured myself back in the UCLA gym at the end of the day with two people left in the gym.

When the announcer said, "From the United States of America, Peter Vidmar," I imagined it was my buddy Tim Daggett saying it. When the green light came on, indicating it was time for the routine, I imagined that it wasn't really a green light but that it was Tim shouting, "Green light!" And when I raised my hand toward the superior judge from East Germany, in my mind I was signaling my coach, just like I had signaled him every day at the end of hundreds of workouts. In the gym, I always visualized I was at the Olympic finals; at the Olympic finals, I visualized I was back in the gym.

I turned, faced the bar, jumped up, and grabbed on. I began the same routine I had visualized and practiced day after day in the gym. I was in memory mode, going yet again where I'd already gone hundreds of times.

I quickly made it past the risky double-release move that had harpooned my chances at the world championships. I moved smoothly through the rest of my routine and landed a solid dismount, where I anxiously waited for my score from the judges.

With a deep voice the announcement came through the speaker, "The score for Peter Vidmar is 9.95."

"Yes!" I shouted. "I did it!" The crowd cheered loudly as my teammates and I celebrated our victory.

Thirty minutes later, we were standing on the Olympic medal platform in the Olympic arena with 13,000 people in the stands and over 200 million watching on television, while the gold medals were officially draped around our necks. Tim, me, and our teammates stood proudly wear-

ing our gold medals as the national anthem played and the American flag was raised to the top of the arena. It was a moment we had visualized and practiced hundreds of times in the gym. Only this time, it was for real.

Vidmar verifies that a person doesn't always get what he wants or what he deserves, but he always gets what he expects. For what a person consistently feeds his elephant mind becomes his expectations and eventually his life's results.

Success through Visualization

Most people fail in life, not from lack of potential, but from lack of planning. Without a plan to feed the elephant mind, he will charge off in the direction of someone else's programming. This focused plan begins the moment a person determines his purpose and dream. The journey of a thousand miles begins with one step, but the first step must be in the direction of one's purpose; otherwise the activity does not lead to results. Invariably, this is one of the most underutilized resolutions in the quest for significance. Most people are busy running in circles or paralyzed by fear because they have not programmed their minds towards their purpose to achieve their destiny.

Author Charles Garfield shared a compelling personal story of how beliefs act on the conscious mind and subconscious mind. Garfield, a former amateur weight lifter, sat down with Soviet sports scientists who mentally prepared Soviet Bloc athletes for Olympic competitions. The Soviets claimed they had tapped into what they called psychophysiology, hidden reserves of energy utilized through mental preparation. Garfield, skeptical of the results claimed by mental visualization techniques, believed that most of the Soviet results were due to steroid use. He listened to the scientists, asking questions to understand the process behind the mental training techniques. The Soviets, in an effort to prove their theories, proposed that Garfield subject himself to their training exercises. The Soviet scientists urged him to attempt a three-hundred-pound bench press—something Garfield hadn't done in several years. He surprised himself as he accomplished the goal, straining every muscle to bench-press three hundred pounds. The Soviets began a series of measurements, blood tests, and calculations designed to measure the full potential inside of Garfield. Finally, they were ready to demonstrate the mental aspects of psychophysiology. Here is Garfield in his own words:

VISION

Eventually we went to the next step. They asked me to lie down on my back. Then they guided me into a deeper state of relaxation. "Imagine your arms and legs becoming increasingly heavy and warm...." Fully awake and alert, I began to feel more at ease.

When nearly an hour had passed, they asked me to get up slowly and gently. They had added 65 pounds to the 300 I had barely pushed off my chest earlier. Any weightlifter knows that you go up in smaller increments; you just don't make a 21% increase all at once. That didn't bother them. Firmly, thoroughly, they talked me through a series of mental preparations. In my mind's eye I saw myself approaching the bench. I visualized myself lying down. I visualized myself, with total confidence, lifting the 365 pounds. I imagined the sounds I would hear, the clink of the metal as I tipped the bar and the weights shifted, my own breathing... Suddenly, I became apprehensive. They actually thought I was going to try and lift 365 pounds! I "knew" I could not do it. I knew my limits. The needles on the monitors jerked back and forth, reflecting my anxiety. Patiently, they talked me through more relaxation, more visualization. They asked me to zoom mentally in and out of the images now becoming familiar imprints in my mind: approaching the bar, grasping, lifting smoothly and confidently. All the while, they checked my responses on their monitors and gauges.

At length, everything began to come together for me, just as it does an instant before you know you are going to succeed in some task for which you have been preparing. One more time they talked me through the lift. In my mind I became convinced I could do it. The world around me seemed to fade, giving way to self-confidence, belief in myself, and then to deliberate action. I lifted the weight. Astounded, exhilarated by the triumph, I wanted to go on, I felt ready to challenge the world record. But more rational minds prevailed.

Garfield, after an eight-year layoff, had achieved his peak bench press through mentally aligning his conscious and subconscious mind—the ant and the elephant. The scientists had united Garfield's conscious beliefs with his unconscious images, creating an unstoppable vision for a successful outcome.

Nearly every world-class athlete has learned the secret of aligning the ant and the elephant, and it's just as effective in other fields. For instance, in 1987, a struggling actor, barely able to pay his bills, drove his old Toyota up Mulholland Drive into the Hollywood Hills. As he stared down at the City of Angels' lights, he ended the internal civil war, aligning his ant and his elephant, once and for all. He wrote himself a check, dated for Thanksgiving 1995, "for acting services rendered," in the amount of $10 million. Few actors or actresses receive checks of this amount, making it especially far-fetched that an unknown actor would believe in so absurd a ritual, but Carrey believed. He was uniting his ant and elephant towards a common goal and dream. When his conscious ant mind wrote the $10 million check, he was purposefully feeding his subconscious elephant mind the vision of his future reality. Today, Carrey, thanks to his united ant and elephant, has surpassed $20 million for acting services. Imagine how many others, however, with practically unlimited talent inside of them, never achieve success because, unlike Carrey, they never align the ant and the elephant.

Many people discipline their conscious ant mind to make a living, but precious few will ever discipline their subconscious elephant mind to achieve their dreams. This can change today for the reader. Determine the purpose, resolve to have character, listen to the positive voice, and align the ant and the elephant. Do this and success is imminent. Remember, the elephant will charge in some direction, but the question is: Is it charging toward one's dreams or one's fears?

VISION

Will Smith

Willard Christopher Smith Jr., otherwise known as Will Smith, is living proof than aligned ant and elephant minds can achieve at the highest of levels. A number one box office phenomenon, Smith has accomplished something that has never been done before: eight consecutive movies grossing over $100 million in revenue. Not surprisingly, he learned to tap into his subconscious mind to achieve these impressive results, sharing, "I don't know what my calling is, but I want to be here for a bigger reason. I strive to be like the greatest people who have ever lived." Still, Smith's isn't a fairy tale story of dream, victory, and he lived happily-ever-after. Rather, it is more like American Dreams of old—a kid with a huge dream has massive struggles and eventually sweet victories, like a modern day Horatio Alger success.

To be sure, Smith didn't start out with a silver spoon in his mouth. He was born to a lower-middle-class West Philadelphia family, but he did start with something much more valuable—a huge dream. This dream to do something great filled him with hope, which led to an unquenchable hunger to fulfill his vision. According to Smith, the turning point in his life occurred when he was sixteen years old when his discovered his first girlfriend was cheating on him. "In my mind, she cheated because I wasn't good enough. I remember making the decision that I will never not be good enough again." Instead of hosting a pity party, in other words, he realized that massive success would be his best revenge. Smith was not the average sixteen-year-old because he began incubating a plan for worldwide success that fed his hunger to learn and grow. Unfortunately, not many sixteen-year-olds respond to rejection by turning it into energy like Smith did.

Smith's ant and elephant mind alignment led him to seek wisdom through reading, understanding the value of borrowing the best ideas from the best leaders who ever lived. He explained:

> *The idea that there are millions and billions of people who have lived before us, and they had problems and they solved them and they wrote it in a book somewhere—there is no new problem that we can have that*

*we have to figure out by ourselves. There's no relation-
ship issue, there is no issue with your parents or your
brother or your government, there is no issue we can
have that somebody didn't already write a thousand
years ago in a book. So, for me, that concept of reading
is bittersweet because you know it's in a book somewhere but you've got to find the right one that is going
to give you the proper information.*

Passing on a prospective engineering career by turning
down MIT, Smith instead partnered with DJ Jazzy Jeff and
released their first album while still in high school. The pair's
PG-rated rap earned them the first-ever Grammy Award for
a hip-hop act. Still, some believed Smith was just lucky, but
he felt otherwise. In an interview with Travis Smiley, he
said, "Just decide, and the universe will get out of your way.
You're in a universe that says 2 + 2 = 4; 2 + 2 is going to be
what I want it to be." After winning his Grammy, however,
Smith, still a teenager, ran into financial difficulties; his
reckless spending led to an Internal Revenue Service audit.
This resulted in an embarrassing and painful tax lien of $2.8
million against his estate! One can only imagine how Smith
felt about this shocking setback as the IRS seized his assets
and garnished his wages. Few people bounce back from challenges of this magnitude, but Smith remained undaunted. If
anything, this merely motivated him further, for his mental
alignment of the ant and elephant simply refused to lose under any circumstances.

Despite facing the derision of friends and impending
bankruptcy, Smith parlayed his rapper popularity into an
NBC sitcom titled The Fresh Prince of Bel-Air. The show
became an overnight hit and Smith's career surged ahead.
Impressively, he erased his financial problems and moved
towards the dreams he envisioned. Smith's troubles were
far from over, however, as he also endured a difficult divorce
during this period, resulting in a $900,000 lump sum settle-
ment to his former wife and $24,000 per month in alimony
and child support. It just didn't seem that Smith could make
enough to outrun his financial challenges. Notwithstanding,
Smith continued to press on. He believed setbacks were just
part of life: "Every once in a while, it's your turn to be broken

VISION

down. And you wait for the tow truck to come. That's how I viewed that difficult time in my life." He understood it wasn't what happened to him but how he handled it that mattered.

Either one of these setbacks, a multimillion-dollar tax lien and a multimillion-dollar divorce, would have knocked down a lesser man, but Smith's failures only fueled his dream to do and become more. This is the power available to anyone who aligns the ant and elephant towards an inspiring vision of the future. The united elephant and ant can turn rejection into fuel for further growth. Needless to say, it takes discipline thinking and actions to create the belief needed for high-end achievement, but this is what every achiever has in common. In fact, it was the size of Smith's dream that determined the size of his comeback. What if Smith had surrendered to bankruptcy? What if he had surrendered to negativity and blamed the world for his problems? Unfortunately, this is exactly what the majority of people do when faced with setbacks—even those setbacks that are minuscule in proportion to those faced and overcome by Smith. The difference was an aligned ant and elephant; otherwise, practically any obstacle can kill a person's dreams if they are in the midst of a mental civil war.

Smith, in contrast, set the goal to become "the biggest movie star in the world." Naturally, to achieve this elephant-sized dream, he had to overcome elephant-sized obstacles. After all, any person who dreams big must also overcome big. This is why a person becomes a champion on the inside long before it's revealed on the outside. Interestingly, with the success of The Fresh Prince of Bel-Air, one would have thought a jump into the movies would be easy. Nothing could be further from the truth, for Smith couldn't buy a meeting with any of the studio directors. In fact, he hustled for over five years before he had his first success. Smith's business partner James Lassiter elaborated upon the reason for the studios' skepticism: "Nobody cared. You're a rapper. You got lucky, and you got this television show, but that's all you can do."

When asked if he ever thought of a plan B during this time, since plan A appeared to be closed, he responded, "I don't want to get too metaphysical, but by even contemplating a plan B, you almost create the necessity for a plan B."

RESOLVED

Clearly, Smith understood the mysterious power of a unified ant and elephant mind to propel a person towards his dream. He remained steadfast in his vision, refusing to even contemplate a plan B, for he knew that opening this door would open up a mental civil war between the ant (let's get reasonable) and the elephant (let's achieve something unreasonable). Indeed, if a person imagines a plan B, his elephant mind becomes confused as to which plan he is supposed to charge towards. This confusion leads to inaction as the paralyzed ant and elephant battle it out in the mental civil war. Not surprisingly, failure is the predictable outcome.

Later in his career, while on the set of the Mohamed Ali movie, Smith described another breakthrough. "When I was doing Ali, I realized that he kept saying, 'I'm the greatest, I'm pretty,' to make himself believe it." Smith elaborated, "He doesn't believe it, but he was dealing with racism. He was reacting to pain and rejection. He said it so much that he started to believe it. That's what I've tried to do for myself." Ali, in effect, used words from his ant mind to speak to his elephant mind, aligning them in the quest to be the greatest. As one can see, Will Smith's success is not by accident, but rather by design—a design available to all who will discipline themselves to align their ant and elephant minds. Smith understood the metaphysical nature of words and taught himself to control his inner voice. He explained, "I think of the universe as this big master computer. The keyboard is inside each of us. I have a keyboard inside of me. I just have to figure out what to type and learn the code to make the things happen that I want." While others may see limits, Smith trained his conscious and subconscious to imagine the limitless. Vision is tomorrow's reality expressed as an idea today and Smith expressed his vision for the future in ideas fed to his subconscious today. He explained to Smiley, "I want to be an idea. I want to represent possibilities. I want to represent the idea that you really can make what you want." Smith created what he wanted through the power of his words as he stated:

I said reading and running and the running aspect is how you can connect with your weakness. When you get on the treadmill you deprive yourself of oxygen.

VISION

What kind of person you are will come out very, very quickly. You're either the type of person who will say you're going to run three miles or you stop the treadmill at 2.94 and you hit it and you call 2.94 three miles, or you get off after a mile. Or you're the type of person that runs hard through the finish line and when you get to 3.0 you realize, "God, I could really do 5," and you go ahead and do two more. And that little person talks to you and says, "Man, do you feel your knee? We should stop. I feel we should stop ourselves right now. This is not healthy anymore." When you learn to get command over that person on that treadmill, you learn to get command over that person in your life.

Smith took command of his positive voice, aligning his thoughts, talk, and, walk toward his goals and dreams—a true example of the ant and the elephant in alignment.

It's been nearly twenty years since Smith had his sitcom splash as the humorous, fast-talking fresh prince. Today, his films gross an average of over $130 million per movie, making him one of movie business' top actors. His biggest grossing films were hits like Bad Boys; Bad Boys II; Independence Day; Men in Black; Men in Black II; I-Robot; The Pursuit of Happyness; I Am Legend; Hancock; Wild Wild West; Enemy of the State; Shark Tale; Hitch; and Seven Pounds. He also earned critical praise for his performances in Six Degrees of Separation, Ali, and The Pursuit of Happyness, receiving Best Actor Oscar nominations for the latter two. He discussed the connection between the proper thinking and hard work necessary to achieve success:

Paulo Coelho in The Alchemist, which is my favorite book, talks about the whole of the universe, and its containment in one grain of sand. For years I've been saying that, and now it's really starting to expose itself to me. My own grain of sand has been my story. The next 10 years will be my peak of innovation in filmmaking and just as a human being. I was reading Malcolm Gladwell's Outliers, and he talks about the concept of 10,000 hours—that you don't really settle into any level of mastery until 10,000 hours, and I feel like I've just completed my 10,000 hours of story structure and filmmaking.

It's difficult to imagine what Smith can do for an encore, but he's probably already on his way to achieving it. By forty-two years of age, he had broken many of the all-time movie records. One thing the world has learned about Willard Christopher Smith Jr. is to not bet against him. He has aligned his ant and elephant and is charging ahead towards his dreams. While others are doubting, he is dreaming; while others are complaining, he is creating; and lastly, where others are surrendering, Smith is just beginning. Everyone can learn from Smith's life, setting one's sails based on our dreams and goals, not just following where the wind takes him. Jesus, in Matthew 17:20, says, "For verily I say unto you, If ye have faith as a grain of mustard seed, ye shall say unto this mountain, Remove hence to yonder place; and it shall remove; and nothing shall be impossible unto you." What mountains need moving in the reader's life? Imagine a world where people removed mountains to achieve their destiny like Smith did in his? The world would be a much different place.

One final thought from Smith: "I consider myself an alchemist—an alchemist who took lead and made it gold." Dismally, so many people see the lead in their lives and avoid their destiny rather than turning it into gold on the success journey. Be that as it may, achievers are modern day alchemists who convert lead into gold. Belief is what makes the difference. Smith's unyielding belief in his mission helped him succeed. "If it was something that I really committed myself to, I don't think there's anything that could stop me becoming President of the United States."

CHAPTER 5

PLAN AND DO
Resolved: To Develop and Implement a Game Plan in Each Area of My Life

*I know that planning and doing are essential
parts of the success process.*
—Orrin Woodward

Now that a person has committed to the mastery of the private achievements, the first four resolutions, he is ready to produce results in his chosen field. To maximize his results, however, he must develop plans, because failure to plan is a plan to fail.

> **Dreams turn into plans, which turn into goals.**

Plan, Do, Check, and Adjust

I learned the importance of the planning process as a twenty-four-year-old engineer working at General Motors. Dr. Edward Deming, a man famous for helping the Japanese turn around their economy after WWII, spoke at a conference on the topic of statistical controls. Naturally, what I learned that day improved my professional life, but even more vitally, it revolutionized how I thought about the continuous improvement for success. Deming stated that experiments are performed to "make predictions" and to "verify predictions based upon data." He went on to explain how running tests help a person determine the accuracy of his predictions. If a theory is correct, he should be able to predict the result of an experiment; but if his results are not predictable, then his theory is not accurate and it requires further thoughts before more testing to tests his new theory.

RESOLVED

Listening to Deming, I realized that his process could be utilized in any area of life, not just for tests at work. Indeed, his methodology, called PDCA—plan, do, check, and act—was designed for testing products and services; but the PDCA process is just as applicable for predicting and testing in life. I adjusted the PDCA wording slightly, making it "plan, do, check, and adjust," and then implemented this methodology immediately in my life.

Every plan must be planned, done, checked, and then adjusted based upon the data to close the gap between predicted and actual results. The gap between the planned and actual results reveals a gap in knowledge that must be closed by further thinking and tests. Each experiment leads to further adjustments until the predicted and actual results align—the theory is proven in practice. Success, in effect, boils down to planning the work and working the plan, checking and adjusting the entire time until the results are predictable. This is why it takes thousands of hours to reach the top in any field, for it takes this long to PDCA to mastery. Gradually, I began to think of life as a series of ongoing tests, opportunities to see if planned behaviors produced the planned results. In other words, the quickest way to sort fact from fiction in one's life is to run PDCAs in the area until the data reveal the truth.

One humorous example is from when I was five years old. I awoke from a vivid dream convinced that I could swim underwater and breathe freely, for this is what I had done in my dream. I announced to my long-suffering mother that I could swim and breathe underwater. My mom patiently explained to me that it was a dream, that human beings cannot breathe underwater because we have lungs, not gills. I ignored he counsel, announcing instead to my brothers and sister that during our swimming lessons, I would prove my hypothesis by breathing underwater. Later that day, after ensuring my mom and siblings were watching, I proceeded to dive underwater, swimming leisurely from one end of the pool to the other. Eventually needing air, I contracted my young diaphragm and inhaled several lungs full of chlorinated water, disproving my prediction amidst flailing arms, gasping breaths, and a reddening face. My predicted result had failed under test conditions and I realized I needed to change—going to the surface for air from then on. By planning and doing, I was able to check the data, no longer believing I could breathe underwater and adjusted my behavior accordingly. This is a simple example of a PDCA. My plan (to swim underwater) was implemented (I inhaled underwater), but after checking the results (nearly drowning), I realized my plan had failed and thus I learned. I made an adjustment (human lungs breathe in air, not water), breathing before going underwater from there forward.

Of course, everyone's PDCAs are different, but each person can improve in any area by following the PDCA process. PDCAs ensure one's predictions/beliefs are accurate, based upon data, not just assumptions. Assumptions, needless to say, are the facts of fools and fools quickly become business failures. Those willing to PDCA consistently, verifying their thinking through data, will quickly move ahead of those who don't. Although everyone uses the PDCA process, at least indirectly, once it becomes the specific intent of all one's actions, the rise to the top and achievement of his purpose and vision is predictable.

PDCA—The Plan Step

Planning without doing is ineffective, but so is doing without planning.

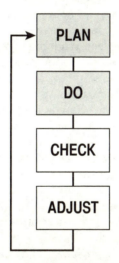

To achieve success, one must plan the work before doing the work, for only then can you check the results and make needed adjustments. A plan is a way to test one's hypotheses, beliefs, or models against reality. For example, if a person wishes to improve as a public speaker, he must plan to speak somewhere and have a few ideas he wishes to test on the audience. He can imagine how the ideas will work in front of the crowd, but won't know for sure until he actually speaks. Perhaps he has a humorous story that ties in with his main message or an analogy he is sure will connect with his audience. In either case, only stepping up to the plate

RESOLVED

and speaking will reveal the validity of his ideas. He has a plan to implement a couple of new items, and now must speak so he can get the valuable feedback on his plan. Thinking alone does not necessarily improve someone for he may be thinking wrong, but thinking (planning) and doing (working) will align one's inner and outer worlds.

One of the first steps to real change is to honestly evaluate where one needs improvement. This is not as easy as it sounds because most people have fragile egos and would rather live with comfortable lies than uncomfortable truths. Indeed, this is why one's purpose and dreams are so vital; they drive a person to change even when it's not comfortable or easy. Ironically, every person misses the mark in many areas. Mastery is so difficult that no one is excellent in more than a few areas of life. Thus, instead of running from painful truth, people would be much better served by changing the truth. When the dream is big enough, the facts don't count, or more accurately, the facts can be changed. For instance, to share a personal story, I was a terrible speaker, receiving zeros in two speeches (one my senior year in high school and the other as a first year masters degree student). This was embarrassing and humiliating as I froze on stage and couldn't even utter a word! Sure I could have avoided public speaking but I would have also avoided my destiny, for Inc. Magazine recently ranked me one of the Top 100 speakers in the world. How is this even possible? PDCA is the answer. Through a series of PDCAs, over a decade plus of speaking night after night, I identified what inspirational stories, logical reasoning, and humorous anecdotes seem to resonate with the audience. I would carefully plan the next speaking opportunity with material I knew the audience would like from previous PDCAs and add new material to test out as well. Gradually, my focus turned from my paralyzing fears to encouraging the audience. Furthermore, I studied all the best speakers and when I was moved, I sought to determine what it was the speaker did to inspire me. I didn't seek to copy anyone's style exactly as each speaker must be authentic to his own personality, but what I learned from others was invaluable on my speaking journey. Between mentoring with great speakers, modeling great speakers, and messaging over and over with the PDCA process, eventually speaking went from something I feared to something I enjoyed. One of my greatest fears, in other, words, was the doorway to my destiny. To this day, I don't speak for recognition or money, but to deliver inspiration and information that can change people lives.

What areas does the reader need to improve in to fulfill his purpose and vision? There is no better time than now to get started

PLAN AND DO

with a plan to improve. Remember, procrastination is the assassination of motivation, so quit procrastinating and start implementing. With a plan and a willingness to work, I believe anyone can improve. Moreover, if it ties in with your passions, potential, and profits (like speaking did for me), one can go from worst to first and fulfill one's purpose. There is no shame in not being good at something. The shame should be in remaining bad when one knows that his purpose depends upon improving in this area. Sadly, too many allow the fears of today imprison them rather than permitting the faith in a better tomorrow to set them free. Write down several areas that one desires to improve in and develop a game plan now. What specific items can the reader implement that he believes will help him improve in this area? If not sure how to improve, then it is time to ask others. Someone has already mastered this field and most winners love to help others who want to win. Moreover, someone has probably

> **Excellence demands consistent planning and testing, and a person must desire the goal more than he desires comfort.**

written a great book and has seminars to attend on the subject. The key is to quit waiting to get better and to start planning and doing now.

PDCA – The Do Step

This leads us to the second step in the PDCA process: Do. The best plans in the world are worthless unless people do them. If the road to Hell is paved with good intentions, then Hell has thickly paved roads. It's been said that the plans to fix the political mess in Washington, DC exist, but plans are worthless without someone willing to execute them. One of the books in the Bible is titled the book of Acts. Notice that it isn't called the book of Thoughts or the book of Best Intentions, but the book of Acts. Greatness begins when a person takes the plan step and has the courage to act on it. "Just do it," as the Nike slogan says. If, in public speaking, a person has identified areas in which to improve, then it's time for him to start speaking. A person simply cannot improve his craft until it is performed correctly over and over, even if he has to make mistake after mistake for an extended period until he becomes good. There simply is no substitute for this. Any person who is unwilling to look bad will never become good. By necessity, the PDCA process pushes a person to failure, forcing him to revise his plans. This isn't actually a failure, however, because what others call failure and winner calls learning, an opportunity to make

119

RESOLVED

adjustments and improve. Regrettably, most people refuse to execute the PDCA process because they fear looking and feeling like a failure more than they fear actually being a failure. After all, the only true failure in the PDCA process is someone who fails to plan and do. Once a person understands the goal of the PDCA process is to learn from "teachable moments" and these moments only occur when one "fails", then he is set free from the fear of failure. Every PDCA leads to learning after failing, which subsequently becomes the knowledge to run an improved PDCA in the future. A person will never get to the check and adjust steps (covered in the next chapter), without the discipline to plan and do.

The PDCA process is so important that I need to share one more personal example to ensure readers are picking up the concept. One of my all-time favorite quotes, a quote I first heard from a professor at GMI-EMI (now Kettering University), a thunderbolt of wisdom that changed my perspective, is, "When all is said and done, much more is said than is ever done." Perhaps the reason it struck me so profoundly is that back then, I was under tremendous financial strain. Having moved out of my parent's house on my 19th birthday and completely oblivious to the cost of living, I was so broke that I could not even afford to pay attention. Seriously, I lived on one hot dog and one potato per night, kept the heat at 50 degrees Fahrenheit in the middle of the winter, and still didn't have enough money for bills and school. Tuition alone cost more than I made as a Co-Op student at AC Spark Plug, forcing me to borrow $17,500 just to continue my education.

Although hopelessly naive and inexperienced in the ways of the world, I vowed to make it without having to run to Mom and Dad for help. Of course, this wasn't easy, but nothing worthwhile ever is. I lived in a dangerous neighborhood in the most wretched of conditions, renting the bottom half of a varmint-infested house that ended up being condemned less than a year after I moved out. Nonetheless, I was not depressed or even fearful, for I had a dream, a plan, and the motivation to escape my poverty and to live my dreams. I quickly realized the key to making my dream come true was massive action! Without this, I would be out of college, out of a job, and practically out of options. Needless to say, my back was against the proverbial wall; however, I believed that if I walked my talk by implementing the game plan, busting my butt at work, and graduating as an engineer, my life would improve.

Reflecting back, I believe the lack of options was a blessing because it narrowed my focus and helped me apply massive action on the one plan I had in front of me. I simply didn't have the time

PLAN AND DO

or money to even entertain other options. This is how I was blessed with FOCUS!

To me, the success process boils down to three things:

1. What do you want?
2. What does it cost?
3. Pay it.

Strangely, however, while the first two questions are talked about incessantly, the third step, the action one, is rarely applied. What gives? Why, in other words, would perfectly capable people, who know what they want and know what it's going to take to achieve it, refuse to do the actions necessary to accomplish it? I believe this is one of the biggest leadership paradoxes facing people moving from the private achievements (I can do this) to the leadership achievements (we can do this).

After all, true leaders are not people who coax people into doing something they DON'T want to accomplish, for that would be manipulation. Rather, leadership is about inspiring people to perform the actions necessary to accomplish what they DO want. Over the next decade, in the process of building leadership communities, I realized just how rare the person is who actually does what he says. If I had a dollar for everyone who said they were going to become a top leader, I could live for the next year! It reminds me of my friend Chris Brady, whose dad told him repeatedly, "Talk is cheap, but it takes money to buy whiskey." Likewise, talk is cheap, but it takes action to buy one's dreams.

The reason I am sharing this is to emphasize to my readers the importance of ACTION! Quit waiting for conditions to be right, for they rarely are; quit waiting for others to lead, for they rarely do; finally, quit waiting for inspiration and focus on perspiration! So many, in other words, wait to feel right before acting right. I have learned, over the years, that a person must start acting right, *then* he will feel right about it. If you have a dream, then act on it, regardless of feelings. Shamefully, most people wait their whole life and accomplish little of substance. This reminds me of the old Chinese proverb which stated, "Man who stands on side of mountain waiting for roasted duck to fly into his mouth waits a long time."

If you have a vehicle to win, then develop a plan, determine the price, and pay it by applying massive action! Everyone wants to live his dreams, but only those who plan and work ever truly will. Yes, my accounting professor at GMI-EMI gave me a priceless nugget and now I am passing it onto you: "When all is said and

121

done, much more is said then is ever done." The world is filled with talkers, but every leader follows the same basic plan—dreaming big, creating the right leadership culture to separate the talkers from the walkers, and learning to love the talkers while leading the walkers. Indeed, the art and science of leadership is nothing more or less than modeling the right behaviors, messaging the right behaviors, and then mentoring those who ACT on the right behaviors. But I am getting ahead of myself and Resolution #9 will cover leadership. Nonetheless, the culture of execution is what every great leader in every field develops to generate lasting success.

Success Never Goes on Sale

Success never goes on sale, but most people spend their whole lives dickering over the cost while never making the purchase. Unfortunately, nine out of ten of the people reading this will not comment and instead will just talk about their dreams, but the one out of ten will comment and ACT their way to their dreams! I encourage the reader to be part of the ten percent because that's what leaders do. Massive action is a price few people are willing to pay for their dreams, but this is why planning and doing is one of the 13 resolutions, for without it, one cannot fulfill his purpose and vision.

The price of success is high, but so is the price of failure, and while the price for success is temporary, the price for failure is permanent. A person's gifts, talents, and energies are only useable during his time on Earth, so don't waste it. Fortunately, every reader right now is applying one of the keys to success; that is, developing a game plan to improve. The previous chapters discussed purpose, character, attitude, and the power of aligning one's ant and elephant towards one's dream. All of these are excellent, but not sufficient for success. Now that we have the inside person right, it's time to act on the outside! Success is a picture backed by a long-term plan and completed through hard work. Five years is a reasonable time frame for the plans of top achievers. Sadly, in today's microwave age, most people expect to see top results in five days. This simply isn't reasonable. The price for success is not purchased in a lump sum; instead, it's paid in daily installments every day. Only after every installment is paid in full does one receive the prize. In fact, many times, one ends up paying more than the asking price; but when committed, he will pay whatever price is required legally, morally, and ethically. Dreams turn into plans, which turn into goals that demand massive action. Develop a plan

PLAN AND DO

for success in each area of life, making every monthly deposit to ensure the price is paid in full.

PDCA and Ten Thousand Hours

With the PDCA process, the more one does, the more he learns. Author Samuel Goldwyn wrote, "The harder I work, the luckier I get." Successful people just appear lucky to those not willing to invest ten thousand hours of painful effort to develop mastery. Luck, in essence, is a loser's excuse not to make a winner's commitment. No one lucks into long-term success. Author Malcolm Gladwell practically explained the PDCA process that all winners use when he referred to K. Anders Ericsson's study:

> *The striking thing about Ericsson's study is that he and his colleagues couldn't find any "naturals," musicians who floated effortlessly to the top while practicing a fraction of time their peers did. Nor could they find any "grinds," people who worked harder than everyone else, yet just didn't have what it takes to break the top ranks. Their research suggests that once a musician has enough ability to get into a top music school, the thing that distinguishes one performer from another is how hard he or she works. That's it. And what's more, the people at the very top don't work just harder or even much harder than everyone else. They work much, much harder.*

Ten thousand hours is the number that appears over and over in the research of top achievers, for it takes years of planning, practice, and improvements to develop the skills that make success look and feel natural. This dedicated PDCA work ethic is what separates those who win from those who lose. Everyone fails, but only losers fail doubly, for they also fail to learn from their failures. Simply logging ten thousand hours won't get it done. A person must endure the pain of "teachable moments" in the PDCA process repeatedly, falling in love with the continuous improvement process. This is why only PDCA hours count towards the ten thousand hours. Dismally, for most people, twenty-five years of experience is actually one year's experience twenty-five times. Since mastery requires ten thousand PDCA hours in a specific profession, focus becomes crucial. There simply aren't enough ten-thousand-hour segments to master every field. As a result, a person can become great in nearly any field, but he cannot become great in all fields. This leads a person back to his purpose to determine which areas he should focus his time in to develop mastery to fulfill the long-term vision.

To use a popular example, the Beatles didn't start out as expert musicians; they needed to invest ten thousand PDCA hours to develop mastery like everyone else. The key was they focused in the field of music until they did so. Many believe the Beatles were just incredibly talented musicians and that talent catapulted them to the top. While it's true they had talent, author Philip Norman set the record straight when he described the group's eighteen months of live performances in Hamburg, Germany: "They were no good onstage when they went there and they were very good when they came back. They learned not only stamina. They had to learn an enormous amount of numbers—cover versions of everything you can think of, not just rock and roll, a bit of jazz too. They weren't disciplined onstage at all before that. But when they came back, they sounded like no one else. It was the making of them." Remarkably, the Beatles performed 270 times in eighteen months, many times for eight hours a night! Is anyone shocked that the musical skills and showmanship of the Beatles improved dramatically when the thousands of hours of PDCA time in in Hamburg, Germany, are thrown into the equation?

The truth is, by the time Beatlemania exploded in the USA, the Beatles had already performed "live" over 1,200 times, more than most bands do in their lifetimes. Needless to say, the Beatles worked harder than other bands by improving their skills through the PDCA process. Gladwell reflected, "The Hamburg crucible is one of the things that set the Beatles apart." In a similar fashion, every achiever needs his Hamburg crucible, practicing while others are playing, dreaming while others are dreading, enduring while others are ending. No extraordinary achievement is accomplished without great sacrifice, and the ten thousand hours is the sacrifice, the price to be paid for mastery.

Deliberate Practice

Abraham Lincoln, amidst many trials and tribulations, invested his ten thousand hours in leadership, and once remarked, "I will work, I will study, and when my moment comes, I will be ready." Lincoln set out to deliberately build his leadership by working, studying, learning, and improving—all parts of the PDCA process. Geoff Colvin called it deliberate practice, which is PDCA by another name: "Deliberate practice is characterized by several elements, each worth examining. It is activity designed specifically to improve performance, often with a teacher's help; it can be re-

PLAN AND DO

peated a lot; feedback on results is continuously available; it's highly demanding mentally, whether the activity is purely intellectual, such as chess or business-related activities, or heavily physical, such as sports; and it isn't much fun." Deliberate practice separates the amateurs from the professionals. Whereas amateurs practice skills that they are comfortable with, the professionals practice skills they are uncomfortable with, pushing past failure to learn, for mastery is on the painful side past routine competence and comfort. Few are willing to endure the painful "teachable moments" and

> **Only through pushing past one's comfort zone will a person improve his level of skills.**

this is why so few master any field. Deliberate practice demands a level of focus and endurance to withstand the constant assault on a person's current skill limits. Not surprisingly, this is why knowing one's purpose is so vital since only one's purpose give the person the persistence to endure the pain. Colvin emphasized the importance of pushing past the comfort zone:

> *Great performers never allow themselves to reach the automatic, arrested-development stage in their chosen field. That is the effect of continual deliberate practice—avoiding automaticity. The essence of practice, which is constantly trying to do the things one cannot do comfortably, makes automatic behavior impossible....Avoiding automaticity through continual practice is another way of saying that great performers are always getting better.*

As stated previously, no one lucks into long-term success. LUCK, properly defined, is "laboring under correct knowledge." Consistently hard and painful PDCA work is the only recipe for developing mastery.

Success—the Pain of Greatness

Just as a mother delivering a baby must endure the pain before receiving the prize, so too must achievers in any field. When the going gets tough, in a word, the tough get going. Winners get better and whiners get bitter. The PDCA process reveals shortcomings in a person's thinking and actions and this is painful. Professor Robert Grudin pinpointed the role pain has in creativity:

125

RESOLVED

To be truly open to any experience, the mind must be open to all. The willing endurance of pain is a key factor not only in human dignity, but also in human creativity. It would seem to follow that individuals who spend their lives in the persistent avoidance of pain are not likely to amount to much...The process of achieving their professional level is usually full of pain. Such mastery demands endless practice of technical operations, endless assaults on seemingly ineluctable concepts, humiliation by teachers, anxious and exhausting competition with peers. To gain such mastery, one must face the sting of pertinent criticism, the shock of a thousand minor failures, and the nagging fear of one's own un-improvable inadequacy...A tiny minority gets through to the top, to memorable excellence or profound understanding. The rest of us stop along the way, perhaps for a temporary rest, perhaps for a period of reassessment. But once we stop, we are unlikely to start up again. Security is suddenly far sweeter than enterprise.

Grudin is describing the PDCA process that separates the achievers from non-achievers. While non-achievers settle for mediocrity, valuing comfort over knowledge, achievers strive for excellence, valuing knowledge over comfort. The highest achievers, because they admit when they don't measure up, work hard to close the gap. In fact, one of the biggest motivators for winners to endure the pain of the PDCA process is the criticism from others who mock them, seeking to make them feel inferior. Winners, however, have learned to turn rejection into energy, as psychologist Henry Link described:

> *A sense of inferiority, we find, is not a disease. I have told hundreds of complaining parents: You should be thankful that your child has a sense of inferiority. The children to worry about are those who always think they are smart, who know better than their elders, who see no reason for painful practice or humble effort. The child, however, who feels inferior, can usually be trained to develop abilities which in time will make him truly superior. All genuine superiority grows out of a sense of inferiority.*

Will Smith elaborated on this in an interview: "I'm not afraid to die on a treadmill. I will not be outworked. You may be more talented than me. You might be smarter than me. And you may be better looking than me. But if we get on a treadmill together, you are going to get off first or I'm going to die. It's really that simple. I'm not going to be outworked." Feeling like others are better is not only not a problem, it actually can be an advantage because it

PLAN AND DO

drives a person to work harder. Inferior thoughts can lead to superior actions with the PDCA process.

Work as a Game

The work demanded to win is tough, but it can be developed by anyone. Thankfully, while there isn't a shortcut past the ten thousand hours for mastery, there is a shortcut for the monotony of it. That is to say, when work becomes a game; the work becomes fun. Many times a person playing a game doesn't even realize the pain he is enduring to develop skills because he is competing against himself or others. The enjoyment of the contest, in a word, lightens the load. The secret to mastery, as a result, is learning to make the PDCA process a game one competes in. To illustrate, imagine a hot autumn day when a man must choose between playing tennis or raking the lawn. On one hand, in the game of tennis, he can play for hours, sweating profusely, but enjoy the entire experience. On the other hand, he looks at the rake with dread, procrastinating as long as possible and only completing the task through sheer strength of will. What's the difference? The temperature is the same, it requires the same amount of time, and the effort is the same, but the enjoyment is night and day. One is perceived by the mind as play and fun whereas the other is viewed as work and drudgery. A person who views his work as a game no longer is working; instead, he is playing a game. This is one of the secrets to top performers—they make the PDCA process a game to play. Work isn't work anymore; rather, it's part of the fun of competing to win the game by improving his skills. Weekend warriors are similarly motivated, giving 100% effort to a sport they will never receive a dime of pay for. They do it for the love of the game. Highly successful people have tapped into this reservoir of energy, creating a game out of their work, thus falling in love with the PDCA process in the quest for excellence and mastery. Imagine the productivity in the world if all people worked as hard in their professions as they do in their hobbies. Better yet, imagine if everybody's profession were his passion.

Ozzie Smith, a baseball Hall of Famer, exemplifies turning the PDCA process into play. Ozzie loved playing baseball, but he grew up in poverty that didn't give him access to the best equipment. Nonetheless, he wanted to play so he used his imagination. He created a game where he bounced a tennis ball off his cement porch. He challenged himself daily, moving closer and closer to the porch, testing his ability to field the tennis ball cleanly into his glove. The goal was to field as many balls rebounding off the porch as he could. Naturally, this was challenging, but it developed his hand-eye coordination beyond anyone else and by making it a game, Ozzie could play for hours on end. He attempted to field the ball again and again relentlessly. He practiced more hours of fielding than any coach would dream of practicing his team. Ozzie's discipline was amazing, but since it was a game, it didn't feel like discipline at all. Smith's love of play allowed him to stay focused while enduring hours of deliberate practice PDCA, developing mastery as a baseball infielder. Not surprisingly, Ozzie became a perennial Gold Glove winner at shortstop and later entered the baseball hall of fame. Indeed, he made the tough plays look easy, amazing fans with his highly developed hand-eye coordination. He made it look easy because of his thousands of hours of PDCA playing his game. Ozzie credited his childhood game for developing his fielding skills and encouraged others to use their imaginations to do similarly. Make PDCA fun, and like Ozzie, the pain of the process will become the joy of the game while skills are developed.

Quitters, Campers, and Climbers

Another lesson in pain in the journey to mastery is the envy of others who refuse to endure the PDCA process. Today's envious age even has a name for it—HATERS. What is it about these haters that make them hate on winners? Author George Roche termed haters anti-heroes, and observed:

> *The anti-hero dismisses all-purpose as illusion. It sees us as helpless pawns, unable to act or even think on our own, fully shaped and determined by outside forces. It reaches this position with tortuous chains of inference, with misused "scientific assumptions" and fanciful formulas that dare to tell us what we can and cannot know, what is and is not real. But all this is contrivance, serving not the search for knowledge and truth, but the rebel's own dark purposes. And it is all belied in an instant by that one purposeful, death-defying act of a hero. That act, a reality known to us all, tells us more about the human condition than all of the empty and life-hating mutterings of modernist philosophers. It serves a Good we all may turn to for fulfillment in our lives.*

To succeed in today's world, a person must not only endure the price of success, paying the same price that Washington, Franklin, and Edwards paid, but must also pay a further price in an antihe-

PLAN AND DO

roic age – the price of unjust criticism. Critics will throw tomatoes at achievers because achievers remind them of what they could have been. Author Marc Simmons, addressing the Western writers of America, said, "You see they must discredit the Western hero because if just one person can be shown to have achieved wholeness, then it becomes evident that the possibility is open to all."

> **When a person develops mastery today, he must expect the pain of the process along with the pain of criticisms from the anti-heroes.**

But if success is open to all, then people would have to take responsibility for their lack of success. This is not easy to do and most would rather blame others to make them feel better. Dr. Paul Stoltz described three types of people staring at the mountain of life—quitters, campers, and climbers. Even though every human being is born with the urge to climb, and there are billions of people in the world, the mountaintops remain practically empty. What happened to all of the mountain climbers? In a word, compromise. Most compromise their convictions for their conveniences, eschewing the pain of the climb, and become "given-ups" instead of grownups.

Life's quitters see the mountain's jagged cliffs, threatening storms, and dangerous paths as risky and settle for safety. Of course, by avoiding failure, they neglect the PDCA process needed to grow and become. By denying their God-given urge to climb, they compromise and rationalize away their lives. Quitters entertain themselves to death, escaping into drugs, sex, or other recreational time-consuming activities. They keep themselves busy doing nothing in order to avoid the mountain they no longer wish to climb. Nonetheless, they suffer a worse pain than the pain of climbing—the pain of regret—a life spent in service to self rather than others. If their conscience confronts them with the truth of their pitiable existence they obfuscate the facts, attempting to justify the unjustifiable, pointedly, they never gave life a chance. Fortunately, light can shine into darkness and I have seen quitters start climbing and produce amazing results for themselves and their families.

Campers, on the other hand, start climbing the mountain by learning and growing (the PDCA process). They are excited about opportunities on the mountainside and begin life's climb enthusiastically. However, at some point, through a combination of successes already achieved and the pain associated with further climbing, they cease the PDCA process, compromising their ideals for the comfort of camp. They may have a nice mountain view, but

129

RESOLVED

their best days are behind them because they surrendered their future significance for doing "pretty good." Though the campers know the price of the climb, they no longer are willing to pay it. Many convince themselves that they are resting for a season, but few seem to ever climb again. Some of the most talented people, with the most to contribute to others, have settled for good and the comfort in camp rather than the power in purpose. Please don't misunderstand, everyone should take a vacation and refresh once in a while (see Chris Brady's *A Month in Italy*), but not take a vacation for life. The intent of vacations is to recharge one's purpose, not avoid it. Purpose, that is to say, is a lifetime calling.

Climbers are the last group. These are people who refuse to compromise their calling, deciding to press on in the PDCA processes. They enjoy the game of life and press on through the pain to see what the next turn in the mountain brings. They know they were called to climb the mountain and are willing to do the work to accomplish it. Climbers are a rare breed—they refuse to sacrifice their convictions for conveniences. For them, life isn't about obtaining the best camping spot or accumulating the most items in their tents. Life isn't graded upon possessions, but rather on purpose—it's about the climb. Climbers know that happiness is in fulfilling one's purpose, becoming who we were intended to be. Not everyone reaches the mountaintop but everyone can reach their potential to serve others and that is the true victory. A climber enjoys the climb up his mountain, and in the process, he conquers himself. His climb leaves a path for others to follow in pursuit of their purpose. Moreover, he teaches other climbers the lessons he has learned climbing his mountain. Each person staring at the mountain is accountable for his personal climb. Will he quit, camp, or climb? If he chooses to climb, the PDCA process will be his invaluable aid in the journey to improve, helping him learn lessons to pass onto others just as I desire to do in writing this book. To sum up, success is the journey, not the destination.

130

PLAN AND DO

Lou Holtz: Planning and Doing

How does a young man from a broken home (his parents separated while he was in college), who didn't come from money or have any special connections, become one of the all-time coaching greats? Moreover, how did he do this despite suffering from a lisp, an undersized physique, and low self-esteem? Needless to say, Lou Holtz's rise to success in football coaching is one of the most surprising and inspiring stories of overcoming adversity in America today.

Holtz was born in 1937 in the small town of Follansbee, West Virginia. He once described his family's dismal financial situation as he was growing up: "We needed a raise to be considered poor. Every day we awoke to hardship, and every night we fell asleep thankful for one more day of sustenance." Holtz, unlike most, did not seek a life of ease by avoiding challenges. Instead, he learned from challenges, developing the ability to persevere no matter what. The Holtz family men worked as manual laborers in either the coal mines or the steel factories. No one in the family had attended college—not his dad, who quit school in the third grade, nor his mom, despite her graduating as valedictorian of her high school class.

Not surprisingly, then, when Holtz's high school coach visited his parents and suggested that he attend college to become a coach, the parents' response was hesitant at best. Moreover, he lacked the grades and the funding to pay for tuition. Even Holtz, at first, thought the idea was ludicrous, but he later warmed to it, noting, "I was not a good student, but I received a good education, not only academically but also in the intangibles everyone must have to succeed." Thankfully, due to the sacrifices his mom made, taking a night job to help pay for school, plus Holtz joining ROTC, he was able to enroll at Kent State.

Strikingly, one of the turning points in Holtz's life occurred shortly thereafter, transforming an academically unmotivated kid into a focused freshman. It occurred in a local grocery store, where Holtz was shopping for several items for his family. He heard two ladies the next aisle over in a conversation. Holtz recalled:

131

RESOLVED

Mrs. Hoback said, "I can't believe Anne Marie Holtz is wasting her money sending that boy Lou to college."

Mrs. Toft then said, "I know what you mean. She took a night job and everything. It's such a waste."

They didn't know I'd overheard them, since I was one aisle over, but those comments cut me deeply and burned inside me throughout my freshman year. I knew that my mother was sacrificing for me, but to have her friends, the people in my town, think that I was not worth the effort, that I was bound to fail, turned my wounded feelings into something quite different. My "want" to do well became a fiery determination. I would do whatever it took to pass, especially as a freshman, a year when the adjustment to college life can take its toll.

This incident awoke the sleeping giant, setting Holtz on fire to follow through on his plan. Notice how he responded to negativity by converting it into positive action. This is a crucial point in goal setting because many others will laugh at one's plans and goals, especially if they are bigger than everyone else's. Nevertheless, the more the critics laughed, the more determined Holtz became to finish what he started. He refused to let his mother's sacrifice be in vain. This provided the motivation to actually do his plan versus just think about his plan. Holtz, needless to say, did finish college and begin his coaching career. Initially, he didn't set the world on fire, working as an assistant coach at several schools and in 1967, unceremoniously, Holtz was fired, along with every other South Carolina assistant coach, when the head coach exited the program. Holtz was at a fork in the road. To make matters worse, he had recently bought a house in South Carolina, so his funds were even lower than his opportunities. His wife, Beth, in a gesture of confidence and love, bought him the classic book The Magic of Thinking Big, which he devoured in a matter of days. Being the hungry student he is, he followed the instructions by writing out his goals, identifying 108 bucket list goals, some of them absolutely crazy given that he didn't even have a job at the time.

Be that as it may, that is how big dreams work. First, one gets the vision, then he develops the plan to make that

PLAN AND DO

vision a reality. True, a fired assistant coach will not achieve all these dreams but a person on fire for his dreams will not remain a fired assistant coach. After all, the dream leads to goal setting, then the commitment to achieve the goals by launching the PDCA process. Few people planned as clearly and lived the plan with as specific intent as Holtz did. He shared how goal planning and action transformed his life: "I've been amazed at how many people have wanted to talk about my list over the years. I can't believe more people don't have a similar list of goals." Indeed, it's the dream that creates the passion and energy needed to do the task, accomplish the goal, and live the dream. Holtz constantly exhorted his teams: "Be a participant; don't be a spectator. Do things. Just decide what you want to do and then ask the question, 'What's important now?' Now what do I have to do to accomplish such and such? And that will tell you the action you have to take. It's not a wish list, it's a set of things I wanted to accomplish and it really hasn't changed that much."

Plans, to be sure, are important, but once the plan is in place, it takes massive action to achieve them. As golfing great Ben Hogan once said: "Playing a tournament is almost an anticlimax. Tournaments are won and lost in preparation. Playing them is just going through the motions." Similarly, plans fail unless they are backed by massive work. Holtz explained:

> *You work hard and suffer because it makes you a better man. If the rewards you seek are found in the praise and adulation of others, you are destined for disappointment, because the moment you drop one pass, or lose one game, the cheering stops and the praise goes away. Internal rewards, the ones you gain from pain, sweat, and tears, stick with you forever... People perform to the level expected of them...If I had expected the scout squad to go through the motions and pump up the egos of our starters, that's exactly what they would have done. But because I demanded nothing short of greatness, the players elevated their performance far beyond anyone's expectations. This is*

the way I was coached and the only way I know how to coach.

Holtz would have never achieved excellence without setting goals and following through with maximum effort to achieve them through following his version of PDCA process. Nonetheless, the PDCA process doesn't promise an easy road or overnight success. Holtz's life, in reality, is a model of the ups and downs that occur even when someone is as hungry as he was. Regardless of the price, though, Holtz always accepted responsibility for the outcomes and continued to apply the PDCA process to improve. Remember, a person doesn't fail unless he blames someone else for his results because only then does he surrender his ability to PDCA to eventual victory. Holtz refused to play the blame game by making excuses; on the contrary, he built his life around personal responsibility to make the choices that create one's life. He wrote, "The choices we make determine how successful we are. When you acknowledge that you and only you are responsible and accountable for the choices you make, and when you refuse to blame others for the choices you have made, you have in your hands the blueprint for success. When you allow others to choose your path so that you can then blame someone else when things don't go your way, you are fooling no one and cheating no one but yourself." Holtz emphasized that when people make choices, they make their beds and must lie in them. Accordingly, if a person desires better results, then he must develop better plans and do the work to change the results. While we may not have complete control over everything that happens to us, we certainly control how we respond to what happens to us. Holtz's life verifies that better plans and hard work do pave the way for better outcomes. This is the secret of high achievement —rigorous planning and doing to launch the PDCA process, followed by checking and adjusting steps discussed in the next chapter. Lou Holtz modeled all of these and this is why he has become a coaching legend. He has set numerous college football records and has helped four schools finish in the top 10 rankings, a feat still never matched.

Not surprisingly, like all achievers, Holtz received his share of criticisms as all great achievers do. Strangely, many

PLAN AND DO

people see life as a competition where the goal is to knock others down to lift themselves up. Since criticism is viewed as the easiest way to knock someone off the top, requiring little effort and not results, this, evidently, is the preferred method of non-achievers. They seek equality with winners, without having to perform, by knocking winners down to their level. The smallest minds with the smallest ideas criticize the biggest minds with the biggest ideas. For instance, imagine if Holtz shared his 108 dreams or plans with his critics. They would have laughed at the fired assistant coach's hubris for daring to plan such audacious goals and told him to get a job. Thankfully, Holtz did dare to dream, ignoring his critics and, in the process, achieving his dreams. Holtz once commented on critics: "The only people who aren't going to be criticized are those who do absolutely nothing. And the critics, the people who just observe, are never on the inside, never really had to make decisions that affect people's lives." Holtz learned, as all successful people do, that tearing down others is easy but valueless while learning from others is difficult but invaluable. He said, "I welcome all the suggestions in the world from people who have been involved in doing something... but somebody who has never done anything except observe and criticize, I don't weigh that at all."

The key lesson here is for a person to live his life based upon his resolutions and not to listen to the dogs barking on the side of the success road. Holtz summed it up well: "The higher up you go and the more things you try to accomplish, the more people try to find fault. There are so many things in life that are not fair. You work all your life to do something and people try to tear you down. You can't control it or do anything about it. When you look at the options of dealing with criticism, there's really only one option—to pray to God that you have the courage and the strength that you won't become bitter and move on with your life." Such wise advice from a man who planned and lived life inspiring others by his model and message. In sum, life only changes direction when, like the captain of a ship, a person seizes the helm and starts steering. Perhaps it's time to take one's goal setting to the next level. If the reader has written goals, maybe now is the time to dust them off. Or better yet, start with a fresh piece of paper and dare to dream again. Decide to do whatever it

RESOLVED

takes legally, morally, and ethically to achieve them by following the PDCA process, like Holtz, once more, expounded:

Every athlete who has ever played for me has heard me preach against the pitfalls of entering anything halfway. In my mind, a half-hearted commitment is worse than no commitment at all...If you're on a team, you owe your coaches and teammates your total commitment. If you don't—if you're unhappy because the coach doesn't start you, or because you aren't getting as many touches as you think you should—you are hurting yourself and the entire organization. You and the team would be better off if you played somewhere else...Commitment is the most critical component in any relationship. A marriage based on the premise, "Well, let's give this a shot, and if it doesn't work out, or if we 'grow apart,' we can always get divorced," is doomed before the vows are complete.

Goal setting and the PDCA process works when the person does. Lou Holtz's life is a living example of the power of goals and work ethic to achieve one's dreams. When a person makes a 100% commitment, backing it up with 100% effort, he will achieve the goal and learn through perseverance. Success is an inside job, just as it was for an unemployed assistant coach who dared to dream and do until he became a household name.

CHAPTER 6

SCOREBOARD
Resolved: To Keep Score in the Game of Life

I know that the scoreboard forces me to check and confront the results and make the needed adjustments in order to win.

Defeats are merely repeats with better information.
—Orrin Woodward

To go further into the PDCA process, even people who plan and do are not finished yet. They must also check the results compared to the goal and then make the necessary adjustments in order to make the predicted results closer to the actual ones. It's been said that airplanes are off course over 90% of the time and yet they land at their destination nearly 100% of the time. They do so through applying a type of PDCA where they set (plan) the destination, fly the plane (do) towards the destination, check the plane's location with respect to destination, and, finally, make adjustments to arrive at proper location. This is the secret to PDCA—fail your way to success. Why not use the same process in living one's life? Interestingly, without the check step, the necessary adjustments cannot be made and a plane, or one's life, will never arrive at the desired destination. For most people, the check step is very difficult because they have to honestly review their current results. As Ronald Reagan once said, "Trust but verify." A person must not only trust his plan, but also verify it's working as designed. If not, then adjustments need to be made. Absurdly, many people are afraid to check their plans for fear they will feel like a loser if it isn't working. This would be like pilots flying a plane while refusing to check their location against the flight plan for fear of feeling like inadequate pilots. Naturally plans fail, but this doesn't make people failures unless

RESOLVED

they refuse to make adjustments. After all, just as a plane cannot expect to reach its destination without applying the PDCA process, people cannot expect to reach their purpose without it either. This is why the check and adjust steps are one of the 13 Resolutions.

The check step is the scoreboard of life.

The check step is similar to the scoreboard at sporting events; a person can quickly look at it to determine who is winning. Without the check step, he cannot identify the areas in life he needs to improve. A good coach consults the scoreboard and halftime data to make adjustments. On the same basis, a leader should also consult his scoreboard and data to make adjustments. To reject the check step is to reject the potential to grow because one cannot change course until he knows where he is. Nevertheless, many people, who had the courage to plan and do, still won't check the results and make adjustments. Usually this is because a person cares more about preserving his ego than successfully completing the task. Sure, it's embarrassing to discover gaps between current skills and the needed ones, but it's even worse to have a gap and not know it. Most people, strangely, would rather hide from negative data that indicate a lack of skills rather than confront the data to grow skills. Avoiding negative data, however, doesn't change them, but only ensures the person's mediocrity. This is like the story of the ostrich sticking its head into the sand to avoid seeing the lion. While it's true he can no longer see the lion, it certainly doesn't change the lion's dinner plans. Achievers must check results, identifying gaps between the current reality and the future goal to make the needed changes and run the PDCA process again. How many times should an achiever PDCA? The answer is as many times as it takes to achieve, master, and fulfill his purpose.

One of the secrets the PDCA proves is to find a defeat in every victory (to remain humble to improve) and a victory in every defeat (to maintain hopeful while losing). Now, regardless of whether one is winning or losing, he is both humble and hopeful for the future. This balance, whether winning or losing is what separates long-term winners from those who rise and fall. Insofar as there has never been, nor will there ever be, a perfect performance, the key is to identify where one can improve and do so. Winners seek areas to improve because those who refuse to stay down usually wind up on top. Learn to study the data in one's field to reveal where one can improve. Great leaders in business, sports, or volunteer communities study data daily to identify what is going right, what is going wrong, and suggest methods to improve. Then, naturally, it's onto the next PDCA to see how one's predictions worked out in practice. It takes courage to make adjustments, especially since most people value comfort over change, but leaders have the courage to change because they want to win.

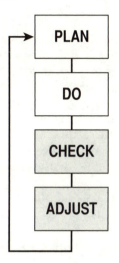

Once the adjust step is completed, the achiever has performed the full PDCA loop. Now, it's time to start over with the new information and run it again with better plans. Success is practically ensured when a person realizes that he is responsible for his own perpetual personal development improvement process. This indicates that anyone can win in life so long as he is willing to humble himself before the data learned in the PDCA process. What makes PDCA such an effective process is that it exposes a person's (and company's) weaknesses to himself (or the leadership team). This forces the person to either change or quit, running from the process and denying the revealed data. Invariably, leaders sacrifice their egos to protect excellence where the rest sacrifice excellence to protect their egos. Success, then, is only for the few—not the talented few but the courageous few, the ones who deal in truth about themselves and their organizations.

> **Success is practically ensured when a person realizes that he is responsible for his own perpetual personal development process.**

PDCA Family Basketball Example

The PDCA process can be used to improve practically anything. For instance, years ago, when our children were still at home, our family started playing Sunday afternoon basketball games. One of the weekends, our team (because of my poor performance) lost all of its games. I was hitting the front of the rim with my shot so I adjusted strategies and started driving to the basket, but when I did this, my knee kept hyper-extending. I didn't make any excuses as we certainly earned our losses, but I did want to improve by making some adjustments for the following week.

In the scale of things, winning or losing the Sunday afternoon basketball games is not one of life's biggest issues; however, once in the habit of utilizing the PDCA process, it's difficult not to use everywhere. Accordingly, I came in after our drubbing and launched a PDCA. First, I asked Laurie to pick me up a knee brace since this would keep the knee in place and allow me to drive to the basket if the other team tried to defend my three-point shot. Second, because the kids were in school, Laurie and I practiced several times the next week during the day. One of us would pass the ball while the other would take a shot, then run to a new position for another shot until exhausted. In other words, shoot and move.

After a couple of practices, I realized what I was doing wrong; shooting the ball at the rim versus arcing the ball to go over the rim and into the net. Being an engineer by training, I did some quick research online and determined the proper arc angle for basketball. At the last practice, I nearly doubled my shooting percentage. This, along with my knee brace, built my confidence going into the next Sunday's game. Moreover, all week long, when taking breaks from reading and writing, I invested mental energy envisioning (The Ant & Elephant Resolution) the high arc of the ball as it swished through the net. Needless to say, I couldn't wait for the next basketball game to help redeem our team's poor performance.

SCOREBOARD

The next Sunday, minutes after the game started, I could tell things had changed. My shot was dropping and I could drive to the hole without pain. No, I'm not going to make the NBA nor even the YMCA teams, but we won both games and we looked like a completely different team. This is the power of the PDCA process. Of course, the other side applied PDCAs the following week and the games became more enjoyable as the strategies unfolded. That, in a nutshell, is the game of life—constant adjustments from all participants to improve outcomes. Never, in other words, rest with good when a few adjustments can make great possible!

Why do so many people continue to repeat the same mistakes in their careers, relationships, hobbies, etc. when the PDCA process is so effective in creating change and improvement? Indeed, if a person will honestly address his shortcomings, applying the PDCA thought process to it, he can and will improve in nearly any area. To be sure, the creativity to develop plans to improve is not the challenge, for everyone is creative. The only question is: Is he creative in making adjustments to win or in making excuses to lose? If you don't like the results in an area, then change by applying the PDCA process. To do so, however, one must care are results more than one's ego.

The Emperor's New Clothes

An excellent example of ego over excellence is found in Hans Christian Anderson's short story, "The Emperor's New Clothes." The wayward emperor cared more about his clothes and status than the people and truth. Indeed, he was so obsessed with his attire that he changed suits every hour, flaunting his wealth and prestige to his subjects. One day, two shysters, pretending to be weavers, presented themselves to the emperor. They bragged about their ability to weave the finest clothes with the most beautiful colors and elaborate designs. The clothes, according to the charlatans, were invisible to any simpletons or anyone unworthy of his office. The emperor, seduced by their claims, paid large sums of money to the weavers for new clothes. The two weavers, requesting the most expensive fabrics and threads, set up two looms, pretending to weave on the looms night and day while placing the materials inside their sacks.

The impatient emperor sent one of his loyal ministers to examine the clothes. The minister, discovering nothing, not even a single strand on the loom, feared that he must be a simpleton. He listened to the impostors describe the beautiful colors and patterns, but he only saw them working on empty looms. Still, not wishing

141

to appear unworthy of his office, the minister reported back to the emperor what a genius the king was for hiring such competent and capable weavers. The emperor, after further delays, sent another official, hoping to encourage the completion of his suit. The official also saw nothing but, fearing the emperor's wrath, reported to the king in a similar manner as the first minister did.

Finally, the day arrived for the emperor to preview the weavers' work. The emperor, seeing nothing, but fearful of being considered unfit for his kingdom, played along with the deceit, proclaiming his love for the patterns and colors in his new outfit. The two con men proceeded to ask the emperor to remove his clothes, raising their arms as if holding something to put on him. The court officials, scared to speak the truth, pretended to agree with the emperor, lauding his genius and the weavers' design. The people, in anticipation of the king's most expensive and wondrous clothing to date, gathered for the parade to view the new clothes.

The emperor paraded through his capital city, listening as the people lavished compliments on him and his new clothes. Nearly all were spellbound by the king's new clothes, but over the din of praise could be heard the cry of a child, shouting, "The emperor has no clothes on!" The father quickly reprimanded his son, but everyone around the boy heard the truth. The emperor, although secretly agreeing with the child, continued the parade as the crowd fawned in endless adulation because his new clothes were only seen by those with intelligence, worthy of their high offices.

Confronting Reality

The story highlights how easy it is for data to be ignored when false beliefs cause one to reject real data. Moreover, it reveals how most people prefer comfortable lies over uncomfortable truths. Leaders, however, are different. They demand truth, for they know only with truth can a person or business thrive. It's vital at the check step of the PDCA process that a person confront reality (the king has no clothes) rather than go along with conventional wisdom, company expectation, or peer pressure. The facts are the facts and the PDCA process reveals whether one is dealing in facts or fantasy. Again, in God we trust, all others must have data. If the person suffers from self-deception, a distortion between reality and his perceptions, he will not confront the data accurately nor adjust his plans to win. The person must choose between comfortable illusions or disturbing realities and only leaders choose the latter.

SCOREBOARD

Why do so many people go through the motions and avoid the PDCA process? They have so much potential and yet so few results. On one hand, winners make changing a habit, choosing to suffer the pain of growth rather than live in mediocrity. On the other hand, losers make lying a habit, choosing to avoid the pain of losing by blaming others. People who lose live lives of delusions (similar to the king), hating to change so badly they distort reality instead. Naturally, this becomes more difficult as life becomes progressively tougher, but for most, this just increases the creativity of the excuses made.

Strangely, both winners and losers escape the pain of losing creatively: one the creativity to change themselves; the other the creativity to excuse themselves. Disastrously, however, the road usually taken, and what at first blush appears to be the easier route, the escape of pain through self-delusion (the emperor's choice), ends up being the toughest road of all. For the pain of change is temporary, but the pain of regret is permanent. Be that as it may, the good news is that a person can get off the road to regret and change his destiny at any time by ending self-delusions. After all, when a person is sick and tired of being sick and tired, he will confront reality and start changing.

Leaders refuse to run from issues. They allow setbacks to build an increasing internal level of frustration, until finally, fed up, they explode past previous limiting beliefs. The pain of defeat has become stronger than the pain of changing. If, at any point in the process, the person chooses any of the escape valves to avoid the mounting pressure (excuses, blaming, or justifications), he temporarily kills the pain but only by passing the buck, denying he is responsible for the problem. Leaders refuse this option because they know they kill the pain only by killing the dream.

Anyone can be a leader, but he must refuse the seductive avenues of escape that lead to mediocrity. Reject completely the temporary mental comfort from avoiding the scoreboard of life. Instead, stare at the scoreboard until one has a plan to change and then DO IT! Don't settle for mental

> **When the going gets tough, the tough get going.**

peace and mediocrity. Rather, embrace the mental tumult of confronting brutal reality to win! Ultimately, there are only two choices in life: surviving or thriving. Start starting and quit quitting for (as I say repeatedly) when the going gets tough, the tough get going.

RESOLVED

How is it possible to confront the brutal facts, both personally and professionally, without losing confidence in the eventual victory? Jim Collins described how great companies do it: "In every case, the management team responded with a powerful psychological duality. On the one hand, they stoically accepted the brutal facts of reality. On the other hand, they maintained an unwavering faith in the endgame and a commitment to prevail as a great company despite the brutal facts. We came to call this duality the Stockdale Paradox." Great companies and individuals confront facts every day, refusing to hide their heads in the sand, regardless of how bad the current scoreboard looks. Nonetheless, they maintain an unwavering belief in their eventual victory, knowing that they will endure the pain to change and win.

Navy Vice-Admiral James Stockdale was a prisoner of war in Vietnam. Even though never given any hope that he would be released, he stated, "I never doubted not only that I would get out, but also that I would prevail in the end and turn the experience into the defining event of my life, which, in retrospect, I would not trade." The optimists, unlike Stockdale, failed to assess their situations properly, suffering from self-delusion of a quick release. They built false hopes (like the emperor's clothes), leaving them exposed when confronted with brutal facts (long imprisonments). Stockdale embodied the quote, "A man who is down need fear no fall," because although down, he was never out due to his unyielding faith. He was in for the long haul, no matter how long it took. Leaders, similarly, are in for the long haul and intend to win, no matter how long this takes.

Developing the Scoreboard

Collins studied great companies and noticed, "The great companies continually refined the path to greatness with the brutal facts of reality." The comparison companies in his study, on the other hand, did not. This is where data is the best friend to the great and the worst enemy to the bad. Bill Gates explained the importance of data: "The most meaningful way to differentiate your company from your competition, the best way to put distance between you and the crowd, is to do an outstanding job with information. How you gather, manage, and use information will determine whether you win or lose." Actually, gathering it isn't enough because unless a company confronts what the data is truly saying, it is still deceived. Collins described the phenomena, "Indeed, we found no evidence that the good-to-great companies had more or better information than the comparison companies. None. Both

144

SCOREBOARD

sets of companies had virtually identical access to good information. The key, then, lies not in better information, but in turning information into information that cannot be ignored." Both points are valid, for Gates's scoreboard, what he calls, "the digital nervous system," is necessary because a company cannot confront data it does not have. This is true both personally and professionally.

The scoreboard for life and business isn't a new concept. Albert Sloan, strikingly, kept score in the 1920's to improve General Motors' performance. Indeed, he created working relationships with the GM dealers nationwide, knowing that his business was not complete when he sold to his dealers but rather when the dealers satisfied the customers by providing the car they desired. He realized his business needed a scoreboard, so he could check the data and ensure the customers were satisfied. This was so important for Sloan that he traveled the country in a private railroad car, visiting GM dealerships, collecting data, and building the scoreboard to make better decisions on real data. If the CEO of the largest corporation in the world traveled extensively to gather the right data, what should people in the digital age do to ensure the right data is collected? As stated earlier, In God we trust; all others must have data, So what is the data that drives the reader's life and business? Start tracking it today and the launch the PDCA process to improve upon it.

> **People must learn to track the score in each area of life because it is an essential step in mastering the game.**

Without data, a business or person is relegated to rumors, opinions, and hearsay. Is this really the way to run a successful business? Michael Dell, early in his career, went through a similar experience and explained, "It was clear that in 1993 we didn't have the information we needed to run our business. We didn't fully understand the relationship between costs, revenues, and profits within the different parts of our business. There were internal disagreements about which businesses were worthwhile and which were not. We were making decisions based on emotions and opinions. In leadership, it's important to be intuitive, but not at the expense of facts. Without the right data to back it up, emotion-based decision making during difficult times will inevitably lead a company into greater danger. That's precisely what was happening to us." Dell was being deceived because he didn't have the data, but after he developed the scoreboard, he quickly sorted out facts from fiction to deal in reality.

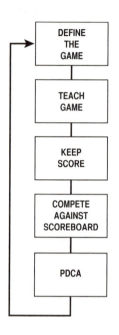

Most people would agree that keeping score in business is a must, but surprisingly, the same people aren't keeping score personally. Leaders, on the other hand, begin with the personal scoreboard to become models of real change, then they build the same principles into the culture of their companies. Non-leaders, in contrast, pass the buck by pointing fingers, seeking to blame others and excuse themselves. Here are three of the most popular methods of self-delusion, which short-circuit the check and adjust steps, thus killing the effectiveness of the PDCA process.

Blame Game and Passing the Buck

The first and most popular way that so-called leaders use to escape a confrontation with brutal reality is to play the blame game. No one likes to lose, but when potential leaders blame others, they abdicate responsibility for the loss to avoid changing. Invariably, however, if a person won't own his losses, he won't own any victories either. Any time a person blames others, whether it be a poor mentor, lazy teammates, a bad economy, etc., he surrenders control to

Real leaders cannot stand the thought of passively waiting for others to improve before their lives do.

SCOREBOARD

that outside influence. Real leaders cannot stand the thought of passively waiting for others to grow so they can. Leaders refuse to pass the buck to release the tension created by the pain of losing, for this tension is what generates the motivation to change. In fact, every minute a person is blaming someone besides himself is another minute spent not leading. Don't fall for the self-delusional blame game. Instead, search for ways to be responsible, working on better skills rather than better excuses. One can make a million dollars or a million excuses, but he cannot make both. Moreover, if a person won't accept responsibility for his current results, then how can he change them? Coach Lou Holtz emphasized, "The person who has never made a mistake in his own mind, who obfuscates and attempts to deflect blame, is someone you should approach cautiously. I've fouled up plenty in my life. In most circumstances, I've done my best to own up to my mistakes and take whatever steps I could to correct them." Don't play the blame game, regardless of the temporary relief provided because in the long run, it only produces a self-deluded loser.

Winning Isn't Worth It

The second way would-be leaders escape confrontation with brutal reality is by denying victory is worth the sacrifice. Statements like, "Well, I'm just not willing to work that hard," or "I'm doing pretty good." Many people seem to forget that hard work is nearly a given in today's work environment. In reality, the amount of hours worked between winners and losers is negligible over their lifetimes, but the mental work through the PDCA process makes all the difference. Society seems to be increasing in abundance and decreasing in happiness. There appears to be two errors when it comes to happiness. First, they believe that by accepting mediocrity, they can enjoy peace and happiness. Second, on the other side of the pendulum, they believe material wealth alone can make them happy. Both sides of the pendulum, in reality, steal true joy—the first with boring complacency and the other with restless discontent. Both err in making self the center of everything vs. the service of God and others. God is infinitely more concerned with the state of your heart than with the state of your net worth. The sacrifices made for others on the journey to success create self-worth, producing happiness (joy) long before the dream is obtained. By taking sacrifice out of success, one also halts the building of self-worth, making the attainment of the dream empty of its true value. The truth is that happiness is not something to be pursued directly; rather, it's the indirect results for striving for a worthy goal, dream, or cause. The people who strive after something significant, serving others in a cause bigger than themselves, end up feeling the happiest even though that wasn't the goal. True success, to be sure, isn't the destination but the journey, and happiness is the by-product in the pursuit of a goal or a dream bigger than oneself.

Vicarious Victories

The third way that people delude themselves is by hiding in the stands of life, vicariously winning through others' score boards and ignoring their own. For instance, nearly everyone loves sports and entertainment as I do. One of the main reasons for this is the scoreboard that provides real-time information and feedback as to who is winning the competition. Without fail, if a person arrives late to a sporting event late, the first thing he checks when sitting down is the scoreboard to determine who is winning. Everyone wants to know the score because the goal is to outscore the other team or beat a personal record. A game without a scoreboard would be laughable, but this is exactly what most people do with their own lives—live life without a scoreboard. Not surprisingly, the fans will berate the players on the field if they are not giving 100% effort. Despite the player on the field having reached one of the highest levels of achievement, playing professional sports, the fan feels justified in criticizing them because he purchased a ticket. Using this same logic, why do employees get upset if the boss criticizes their performance? After all, he is paying money for a job well done, and has a right to expect it just like the fan expects top performance from his team. Better yet, why doesn't the employee hold the bar as high on himself as he holds the bar on his favorite team?

Anyone see the cognitive dissonance here? Isn't it ironic that, many times, the person criticizing the player's performance isn't criticizing his own, even though his personal career statistics are most likely far inferior to the player's? While I agree the players ought to give 100%, I also believe every person in every field should. Why the peculiar double standard? Although living paycheck to paycheck, barely keeping his head above water, he is disgusted if the player does not give 100%. Most fans, evidently, have a performance dichotomy. They have higher expectations for their sports teams (which hardly affects their personal life) than they do their personal careers (which greatly affects their personal life). Imagine

> **Winning and losing can be measured instantly by the scoreboard.**

SCOREBOARD

what would happen if all sports fans, who expect the coaches to lead their teams with excellence, would lead their families with the same level of expected excellence. The world would be radically changed! Of course, the paradox is solved once one realizes that most people have vicariously substituted the passion they ought to have for their personal scoreboard for their favorite sports teams, musical bands, or brand name. Since human beings are hardwired to keep score, they cannot surrender the urge to compete and score in the game of life. Instead, they transfer life's competition from themselves to others, seeking to vicariously live excellence through others' achievements.

What else could explain why a person would spend his time, money, and energy as a fan of someone else's success journey, while claiming not to have time, money, or energy for his own success journey? It appears that people, after years of struggling with little success, surrender the hope for personal victory. Fans, vicariously, feel the thrill of victory and the agony of defeat with no personal growth or results included or required. The people stuck in a vicarious victory cycle are wonderful people with amazing potential and great passion. They are simply missing the connection between the passions they feel and the dreams they once had. Indeed, only by re-awakening the dream and purpose can these people get back to chasing their own scoreboard and using sports teams as a healthy diversion, not the main event in life. I broke out of the vicarious victory cycle by imagining what my God, my wife, and my kids would do if they were watching my complete life in the stands. The last thing I wanted was to be "booed" by those closest to me because I wasn't giving 100% effort. In the end, leaders must either sacrifice their egos on the altar of truth or sacrifice the truth on the altar of their egos. Life is a game, and the game is being played now. Isn't it time to start keeping score?

The PDCA Success Summary

Much of success boils down to applying the PDCA process to learn. No one ever arrives because there is always more learning one can do. Naturally, people suffer setbacks in the PDCA process, but this only reveals false theories in need of more thinking and testing. People disciplined enough to apply the PDCA process to each area of their lives will improve rapidly, leaving friends and family puzzled on how they changed so profoundly. Sam Walton exclaimed, "I've made it my own personal mission to ensure that constant change is a vital part of the Wal-Mart culture itself. I've forced change—sometimes for change's sake alone—at every turn

149

RESOLVED

in our company's development. In fact, I think one of the greatest strengths of Wal-Mart's ingrained culture is its ability to drop everything and turn on a dime." One final note: be patient with the PDCA process, for most people overestimate what can change in one year and underestimate what can change in ten. Rome wasn't built in a day, oak trees do not mature overnight, and success will take time. Nevertheless, the PDCA process is a hungry person's best friend to change and achieve over time.

SCOREBOARD

Sam Walton: Tracking the Scoreboard

The year was 1966. Little did the world know that a small-time merchant from Arkansas, enrolled in an IBM school for retailers, was about to change the face of American shopping. One of the speakers was Abe Marks, the first president of the National Mass Retailing Institute (NMRI) trade association. Marks recalls the first time he met Sam Walton:

> So he opens up this attaché case, and, I swear, he had every article I had ever written and every speech I had ever given in there. I'm thinking, "This guy is a very thorough man." Then he hands me an accountant's working column sheet, showing all his operating categories all written out by hand. Then he says: "Tell me what's wrong. What am I doing wrong?" I look at these numbers—this is in 1966—and I don't believe what I am seeing. He's got a handful of stores and he's doing about $10 million a year with some incredible margin. An unbelievable performance!

Of course, Walton's stores would go on to much better performance than Marks observed, but the foundation was already in place for his Wal-Mart revolution. Not surprisingly, Walton had enrolled in the IBM school seeking to learn how to use computers to manage his product inventory and meeting Abe Marks was part of his plan to improve.

Walton seemed to intuitively understand that computer tracking was the key to future growth since he could not personally be on hand to track the scoreboard at each store. The goal, in other words, was to create a culture of local leadership with centralized oversight. Marks elaborated upon Walton's philosophy: "He knew that he was already in what the trade calls an 'absentee ownership' situation. That just means you're putting your stores out where you, as management, aren't. If he wanted to grow, he had to learn to control it. So to service these stores you've got to have timely information: How much merchandise is in the store? What is it? What's selling and what's not? What is to be ordered, marked down, replaced? The more you turn your inventory, the less capital is required." This is one of the keys to Walton's explosive growth—keeping score. After all without a scoreboard

151

RESOLVED

for each store, how is an offsite leader to know which stores are executing the play properly and which need further PD-CAs? Walton refused to run his business on expectations alone; instead, he inspected what he expects by allowing the data to point out where expectations were not being met and adjustments were necessary.

Walton understood that keeping score was vital to Wal-Mart's success because as Marks explained, "He couldn't expand beyond that horizon unless he had the ability to capture this information on paper so that he could control his operations, no matter where they might be. He became, really, the best utilizer of information to control absentee ownerships that there's ever been, which gave him the ability to open as many stores as he [opened], and run them as well as he [ran] them, and to be as profitable as he [made] them." Walton utilized computers to help track the scoreboard used by both the local stores and Walton's leadership team to study and make adjustments. This created a culture in which local managers were responsible for store results and the central leadership team offered suggestions and feedback based upon the results at the best stores. While it's true that Walton could not have grown Wal-Mart into the business success it is today without the advent of the computer age, he, nonetheless, developed the culture of inspect and expect beforehand to capitalize on the new technology. Marks recalled, "He was really ten years away (in 1966) from the computer world coming. But he was preparing himself. And this is an important point: without the computer, Sam Walton could not have done what he's done. He could not have built a retailing empire the size of what he's built, the way he built it. He's done a lot of other things right, too, but he could not have done it without the computer. It would have been impossible."

Once Walton had the scoreboard in place, he leveraged it to teach each store's leadership teams. For one thing, he implemented a Saturday morning meeting to share ideas, confront brutal reality, and make needed course corrections. Everyone studied the same scoreboard data so no one could hide from the facts. This ensured both local leadership and top management examined the same data to celebrate victories, and learn from defeats. Walton explained: That's why I come in every Saturday morning usually around two or

SCOREBOARD

three (a.m.), and go through all the weekly numbers. I steal a march on everybody else for the Saturday morning meeting. I can go through those sheets and look at a store, and even though I haven't been there in a while, I can remind myself of something about it, the manager maybe, and then I can remember later that they are doing this much business this week and that their wage cost is such and such. I do this with each store every Saturday morning. It usually takes about three hours, but when I'm done I have as good a feel for what's going on in the company as anybody here—maybe better on some days.

No one understood more than Walton that you have no right to expect what you are not willing to inspect and Walton expected a lot from his leaders. He trusted them to achieve excellence, but verified his trust by studying the scoreboard. A. L. Johnson, a former vice chairman of Wal-Mart, said, "As famous as Sam is for being a great motivator—and he deserves even more credit than he's gotten for that—he is equally good at checking on the people he has motivated. You might call his style: management by looking over your shoulder." Because Walton was expanding so fast, he was constantly on the lookout for leaders to run his local stores. This forced the new leaders to prove themselves quickly because each store depended upon their ability to execute. Still, thanks to his scoreboard, Walton could quickly identify the leaders who were in over their heads as Ferold Arend, former president of operations at Wal-Mart, said:

> *Sam would take people with hardly any retail experience, give them six months with us, and if he thought they showed any real potential to merchandise a store and manage people, he'd give them a chance. He'd make them an assistant manager.... In my opinion, most of them weren't anywhere near ready to run stores, but Sam proved me wrong there. He finally convinced me. If you take someone who lacks experience and the know-how but has the real desire and the willingness to work his tail off to get the job done, he'll make up for what he lacks. And that proved to be true nine times out of ten. It was one way we were able to grow so fast.*

RESOLVED

Walton's delegation of responsibilities, coupled with his zeal for inspecting the scoreboard, was a key aspect of his leadership development. As a result, he produced leaders who confronted reality based on data, not daydreams. Walton developed a culture at Wal-Mart in which high achievers were rewarded and low achievers were replaced. He created a winning business game around the equation: low prices + good quality + friendly service = high value and satisfied customers. Each Saturday morning, the game participants would gather to review the scoreboard and identify areas where they achieved goals (in which case, they celebrated) as well as areas where they fell short of the mark (in which case, they made adjustments). The objective for store leaders was to produce results that would be recognized at the Saturday-morning meeting. Walton's purpose for studying the data was to identify the gap between good and bad results in each category. Naturally, this led to praise for the good and "teachable moments" for the bad. Walton's competitive drive made losing intolerable and drove change whenever the scoreboard identified a weakness in their strategy.

The highly competitive game measured store profitability, and when individual stores improved, so did the total profitability of Wal-Mart. Some will say that money is not a proper measurement of success, but they seem to forget that a customer only gives his money if he is satisfied, for an unsatisfied customer gives his money to someone else next time. Therefore, long-term profitability indicates the store is satisfying the customer and is returning to do business again. That is to say, customer satisfaction is measured in long-term profitability. Walton's simple equation—low prices + good quality + friendly service = high value and satisfied customers— was the only constant. To achieve progress, innovative leaders must effectively implement plans the produce happy customers. Wal-Mart was difficult to beat because any competitor that started to make progress against them would be revealed by a loss in sales, which would launch a plan for improvement. This adjustment in the PDCA (plan, do, check, and adjust) process would surge Wal-mart even further ahead. Wal-Mart's culture simply refused to lose. No other

SCOREBOARD

organization had such unit discipline to allow data to speak truth to the entire leadership team.

Needless to say, most management teams avoid negative data like a person avoids the plague. Walton, in contrast, was more interested in results than his or his management team's ego. David Glass, former CEO of Wal-Mart, shared, "Two things about Sam Walton distinguish him from almost anyone else that I know. First, he gets up every day bound and determined to improve something. Second, he is less afraid of being wrong than anyone I've ever known. And once he sees he's wrong, he just shakes it off and heads in another direction." Walton, because he was one of the world's greatest optimists, never allowed data to reduce his confidence in ultimate victory. Rather, he allowed it to help him improve his methods and processes to improve faster. His ego, in other words, was not attached to the current process but instead focused upon improved results. For example, if customer satisfaction is the ultimate reason for a company's existence, then all processes should be studied to determine whether they help achieve that end. In contrast, if the boss's ego, salary, or power-base are the ultimate reasons for existence, then customer satisfaction and the company's health will be sacrificed to these ends. Needless to say, the altar of pride and self-preservation was not a shrine Walton worshiped at.

Once the data are gathered, Walton's secret was to turn the business into a game. He did this in a variety of ways, and one of the best was by using the Volume Producing Item (VPI)—a merchandising program designed to encourage different regions and stores to compete based upon the amount of merchandise sold. Walton wrote, "We have a lot of fun with all this item promotion, but here's what it's really all about. The philosophy it teaches, which rubs off on all the associates and the store managers and the department heads, is that your stores are full of items that can explode into big volume and big profits if you are just smart enough to identify them and take the trouble to promote them." Competition amongst the stores created cooperation within them as they pushed each other to reach for levels of sales previously thought impossible. The scoreboard made the game effective by providing real-time sales data from each store.

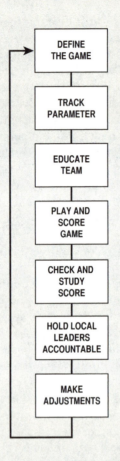

Finally, anything that improved performance was cross-pollinated into other stores, recognizing the creators of the innovative promotion in the process. Walton developed competition through the games to a fine art, helping his stores track the numbers, reduce costs and increase sales. Perhaps the most visible of Walton's competitions occurred in 1984 when Walton agreed to wear a grass skirt and do the hula on Wall Street if the company achieved a pretax profit of eight percent. This goal energized the entire Wal-Mart team, who wanted to see if the store's conservative founder would really dance the hula in front of the financial cronies of Wall Street. Not surprisingly, Wal-Mart hit the target, and Walton followed through on his word, dancing on the front steps of Mer-

SCOREBOARD

rill Lynch in a grass skirt and Hawaiian shirt with real hula dancers and ukulele players. Walton said, "It was one of the few times one of our company stunts really embarrassed me. But at Wal-Mart, when you make a bet like I did—that we couldn't possibly produce a pretax profit of more than eight percent—you always pay up....

> **Any friendship that cannot laugh at itself isn't real.**

Most folks probably thought we just had a wacky chairman who was pulling a pretty primitive publicity stunt. What they didn't realize is that this sort of stuff goes on all the time at Wal-Mart. It's part of our culture, and it runs through everything we do....We always have tried to make life interesting and as unpredictable as we can, and to make Wal-Mart a fun proposition." Games are fun, and this was Walton's specialty, namely, making business fun. He explained, "If you are committed to the Wal-Mart partnership and its core values, the culture encourages you to think up all sorts of ideas that break the mold and fight monotony."

To be sure, the bigger Wal-Mart grew, the more important it was for individual stores to keep score since the total sales and volume of the company grew so large it could hide bad stores within the total. To accomplish this, each store needed information in a timely manner, studying and adjusting at the local level rather than waiting for the corporate leadership to issue directives. Walton emphasized, "Sharing information and responsibility is a key to any partnership. It makes people feel responsible and involved. In our individual stores, we show them their store's profits, their store's purchases, their store's sales, and their store's markdowns. We show them all that on a regular basis, and I'm not talking about just the managers and the assistant managers." Walton understood in building an absentee ownership enterprise; local leaders must have access to the scoreboard to hold them accountable to the results. Leaders who accomplished objectives moved up; those who didn't had "teachable moments" to improve. In Wal-Mart's culture, due to the constant focus on results rather than mere talk, managers either improved or were removed since hiding was impossible because of the store-based scoreboard culture.

RESOLVED

Through tracking the scoreboard and traveling to local stores, Walton created more "teachable moments" than any other retailer. This allowed his stores to learn faster from the PDCA process than its competitors. After all, without an accurate scoreboard, people can spin stories to suit their own liking while avoiding uncomfortable data. However, when one tracks the scoreboard, holding those who are in leadership positions responsible, the company's culture is changed. Now, conversations occur on the brutal facts and plans are put into place to change them. Eventually, this becomes the standard operating procedure hardwired into the company's DNA. Sam Walton followed a four-step process to create a scoreboard culture that led to massive success for his company. Fortunately, every other business leader can do similarly by developing the proper criteria to play his company's game. In reality, the steps are easy (define the game, play the game, analyze the game, and execute the plays that win); however, developing the leadership culture to focus and execute the plays to win the game is what separates Walton from the rest of the field.

CHAPTER 7

FRIENDSHIP
Resolved: To Develop the Art and Science of Friendship

I know that everyone needs a true friend to lighten the load when life gets heavy.
—Orrin Woodward

True friends give the most when they receive the least. Friends serve one another with brotherly (and sisterly) love. Interestingly, love is a word that has several different meanings. For instance, the Ancient Greeks had four distinct words to communicate the concept of love: agape, eros, storge, and philia. Agape embodies sacrificial love; eros describes sensual love; storge pertains to familial love; and philia, the subject of this chapter, symbolizes brotherly love (like Philadelphia, "the City of Brotherly Love"), the love between friends.

Aristotle described philia love as the love displayed between two longtime friends, serving each other with a mixture of virtue, equality, and familiarity. Regretfully, however, philia-type friendships are not prospering today. In fact, the quality and quantity of friendship, according to the 2006 study of the American Sociological Review, is declining precipitously. In a survey of 1,467 people, data was collected and compared to an earlier survey from nineteen years ago. The survey revealed, dismally, that the average number of people with whom Americans can discuss matters of importance had dropped by nearly one-third, from 2.94 people in 1985 to 2.08 in 2004. Researcher Professor Lynn Smith-Lovin commented, "The evidence shows that Americans have fewer confidants and those ties are also more family-based than they used to be. This change indicates something that's not good for our society.

RESOLVED

Ties with a close network of people create a safety net. These ties also lead to civic engagement and local political action." The study also revealed that people with no one to discuss important personal matters more than doubled to almost 25% of survey respondents. That's one out of four people who do not have a true friend to confide in! Sociologists affirm the need for social discourse, a person's network of friends and family, to provide encouragement, counseling, and support.

Some may believe that online networks (like Facebook and Twitter) can fill the void in social discourse and friendship, but the high-tech world cannot replace high-touch relationships. In fact, author Robert Putnam asked, "What is the single most common finding from half a century of research on the correlates of life satisfaction?" His extensive research can be summarized in one sentence: "That happiness is best predicted by the breadth and depth of one's social connections." Putnam, who has spent his life researching communities, didn't say a person's happiness was based upon his wealth or status, instead he concluded it's based upon his friendships. I could not agree more wholeheartedly. C. S. Lewis noted the shift in friendships years ago: "To the Ancients, Friendship seemed the happiest and most fully human of all loves; the crown of life and the school of virtue. The modern world, in comparison, ignores it.... It is something quite marginal; not a main course in life's banquet; a diversion; something that fills up the chinks of one's time." The modern world, in other words, is caught up in the pursuit of wealth and status while turning away from the true happiness offered in servant-based relationships. Indeed, this is why friendship is one of the 13 Resolutions, for a restoration in friendship is vital for a restoration in healthy communities within society.

The Eight Principles of True Friendship

After enjoying decades of true friendships, living and breathing the principles into a thriving community, and doing extensive personal research, I have identified eight essential principles for building and maintaining long-term philia-friendships:

1. True friends form around shared insights, interests, or tastes, enjoying the common bond uniting them.
2. True friends accept one another, loving each other despite their human imperfections.

160

FRIENDSHIP

3. True friends approve of one another, protecting each other's weaknesses while enhancing each other's strengths.
4. True friends appreciate one another, encouraging, nurturing, and believing in one another's gifts and talents.
5. True friends listen with empathy, understanding each other's hopes, fears, and struggles.
6. True friends celebrate one another's success, proud of each other's accomplishments without envy.
7. True friends are trustworthy, maintaining everything shared in confident with honor and self-respect, knowing that gossip separates the best of friends.
8. True friends are loyal, respecting and defending one another's character, reputation, and motives as far as truth allows while addressing any issues between them promptly and privately.

1. True Friends Form around Shared Insights

True friends begin as companions, but soon go further, developing a mutual love and respect for one another. Author Fred Smith shared a poignant description about love: "Love is willing the ultimate good for the other person." Only a deep friendship, one that truly desires the best for the other person, will build bonds of this magnitude. C. S. Lewis depicted the feeling experienced amongst true friends when he wrote:

> *Friendship arises out of mere companionship when two or more of the companions discover that they have in common some insight or interest or even taste which the others do not share and which, till that moment, each believed to be his own unique treasure (or burden). The typical expression of opening Friendship would be something like, "What? You, too? I thought I was the only one"...In this kind of love, as Emerson said, "'Do you love me?' means 'Do you see the same truth?'—Or at least, 'Do you care about the same truth?'" The man who agrees with us that some question, little regarded by others, is of great importance, can be our Friend.*

There is an indescribable joy in the discovery of, and in being discovered by, another human being, providing a brief respite from the loneliness of life. Emerson once shared: "The glory of friendship is not the outstretched hand, not the kindly smile, nor the

161

joy of companionship; it is the spiritual inspiration that comes to one when you discover that someone believes in you and is willing to trust you with a friendship." Aristotle distinguished between a genuine friendship and two counterfeit types—one founded on utility, the other on pleasure. A friendship based solely on utility, like a mailman, survives only as long as both parties receive benefit, while a friendship based only on pleasure, like golfing buddies, ends when one party no longer finds the activity pleasurable.

Genuine friendship, on the other hand, is more enduring. According to Aristotle, "It is those who desire the good of their friends for the friends' sake that are most truly friends, because each loves the other for what he is, and not for any incidental quality." Genuine friendship, then, will last as long as both parties are committed to virtue, since a virtuous person desires good for his friends as much as for himself. Virtue, however, doesn't mean lack of fun.

> **Any friendship that cannot laugh at itself isn't real.**

The best of friends laugh often and heartily. Just as one can tell a man's character by his ability to laugh at himself, so in a friendship, one can tell the quality of one's friends by their ability to laugh at each other—not a derisive or condescending laughter, but simply one that acknowledges the imperfections (faults and foibles) inherent in the human condition. Any friendship that cannot laugh at itself isn't a full friendship, just like a person who cannot laugh at himself isn't a full person. True friends enjoy one another's company, while helping each other become better. My insightful wife called it "friendtor", the combination friend and mentor. Everybody ought to be this type of friend to others and seek friendships of this caliber, magnifying blessings by giving and receiving true philia-friendship.

2. True Friends Accept One Another

The value of a true friend is immeasurable. Everyone makes mistakes, but "love covers a multitude of sins" (I Peter 4:8). As such, a friend loves his friends enough to see past their faults and foibles and recognize the talents and treasures buried within. Friends have built bonds of trust that cannot be broken easily, especially when the relationship is coated with love, forgiveness, and grace. Friends offer one another grace when they make mistakes, recognizing their own faults, while forgiving their friends. True friends both need and give grace while steering each other back to light and away from darkness. They see the hidden hurts, fears, and vulnerabilities but love each other, warts and all, anyway.

162

FRIENDSHIP

Author Les Giblin shared a Triple A Formula—accept, approve, and appreciate—that, if practiced from the heart, builds strong and lasting relationships. Acceptance from one human being to another helps creates peace within, which allows a person to relax and share openly. In contrast, when someone is constantly judging what another person says or does, he isn't creating a safety zone for the other person to relax and share, making true friendship impossible. Acceptance doesn't mean one approves of everything his friend is doing, but it does mean he accepts his friend as a human being making human mistakes. A friend's acceptance stills troubled waters, allowing a person space to reflect and grow. Acceptance by another human being frees the person to look at his actions honestly without having to defend them since he is accepted either way. Acceptance is to the soul what food is to the body, providing nourishment and energy to act and change.

Accepted people seek more of that feeling of peace that leads them onward to seek approval from their friend. Curiously, many people get this wrong, thinking that they cannot accept someone until he does everything right. But how could this be since none of us does everything right? If this was truly the standard, no one would ever be accepted (outside of divine intervention) and the world would be a lonely place. Everyone needs to grow and change, and it's only through acceptance that the soul is nourished enough to pursue further change by moving to approval and appreciation. Moreover, a person shouldn't judge others' faults too critically since he has a full-time project working on himself. As the humorous proverb says, "Blessed are the flexible, for they shall not be bent out of shape." The following story displays the power of acceptance:

A water bearer in China had two large pots, each hung on each end of a pole, which he carried across his neck. One of the pots had a crack in it, while the other pot was perfect and always delivered a full portion of water. At the end of the long walk from the stream to the house, the cracked pot was only half-full. For a full two years, this went on daily, with the bearer delivering only one and a half pots of water to his house.

Of course, the perfect pot was proud of its accomplishments, perfect for what it was made to do. The poor cracked pot, on the other hand, was ashamed of its imperfection. It was miserable that it was able to accomplish only half of what it was made to do.

After two years of feeling a bitter failure, the poor cracked pot spoke to the water bearer one day by the stream.

"I am ashamed of myself, and I want to apologize to you. I have been able to deliver only half my load because this crack on my side causes water to leak as you walk all the way back to your house. Because of my flaw, you have to do all of this work, and you don't get the full value of your efforts," the pot said.

The bearer said to the pot, "Did you notice that there are flowers only on your side of the path, but not on the other pot's side? That's because I have always known your flaw. So I planted flower seeds on your side of the path, and every day, while we walk back, you water them. For two years, I have been able to pick these beautiful flowers to decorate the table. Without you being just the way you are, there would not be this beauty to grace the house."

Every person has imperfections, and it doesn't take a genius to find them since everyone is a proverbial cracked pot. Gaining acceptance, despite one's flaws, from others is the base from which to change. For when a person is accepted, he has no need to deny his present reality; therefore, he can confront the uncomfortable facts and change them, knowing either way he is loved and accepted as is. This inspires a person to seek approval because he loves the feeling of being accepted. Not surprisingly, when a person is accepted by others, it allows him to accept himself, which leads to honestly looking at his imperfections (for the ego is not in self-protection mode), not for negative self-criticism, but rather for self-adjustment to improve. All of this occurs because someone simply accepted another human being as he is, freeing him to become what he ought to be.

3. True Friends Approve of One Another

If acceptance is described as withholding criticisms, then approval can be viewed as giving commendations. A true friend approves his friends' gifts and talents. But how can one approve of others when he doesn't feel approved by them? Many times this is the case amongst new friends where they attempt to one up the other's accomplishments, but the best policy is to first be impressed before trying to impress. By providing relationship oxygen to one's friend, he can breathe easier knowing he is accepted. Now, he is in a much better state of mind to approve other's accomplishments. Seek first to understand and then to be understood is the key principle in all relationships. After all, seeking to understand costs a person nothing (unless self-pride is more important than others' self-worth),

FRIENDSHIP

but it makes a huge deposit in the relationship. Approval moves beyond mere acceptance of another person and moves into acclaiming specific abilities and actions and talents. To approve of others, a person must look for the qualities and attributes he respects in them and then point them out. Sadly, this is rarely done because so many are so focused on themselves and their actions. This is one of the reasons leadership is so rare, because they are the few who have gotten over themselves so they can focus on others. Imagine the friendship revolution possible if more people focused on feeding approval to others rather than constantly hungering for it. Find what one respects in others and let them know. It costs nothing but it provides immense value and untold joy to the other person. approval food from others? Regretfully, some of the best words spoken of others are at a person's funeral. Although this is nice to do, I suggest not waiting for people to be deceased to express what one approves in them.

Just as oil works in an engine, approval makes relationships run smoother, with less friction. Interestingly, approving a friend's strengths that are less obvious is more impactful than approving the ones that are easier to notice because they display a person cared enough to look for them. For example, a professional driver is aware he has good racing skills, but if someone notices he also is a loving parent who has raised well-mannered children, he will never forget the kind words of approval. Be a professional observer, and approver, of excellence. The oil of approval reduces the heat and friction that is predictable in any relationships, strengthening the bond of friendship and the resolve of both to fulfill their purpose. In fact, a New York Times article on friendship revealed, "Last year, researchers studied thirty-four students at the University of Virginia, taking them to the base of a steep hill and fitting them with a weighted backpack. They were then asked to estimate the steepness of the hill. Some participants stood next to friends during the exercise, while others were alone. The students who stood with friends gave lower estimates of the steepness of the hill. And the longer the friends had known each other, the less steep the hill appeared." Friends lighten life's load. Researcher Karen Roberto noted, "People with stronger friendship networks feel like there is someone they can turn to. Friendship is an undervalued resource. The consistent message of these studies

> **Approval is the shining of one's light into another's darkness; although the words cost one little, their value to others is priceless.**

is that friends make your life better." Notice that the friends didn't carry the load or physically help in any way, but only encouraged the participant with approving words, building the friend's belief that they could climb the hill. This matches what Greek philosopher Epicurus noted, "It is not so much our friends' help that helps us, as the confident knowledge that they will help us." Approval is the shining of one's light into another's darkness; although the words cost little, the value to others is priceless.

4. True Friends Appreciate One Another

If acceptance is the appetizer and approval is the main dish, then appreciation is the dessert in the friendship buffet. A person who appreciates a friend communicates to him that he is unique and is not just another face in the crowd. Depreciation indicates a loss in value; conversely, something that appreciates gains in value. Therefore, appreciation adds value to others' lives. This is why when a person sets appointments, he should be on time or a few minutes early because this communicates a person appreciates and values another person's time. To really appreciate people, one should share all the good he finds with them and with others about them. Appreciation is great directly from one person to another, but sometimes it's even more impactful if they hear from a third person the kind words said about them from their friends. This is the good form of talking behind someone's back—sharing all the good that one knows about a person to others. Author Fred Smith wrote, "Another characteristic of friendship above acquaintance-ship is the genuine desire of friends to help each other. They really want others to do well and are happy to contribute to that welfare. Friends look for ways to help each other. They think of each other when opportunities arise."

Every day, inside of every person, a battle wages over whom to listen to. One of the greatest things that true friends can do for one another is help each other turn up the positive voice and turn down the negative one. Friends help friends think more positively about themselves and their opportunities by pointing out positives and minimizing negatives. Indeed, a true friend helps his friends gain a positive attitude (Attitude Resolved) and victory in the mental civil war (Ant and Elephant Resolved) to move on towards his purpose and destiny. Now the reader knows why friendship is its own resolution for it vital to the completion of several others. Bad association, in contrast, turns up the negative voice, leading to bad attitudes a mental civil war and an uncompleted purpose. Choose friends wisely because a person becomes like those he as-

FRIENDSHIP

sociates with. True friends magnify each other's positive voice because friends accept, approve, and appreciate each other's gifts, providing the positive volume to drown out the negative voice. An individual should not complain, condemn, or criticize his friends; they do enough of that to themselves already. Remember, a person catches more bees with honey than vinegar so put away critical vinegar and replace with appreciation honey. A true friend should never forget someone who helped him believe in himself. This poem sums up the essence of how true friends help one another: *A friend is someone who knows you as you are, understands where you have been, accepts who you have become, and still gently invites you to grow. —Unknown*

5. True Friends Listen with Empathy

One of the best ways to show acceptance, approval, and appreciation is through listening. A person has two ears and one mouth, and they should be used in that proportion. People learn more from listening than from talking anyway so cultivate the art of listening. Not surprisingly, people can tell when someone is truly listening or just going through the motions, waiting for the other person to pause long enough for him to speak again. Active listening, by contrast, requires discipline, allowing others to share until the true meaning and feelings are mutually understood. One of the biggest compliments a person can give another is to genuinely listen to him. Abraham Lincoln, for example, in the midst of the Civil War emancipation question, sent a telegram to Leonard Swett, a longtime friend, stating, "I need to see you." Swett, having earned Lincoln's trust, accepted the president's request, packed his bags and took the train from Illinois to Washington D.C. Author Douglas Wilson shared, "Lincoln asked Swett to listen as he read from letters and position papers and then laid out, in his own words, various arguments both for and against issuing a policy of emancipation. Swett was an old friend and close confidant, and he was surely expecting Lincoln to say, 'Now, what do you think?' But he didn't. Instead, when he finished he said, 'Tell all the folks 'hello' when you get back to Bloomington, and I really thank you for coming.' He asked Swett to come to Washington simply to listen." Swett was a true friend, with whom Lincoln trusted to unburden his heart. In the process, Lincoln solidified his thinking on his momentous proclamation. Of course, many times a friend will ask for advice, but either way, a friend is a trusted person who listens to others so they can unburden their hearts. Poet Dinah Maria Mulock Craik described the joy when a friend truly listens: "Oh, the

167

comfort—the inexpressible comfort of feeling safe with a person, having neither to weigh thoughts nor measure words—but pouring them all right out—just as they are—chaff and grain together; certain that a faithful hand will take and sift them—keep what is worth keeping—and then with the breath of kindness blow the rest away." What a beautiful picture of true friendship and the joy of being truly understood by a friend!

6. True Friends Celebrate One Another's Success

True friends celebrate each other's victories. This is essential for true friendships as friends should be one another's greatest cheerleader. Friends refuse to let petty jealousies or envy rot out the core out of a friendship, because each friend desires the other's good as much, if not more, than he desires his own. Friends are not competitors; rather, they are cooperators, the biggest fans and partners possible to help achieve each other's purpose. A friend that envies another person is not that person's friend. For when a true friend has a victory, it raises the tide for all ships in the friend's harbor. Even if it didn't, however, a true friend is proud and inspired by his friends' accomplishments. Friends dream, laugh, struggle, lose, cry, win, and celebrate together. A person should be the most enthusiastic cheerleader for his friend's success, even when he is struggling personally. There are seasons in everyone's life, but one's challenges should rain on a friend's parade. Celebrating with friends in this fashion lets them know that their efforts and quest for excellence are making a difference.

> One should be the most enthusiastic cheerleader for a friend's success, even when he is struggling personally.

In reality, there are two ways to react to a friend's success: admire and emulate or envy and denigrate. A true friend admires and emulates where possible while celebrating a friend's accomplishments as if his own. This forms an even stronger bond of fidelity since so few will celebrate another's success genuinely without the smallest hint of jealousy or envy in his heart. Friends lift each other when together and apart. As mentioned previously, talking behind each other's backs is perfectly acceptable, as long as it's all the good qualities one knows. By applauding one another's accomplishments, friends build each other's reputations to match their level of character within the community.

John Maxwell shared a story about how Andy Stanley and his friend Louie Giglio ensured envy and ego did not dampen their

FRIENDSHIP

friendship. Stanley explained, "Louie and I have been friends since the 6th grade...We met at youth camp under a bunk bed while seniors battled it out over our heads. Louie is just a phenomenal communicator. When I announce at our church that Louie Giglio is going to be speaking next week, they all start clapping and we have high attendance on Sunday. And then for four or five days the rest of the week everyone's going, 'Oh, Louie, Louie, Louie.'" If it weren't for the love and loyalty shared between these two stellar performers, jealousy and envy would creep into their relationship, damaging their friendship. Neither friend, however, allows this to occur. Maxwell observed, "When Louie delivers a great message, Andy goes out of his way to praise him and celebrate with him. And Louie does the same with him. Andy said, 'It's not enough to think it. I have to say it because that's how I cleanse my heart. Celebration is how you defeat jealousy.'"

7. True Friends Are Trustworthy

Without trust, a person cannot open his heart to others, making his relationships shallow. But how can one build trust with others? Perhaps the simplest answer is to follow the golden rule: "Do unto others as you would have them do unto you." A friend listens to another's innermost thoughts and protects these with his life. True friends never violate one another's confidences. Indeed, when a person shares his fears, struggles, ambitions, or dreams, a true friend can be counted on to listen without judging, empathize without pitying, and guide without lecturing. Trust is built when one can hear the burdens of another person's heart, listening empathetically and offering earnest advice without looking down upon them. Furthermore, true friends don't exit the scene when life gets tough; instead, they exhibit loyalty and sacrificial love, supporting each other in times of trouble. False friends, on the other hand, may speak a good game, but merely associate for the perceived personal gain by doing so. Naturally, these fair weather friends depart the scene when the storms appear and the benefits end.

Pepper Rodgers, former UCLA football coach, in the middle of a tough season, jestingly said, "My dog was my only friend, and I told my wife that man needs at least two friends. She bought me another dog." Maxwell commented, "False friends are like shadows, keeping close to us while we walk in the sunshine but leaving us when we cross into the shade, but real friends stick with us when trouble comes." As the old saying goes: "In prosperity, our friends know us; in adversity, we know our friends." A person is considered blessed if he has a couple of friends who can be counted on, in both prosperity and adversity, to be faithful to him.

8. True Friends Are Loyal

A trusted friend is loyal when they are together, and even more importantly, when not together. As Martin Luther King Jr. said, "In the end, we will remember not the words of our enemies, but the silence of our friends." Loyalty doesn't mean taking a friend's side on every issue, but it does mean one is a friend regardless of whether he agrees with his friend in that specific instance. Friends protect a friend's character, honor, and reputation as far as the truth allows while resolving any issue privately and promptly. Lincoln said, "A friend is one who has the same enemies as you have." This is true so long as the friends are on the side of truth. The key principle is loyalty to the absent, protecting the character of those not present to stand up for themselves. For example, if a person wouldn't say something about another person if they were in the room, then why should he say it when he's not present? Disastrously, when this principle is abused, the gossiper loses many of his mutual friends who realize if they gossip about one of their friends, he most likely, will gossip about them also. People who spread rumors to third parties seek to lift themselves by lowering others. In reality, however, the talebearer merely loses trust with leaders who follow the correct principles while only fooling non-leaders, who love to get in the mud with the dirty person.

Be that as it may, what if two friends fall into a conflict and a mutual friend is placed in the middle? In this situation, the mutual friend insists the two conflicting parties meet in a spirit of reconciliation. Both parties should follow the conflict resolution principles (to be covered in the Conflict Resolution Chapter) and if either side refuses to follow these principles, then this party is violating the trust of everyone involved. In other words, what good is having the proper principles to live by if one doesn't use them when his feelings are hurt? Emotions lead to self-deception and blindness and the only cure is conflict resolution in which friends speak truth to all parties and bring them back to light from darkness. As Maxwell wrote, "If you are not honest with yourself, you will not be capable of honesty with others. Self-deception is the enemy of relationships. It also undermines personal growth. If a person does not admit his shortcomings, he cannot improve." As a result, if the mutual friend cannot bring both sides together then he must confront the side not willing to resolve the conflict and let him know he is not following the proper principles. If he relents, then one has gained a friend. If

FRIENDSHIP

he refuses, then one has lost a friend because friends cannot follow another one into darkness. They must call them back to the light and break association until they return to light. Simply put, loyalty to a friend ends only when unrepentant untruth begins. Even then, however, the former friends should maintain confidences where possible and hold out hope in a future reconciliation. Despite its rarity today, loyalty, fidelity, and honor are still the foundations of lifelong friendships. With the exception of truth itself, the most valued principle of friendship is loyalty, which forms the glue that holds friendships together during the storms of life.

Summary

True friendship is a lost art in today's "me" generation, but this only increases the value of finding a true friend. The best way to find friends of such caliber is to be one. This is why developing the art and science of friendship is one of the 13 resolutions, for the value of true friendship is immeasurable in the amount of joy it brings to one's life. One must make a commitment to give more to each of one's relationships than one receives. Although this is simple in theory, it is much tougher in practice, because true friends are seeking to bless more than be blessed by their friends. A person's real wealth isn't his net worth but rather in his relationships with God, family, and friends—therefore, nurture all three. No amount of money can buy the joy experienced in true friendships nor cancel the pain of a damaged relationship. Nevertheless, it's better to love others and lose once in a while than to not love at all. Resolve today to be a true friend to others.

C. S. Lewis and J. R. R. Tolkien: Friendship

A couple of unknown Oxford professors, both founding members of a local writing club called Inklings, went on to become two of the best-selling authors of all time. The relationship between these legendary authors exemplifies how the love and encouragement from a person's friends is vital to fulfill his purpose. The bond between C. S. Lewis and J. R. R. Tolkien formed into something special in September of 1931. Tolkien, Lewis, and Hugo Dyson strolled down Addison's Walk on the grounds of Magdalen College in a deep discussion, a discussion that would transform Lewis from a materialist into a Christian. Tolkien and Dyson, both Christians, repeatedly pointed out the inconsistency in Lewis's materialistic worldview because it separated his power of reasoning from his power of imagining. Author Ethan Gilsdorf captured the drama:

> *"Myths are lies," Lewis had said that night. "Myths are not lies," Tolkien countered, among the swaying trees of Magdalen Grove. "Materialistic progress leads only to the abyss," Tolkien said, "but the myths we tell reflect a fragment of the true light." He argued the Christ story functions as a myth, just like the Scandinavian myths they had loved, with one difference: The Christian myth was true.*

As the night wore on, Lewis began to see the hopeless divide in his materialistic mind-set, leading to his eventual conversion. In his book Miracles, Lewis described his conversation with Tolkien and Dyson:

> *The heart of Christianity is a myth which is also a fact. The old myth of a Dying God, without ceasing to be myth, comes down from the heaven of legend and imagination to the earth of history. It happens—at a particular date, in a particular place, followed by definable historical consequences. We pass from a Balder or an Osiris, dying nobody knows when or where, to a historical Person crucified (it is all in order) under Pontius Pilate. By becoming fact it does not cease to be myth: that is miracle. To be truly Christian we must*

FRIENDSHIP

both assent to the historical fact and also receive the myth (fact though it has become) with the same imaginative embrace which we accord to all myths.

Lewis envisioned God as the storyteller who enters his own story, completing the work of redemption according to his plan. Accordingly, God makes all other stories and myths pale in comparison, because his story is myth made real in history by the direct intervention of God through the birth of Christ. Lewis finally realized why fantasy and myth were so popular; mainly because they provide a foretaste, a foreshadowing, of the greatest story in redemptive history: the true story told in the Bible of the birth, the life, the death, and the resurrection of Jesus Christ. After Lewis's conversion, the authors began discussing how they could apply their love of fantasy and myth to lead people to the true myth of Christ. Duriez explained:

The two friends had a tangible confidence that the separation of story and fact had been reconciled, which led them to continue in a tradition of symbolic fiction, telling stories of dragons and kings in disguise, talking animals and heroic quests, set in imagined worlds. For them, heaven at a particular, definable moment in space and time came down to earth, and our humanity subsequently was taken up by the ancient fall of humanity, having met and fused forever because of the heroism of Christ. Their confidence in the reconciliation of myth and fact directly led Tolkien and Lewis to create Middle-earth, Narnia, Glome, and Perelandra, which aim to present a true picture of reality that combines heaven and earth, spirit and nature.

Needless to say, were it not for Lewis's conversion, the Narnia series would not exist since it was his Christian worldview, along with his understanding of the role of fantasy and myth, that inspired him to write the books. Tolkien played such an important role in Lewis's journey because he was able to confront his friend's former worldview while still communicating love and respect for him as a person. Tolkien's friendship, in a word, provided the spark that set

Lewis's soul on fire. He played the key role of a true friend, which is to help sharpen the thinking of his fellow life passengers, while encouraging and feeding the hunger for truth. Although Lewis was brilliant, he had swallowed a poisonous worldview that needed an antidote of faith, and Tolkien provided the antidote. Indeed, for the first time in Lewis's life, he could merge his reason and imagination together, allowing him to write some of the classic works of modern fiction.

The authors' relationship, however, was not a one-way street. Lewis impacted Tolkien in different, but equally important, ways. Just as there would be none of the Lewis classics without Tolkien, the same could be said in reverse: There would be none of the Tolkien classics without Lewis. Without Lewis's constant encouragement of the hyper-critical Tolkien, The Lord of the Rings series would not have existed or, at best, would have existed as a story shared only in the Tolkien family. Tolkien wrote of Lewis's impact on him two years after his friend passed away: "The unpayable debt that I owe him was not 'influence' as it is ordinarily understood, but sheer encouragement. He was for long my only audience. Only from him did I ever get the idea that my 'stuff' could be more than a private hobby. But for his interest and unceasing for more I should never have brought *The Lord of the Rings* to a conclusion." Tolkien found an enthusiastic listener and encourager in the younger Lewis, and this encouragement was regularized with the founding of the Inkling's Thursday-night readings. Lewis and Tolkien sharpened each other, clarifying the thinking of one another and encouraging one another to finish the projects that would ultimately impact the world.

Christian History managing editor Chris Armstrong interviewed author Colin Duriez, seeking the ways these two authors influenced each other. "You have said that if it hadn't been for the friendship between Tolkien and Lewis, the world would likely never have seen *The Narnia Chronicles*, *The Lord of the Rings*, and much else. What was it about 'fairy stories' that led these two men to want to rehabilitate them for a modern audience—adults as well as children?" Duriez answered:

They had both personal and professional reasons for this interest. Personally, they had both read and

FRIENDSHIP

enjoyed such stories as they were growing up, in collections by the brothers Grimm, Andrew Lang, and others. Lewis had also heard Celtic myths—his nurse had told him some of the folk tales of Ireland. Professionally, they studied and taught the literatures of medieval romance and, in Tolkien's case, the background of Norse myth. And they realized that it was only quite recently that such stories had become marginalized as "children's stories." Through much of history these were tales told and enjoyed by grown-ups. Even strong warriors enjoyed them, rejoicing in their triumphant moments, weeping at tragic turns of events. These stories told them important things about life—about who they were and what the world was like, and about the realm of the divine. It dawned on both men that there was a need to create a readership again for these books—especially an adult readership.

Still, it's one thing to recognize the need to build a community of readers who enjoy "fairy stories" or "children's stories," but the odds were against these two academic professors, with no financial backing or worldwide connections, to fill this need and impact culture as significantly as they did. It is truly a fairy tale in itself. Sure, both men were greatly concerned about the rampant materialism of the modern age, believing it divided the mind of humanity by separating man's reason from his imagination, but most professors, when confronted with this dilemma, would express concern, then fold their hands and do nothing. Evidently, Tolkien and Lewis were not like most professors.

Unbelievably, these two visionaries, who had hardly published anything, believed they could reintroduce imagination into the materialistic mind through the use of fantasy and myth. The dearth of good fiction that exemplified the spirit of recovery and escape motivated the authors to write stories with the power of myth. After reviewing various authors and their works, Tolkien and Lewis developed a plan, a plan so audacious in scope that it boggles the mind, especially given the amount of time and effort it would entail. Nonetheless, these professors agreed to write fiction with a purpose, to lead people to truth through the power of myth. They resolved to reconnect reason and imagination again and overcome the division created by the materialistic modern world. Duriez wrote:

> *"You know, Tollers," Lewis says decisively, pipe in hand. "I'm afraid we'll have to write them ourselves. We need stories like your Hobbit book, but on the more heroic scale of your older tales of Gondolin and Goblin wars. One of us should write a tale of time travel and the other should do space travel."*
>
> *Tolkien reminds his friend of a rather similar challenge well over a century ago—Lord Byron, at Lake Geneva in 1816, had challenged Percy Shelley and Mary Shelley to write a ghost story....and Mary, a mere girl at the time, went on to write Frankenstein. "They needed," Tolkien continues, his eyes brightening, "stories today that expose modern magic—the tyranny of the machine."*
>
> *"Let's toss for it, Tollers. Heads, you write about time travel; tails, you try space travel. I'll do the other." Tolkien nods his agreement, grinning. Lewis fishes in the pocket of his crumpled and baggy flannels and a coin spins in the air. "Heads it is."*

Strikingly, these two unknown authors accomplished exactly what they set out to do, creating fiction that captured the profound realities of life that are practically impossible to capture in any other fashion. Lewis wrote many other books on top of his classic Narnia set, while Tolkien focused mainly on his *Lord of the Rings* series. Both authors became famous through their classic fantasy fiction collections. These two friends fueled each other's belief that they could make a difference despite their inexperience and swimming against the currents of modernity. Interestingly, perhaps, it was their inexperience that led them to believe it was possible. After all, history is full of examples of great achievements accomplished by optimistic amateurs rather than by pessimistic experts. Anyone remember the bicycle mechanics (Wright brothers) who created the first powered airplane flight, beating the team funded by the university and military complex?

These two remarkable Oxford professors, who, on a whim, formed the Inklings and changed mythical fiction his-

FRIENDSHIP

tory. Although the Inklings were an informal organization, the members, typically ten or less, perfected their crafts by reading to one another their latest works. Clearly, they did a stellar job of perfecting each other's works, for in a recent survey of the top five best-selling books of all time, Tolkien's Lord of the Rings series was number four, and right behind it, was Lewis's Chronicles of Narnia set. How about that for the success of two friends who fueled each other's dreams in the Oxford Literature Department? On one hand, *The Lord of the Rings* book series has sold over 200 million books, while its movie adaptation trilogy has surpassed $3 billion in box office revenues. On the other hand, Lewis's Narnia series has sold over 150 million books, and its movie adaptation's sales have reached just under $2 billion, with several more movies in the series still to be produced. When these staggering totals are added together, the grand total from the works of these two creative geniuses is over 350 million books sold and nearly $5 billion in movie sales.

It would be hard to fathom a friendship that led to greater results than Lewis and Tolkien's. Two of the top five best-selling books of all time were birthed from a friendship that started in 1926, was nurtured through the Inklings club, and was fueled by constant encouragement and belief in one another. Lewis and Tolkien changed each other internally, providing the world with the external fruits of their internal victories in fantasy fiction classics. Their friendship displays the amazing power to be tapped into through a synergistic friendship.

CHAPTER 8

FINANCE
Resolved: To Develop
Financial Intelligence

*I know that over time, my wealth is compounded when
income is higher than expenses.*
—Orrin Woodward

Financial literacy is as valuable as, if not more so, than the ability to earn income. For once a person moves from private achievements to public achievements, he will discover that his ability to make money increases. Nonetheless, if he doesn't learn to manage his finances, chances are, he won't get ahead financially. For example, ever notice

> **As a person moves from private achievements to public achievements, he will find that his ability to make money increases.**

how many people who make $25,000 per year believe if they made $50,000, their financial issues would be solved. Similarly, people who make $50,000 believe if they just made $100,000, their financial challenges would be over. In reality, it's not just a person's income that determines one's wealth, it's also how one budgets the money one makes. The plan for wealth is actually pretty simple—spend less than one makes and compound it over time. While simple, this certainly isn't easy with advertisers, credit cards and low interest loans. This is principles delayed gratification—the ability to say "no" even when one has the cash to say "yes"—is so vital to financial health.

Financial literacy is the ability to comprehend the financial principles and apply them with wisdom to accumulate wealth. Financial literacy is a key part of success, along with personal and professional development. Financial independence ought to be one of the key goals to obtain one's purpose for it frees people from the urgent (the need of money) to the important (make a difference by fulfilling one's purpose). Debt, therefore, is the enemy of destiny, for it enslaves people to what is urgent, forcing long-term planning and personal development to plummet down the priority list. A short study of the Founding Fathers will reveal nearly all of them had the financial means to divest from day to day work activities in order to invest time in the creation of the United States of America. Can anyone imagine them pulling this off if they had to work 40-50 hours a week to pay of mortgages, car loans/leases, and credit cards? They had the time and money to invest in the things they considered important. Today, less than 1% of the people in the USA, the wealthiest country in the world, enjoy financial independence, even though the principles are readily available. Instead, most Americans burn their most productive years making a living instead of making a legacy.

Without mastery in financial literacy and financial management, it's difficult to outrun the debilitating effects of compound interest working against him year after year. On the other hand, it's easy to get wealthy when compound interest is working for him year after year. The facts, dismally, reveals the average American's (Canadian's and others') is losing the battle against compound interest. For example, 50 percent of Americans have less than one month's savings. This indicates most families are less than 30 days away from bankruptcy and that's just the tip of the iceberg. Here are the top ten disconcerting financial facts compiled from Own the Dollar and Money101:

1. Students graduate with an average of $23,186 in student loan debt and $4,100 in credit card debt.
2. People spend 12–18% more when using credit cards than when using cash. Fast food giant McDonald's found that the average transaction rose from $4.50 to $7.00 when customers were allowed to use plastic instead of cash in its restaurants.
3. A recent study by Harris Interactive found that 57% of households do not have a budget.
4. A Money Magazine poll stated: "43% of readers who lent to family or friends weren't paid back in full; 27% hadn't received a dime."
5. The number of Americans living paycheck to paycheck is 61%, up from 49%in 2008 and 43% in 2007.
6. Personal saving as a percentage of disposable personal income was 3% in August of 2009, compared with 4% in July.

FINANCE MANAGEMENT

7. There were 159 million credit card holders (separate individuals who owned at least one card) in the United States in 2000, 173 million in 2006, and an estimated 181 million in 2010.
8. At the end of 2008, Americans' credit card debt reached $972.73 billion, up 1.12% from 2007. That number includes both general purpose credit cards and private label credit cards that aren't owned by a bank. Average credit card debt per household was $8,329 at the end of 2008. 75% of credit card holders maxed out at least one credit card between 2008 and 2009.
9. In a study analyzing the impact of financial literacy, Annamaria Lusardi (professor of economics at Dartmouth College) and Olivia Mitchell (professor of insurance and risk-management at the University of Pennsylvania) quizzed people on simple calculations such as compound interest and percentages and then compared the participants' knowledge with their net worth. The findings: More right answers matched up with greater wealth. Those who grasped compound interest, for example, had a median net worth of $309,000 vs. $116,000 for those who missed the question.
10. Personal savings as a percentage of personal income declined from 7.5% in the early 1980s to 2.3% in the first three quarters of 2003. According to the Bureau of Economic Analysis, personal savings dropped precipitously from there to a negative 1.5% during the second quarter of 2006.

If anything is clear from this data, it's that most Americans have not learned the importance of financial literacy. The good news is, with a little instruction and discipline; people can overcome past financial mistakes and enjoy the freedom through financial mastery. The objective isn't to die with the largest net worth, but rather learn to live free from financial worries so one can focus on purpose not paychecks. Financial mastery, in a word, helps a person to live the life he's always wanted.

There are ten principles I have learned over the years that have helped us and others achieve financial literacy, which, when rigorously applied, will lead to financial freedom. These ten principles applied to people's lives can overcome practically any financial train wreck, allowing them to regain financial control of their lives. If a person is married, then these principles must be reviewed with one's spouse to get the household on the same page financially. Indeed, mastering the other resolutions without mastering finances is a foolish, because as one's income increases, he will become financial fodder for banks and other lenders.

This would be like pouring buckets of water into a large barrel (increasing one's income) while ignoring the fact that the barrel has a large hole (lack of applied financial literacy) in the bottom. A person must fill the financial barrel, but also plug the holes in the bottom of it. For further information on this resolution see Chris Brady and my books, *Financial Fitness* and *Beyond Financial Fitness*.

1. Identify Net Income/Revenue

The first principle in regaining control of one's finances is to identify what is one's net income. Most people, like the old joke, quoting gross incomes to their friends (I make X amount) and net incomes (honey, I only make X amount after taxes) to their spouses. Taxes are a given so only the net income is left to pay bills, save for the future, tithe, etc. The gross income, as a result, is not really as important as net income after all taxes. This leaves the amount of income

> **The goal is to determine the amount of net income that a person has to make his life decisions.**

that can be used to make budgets and financial goals. For example, a person may have a job income, a 1099 small-business income, or even babysitting income—whatever it is, he must write it down to determine the total inflow of money then subtract taxes because they must be paid. Without this critical first step, a person is running blind financially; a person who does not know his net income is bound to make unwise financial choices because he is estimating, not calculating, his financial position. In essence, the financial plan is another type of PDCA related to one's financial goals; keeping score is a huge part of it, knowing exactly how much one's revenue and expenses are. He should not include "ifcome,"—money from potential raises or bonuses that are not guaranteed because a person must live on his income, not his "ifcome," especially when some of the "ifcomes" never come through. No matter how bad the data looks when a person documents his net income, it must be done since hiding from the data will not change it. The author has witnessed many radical changes from people having the courage to keep score and then make tough decisions they had neglected for years. The government may be able to get away without keeping score (merely printing more money), but most people do not have the luxury of hiding from reality. Get a piece of paper, or get in

FINANCE MANAGEMENT

front of the computer, and start compiling all sources of income, for confronting brutal reality is impossible until one knows the data.

2. Document All Expenses

This leads to the second principle, documenting all expenses. Anything that flows out of a person's income into another entity's hands should be written down: all bills, all after tax expenses— everything that flows out of his money pile into someone else's money pile. He must also determine the amount of miscellaneous expenses necessary to maintain cars, houses, etc. The goal is to get as close as possible to the average monthly expenses one typically has. Remember, revenue minus expenses equals profits. Step One focused on determining all revenues and step Two focused on determining all expenses. Now, after revenue and expenses are accurately tracked, a person can subtract expenses from revenue to calculate monthly profits. Sadly, many people, when performing this exercise, will learn that they have no profits, but rather, are falling further behind every month because they spend more than they make. Like a ship taking on water, this house is about to capsize and is in need of courageous leadership to avoid shipwreck.

If spending money frivolously is an issue, a person should start a cash allowance, setting aside a certain amount of cash for himself and his spouse in order to keep spending within set limits. This improves the ability to budget and reduces wasteful spending. Remember, 57% of people don't have a budget. When a person completes these first two steps, he puts himself in a position to budget, placing him in the top 50% of all people. Needless to say, many people don't like the word budget because it conjures up images of limits and constraints. But in truth, everyone is on a budget; the only question is: Is it self-imposed or other-imposed? Indeed, if a person won't manage his own budget, the banks, credit cards, and other lenders will gladly budget for him as they deny him future credit. There is no escaping from budgeting since money is not unlimited, despite what the Federal Reserve believes.

3. Set a Financial Goal

The third principle is to set a financial goal, focusing on reducing expenses and increasing income to spend no more than 75% of one's net income. Sure, it may take some time to achieve this goal, but the sooner one starts the sooner one will arrive. A person who spends less than he makes is on the right track because, unlike our government, he is disciplined enough to live within his current means. Furthermore, he is growing personal and professionally to expand his income while developing financial literacy to manage his current income and expenses better. Imagine how quickly money could accumulate once one learns to not blow it all the moment it hits the account? People who spend every penny they make are like bobbers on the water—the first financial bite pulls the household underwater. Spending less than one makes, as a result, becomes a form of insurance against the storms of life that predictably come. With every four months that pass, living on only 75% of one's net income creates savings equivalent to a month's income. To be sure, a person must adopt strict financial thinking regarding his current financial position. Does he really need all the toys he has? Does he really need to lease the latest vehicles versus drive a slightly older car he can pay cash for? Does he have to live in as big and expensive a house as he is? The first time he seizes control of his finances, many around him will think that he has gone mad. The Joneses will watch him reduce his lifestyle and think he has suffered a severe financial setback. In reality, however, he is on his way to financial freedom by severing the chains of debt holding him in financial bondage. Like the proverb says—Don't wait till you're thirsty to dig your well. Quit trying to keep up with the Joneses by looking wealthy and instead start becoming wealthy. With time, these principles will increase one's income while decreasing expenses. Eventually, a person will own his assets and can then live on even less than 75%, sometimes even less than 50% of his income. Few things allow someone to sleep better at night than a healthy financial position.

4. Never Finance Anything that Depreciates

The fourth principle, one that would radically change most people's financial position, is to not finance anything that depreciates. People believe they can afford a motor coach because they can afford the payments. However, the fact is that if they have to finance it, they cannot afford it yet. Paying interest on something that depreciates is the classic financial double whammy. One gets to pay for borrowing money while the asset itself loses value. He is a two-time loser on both the interest on money borrowed and the depreciated value of asset. This can lead to situations in which the asset loses half of its value while the person pays half again the original price in interest payments. Needless to say, this is not a good financial move. For example, if a person finances a $30,000 motorcycle for five years, depending upon the interest rate, he could pay upwards of $50,000 while at the same time his $30,000

FINANCE MANAGEMENT

motorcycle has plummeted to under $20,000 in resale value. This creates a horrendous financial position in which one has paid approximately $50,000 for something worth $20,000! With financial logic like that, no wonder most people are upside-down financially! A person should never finance entertainment or toys, for why take a vacation on credit when a person will have to work twice as hard just to pay it off thanks to compound interest working against him? This only increases the financial stress once he returns from his unpaid for holiday. Instead, there are plenty of free beaches, mountain hikes, or walks in the woods to enjoy with the family while plugging the hole in his financial barrel.

I was once asked how I learned about finances. For me, the answer was simple—mathematics. I was dead broke when I started taking my engineering classes, so I had to either learn financial management or starve. Finances are mathematics applied in life and when I saw how fast compound interest worked against a person, I vowed to eliminate this parasite from my finances. Albert Einstein once spent months studying compound interest and summed it up best when he said, "Compound interest is the eighth wonder of the world." Accordingly, even if a person must purchase a house or a car on credit, it is wise to lower the amount borrowed and reduce the length of time it is borrowed for. For instance, on house mortgages, instead of borrowing three times gross earnings for a house, why not just borrow two times earnings and pay the house off in fifteen years instead of thirty? He should also confirm he is buying into a neighborhood where houses will hold their value. One realtor told me the three biggest factors driving a house's price are location, location, and location. Unfortunately, in today's fiat money environment, many houses are depreciating instead of appreciating in value. Remember, the banks want to loan a person as much money as he is capable of repaying; they are not concerned about his purpose but only their profits. Nonetheless, the sooner a person can pay off his mortgage, the sooner he owns the asset rather than merely "renting" it from the bank.

Another deadly interest trap is the lease car option. Whoever conceived of the car lease program was a financial genius. Seriously. In a car lease, the buyer doesn't own anything at all—he is simply paying for the cost of car depreciation, plus a healthy profit thrown in on top—an ingenious method to sell more cars and siphon off more of society's wealth. The banks and car dealerships celebrate their financial wizardry, but the people fall even further into debt and financial bondage. Leasing a car, in most instances, is an acknowledgement that one would rather look successful than

185

be successful. Further, it's one of the biggest drains on a person's take-home income after one's house. Fortunately, thanks to the Financial Fitness Program, thousands of people have delayed gratification and driven older cars they own outright and saved the huge lease payments on their way to financial freedom. This generates hundreds, and in some cases, thousands of extra dollars that go into savings. Of course, this doesn't even include the added "gotchas" the dealer charges when a person goes over the mileage limits. Sometimes people cannot even return their leased cars because they cannot afford the penalties assessed from exceeding their mileage limits.

5. Set a Price Limit on Spontaneous Purchases

The fifth principle is to set a price limit on spontaneous purchases. Any item above a certain amount must not be purchases until a person sleeps on it. Spontaneous purchases destroy most people's budgets because they are bought on emotion without giving time for the rational mind to think through the value of the purchase. Billions of dollars are lost every year by undiscerning buyers who make emotional decisions, only to pay for them for years to follow. This single principle helped Laurie and I get our finances under control because spontaneous buys were killing our ability to make ends meet. When a person sleeps on it, he awakes with the spell broken, realizing his earlier desire to purchase the item was simply a want, not a need. After all, a person should desire financial freedom more than material things. Sleeping on his higher-end purchasing decisions gives him time to discern if the item is really necessary. The price limits may vary, but $100 isn't unreasonable to start a new family down the road of a new financial behavior. The goal is to help them determine whether an item is really needed or if it is just another item that will wind up in the garage or storage. Look at all the rummage sales where items are sold for a tenth of the original price. These families have lost 90% of the purchase value in just a few short years. It's difficult to get free when these type of financial choices are being made.

6. Pay Off Credit Card Debt and Use Cash Whenever Possible

The sixth principle is to use cash instead of credit cards if one discovers he spends more when using a credit card. Credit cards have been found to increase a person's spending, which can cause debt to accumulate that he cannot afford. Only when he can pay

FINANCE MANAGEMENT

his credit card balances in full each month while still building his savings should he consider using a credit card for personal convenience. Otherwise, if spending is out of control, consider a personal convenience one cannot afford to indulge in. The key to regaining control of a person's finances is to pay as he goes, no longer living today on next month's (or year's) income. The goal, in contrast, is to live today on money earned last month and eventually last year. Furthermore, credit cards usually have high interest rates, so they can quickly wipe out a person's net worth if he lacks discipline when a piece of plastic is all that separates him from his desire. As a result, the person makes the purchase and hardly comprehends that he has sold himself into financial bondage due to using a credit card versus using cash. Imagine how good it will feel to go to be debt free, resting easy knowing compound interest is working for him, not against him, while he sleeps. Above all, it will take guts to leave the financial ruts; however, the joy a person experiences the first day he has no debt makes it all worthwhile.

7. Wipe Out All Consumer Debt Before Starting to Save

The seventh principle is to wipe out all consumer debt using the 10% paid to self. This principle is similar to calling all hands on deck when a ship is taking on water—everyone on board must help bail out the water to keep the ship from sinking. In a financial sense, every dollar of income coming in is needed to help bail out debt off the ship before it sinks. The 10% savings is converted into debt reduction since savings are typically at 2% or less while debt can be anywhere from 5% to upwards of 20%! For instance, if a person is saving money is at 2 % interest while he pays 20% interest on his credit card debt, then it doesn't take a rocket scientist to realize that his savings account is costing him 18% interest. Why not take the money in savings and hammer the credit card payment down or out completely? Wipe out all credit card debt as quickly as possible by selling the toys, turning in the leased cars, or stopping the high-priced vacations. Unless the savings account makes significantly more interest than the debt is costing, it's best to just wipe out one's debt. Not to mention the fact that most of the money earned to pay interest (except house interest in America) is still taxable so there aren't any tax benefits for servicing most debts. Remember, debt is cancer. When someone has cancer, the goal is to remove it; likewise, when someone has debt, the goal is to kill it.

After debts are eliminated, now start saving money, setting aside a minimum of 10% per month that is set aside for potential financial storms. Tithes to a local church are not included as part of

RESOLVED

a savings plan because they are given to God, not saved. Savings, in other words, is money not spoken for and used to build a nest egg for the future.

8. Know the Difference Between an Investment and an Expense

The eighth principle is to understand the difference between an investment and an expense. An investment has a return on the principal, while an expense is just consumed money. For instance, if a person invests in new marketable skills, there would be a return because his income making potential has increased. Learning is an investment of money into a person's future for a return in the future through improved performance and results. As Ben Franklin once said, "An investment in knowledge always pays the best interest." Whereas people should cut all unnecessary expenses, they should not cut out personal investment in improved skills. This would be throwing the baby (investments) out with the dirty bathwater (expenses). The old joke, "Due to recent cost cutting measures, the light at the end of the tunnel will be shut off until further notice" drives home the point to not turn off the light when times are tough; otherwise one will be groping in the darkness. Great companies understand this; even when cutting back on expenses, the best companies continue to research, investing in future technologies. An individual must do the same if he intends to improve his circumstances in the future. On one hand, without continued investment in personal development, a person is as good as he will ever get. On the other hand, when he invests in improved leadership and skill sets, the only limit on the horizon is the size of his dream. A person should never use lack of money as a reason to not invest in himself since this is the conscious (ant) brain is telling the subconscious (elephant) brain that it is not worth the investment. This launches the civil war because the conscious and subconscious minds are not aligned. Absurdly, this is what most people do, thinking they are saving money when they are actually shutting off any hope for personal change and a better tomorrow. After all, no economic downturn can take away improved leadership abilities, better communication skills, and improved attitudes.

> **Without investing in personal development, a person is as good as he will ever get.**

FINANCE MANAGEMENT

9. Focus on Quality of Life and Peace of Mind

The ninth principle is to focus on quality of life and peace of mind when one becomes wealthy. Too many people spend all their time seeking to increase wealth, leaving their families, friends, and internal peace neglected. For example, John Rockefeller, one of the wealthiest people in the world when he was alive, lost money in nearly every investment outside his own business. He knew how to make money in his business but lost millions investing in others' businesses.

> **A person should give to causes, charities, and organizations that he believes in, providing others the opportunity to strive for accomplishments.**

A simple principle to remember is that it's easier to convince others that a business is good than it is to run a good business. Why lose time and money investing in business when one doesn't need the money and it only deflects one from his true purpose? A person should never invest more money in someone else's business than he can afford to lose without any stress. Otherwise, he is setting himself up to lose his money and his quality of life. Steel magnate Andrew Carnegie, said it best: "Put all your eggs in one basket, and protect the basket." Whereas many people talk about diversification, Carnegie, on the other hand, talked about focus. One can be good at nearly any business, but he cannot be good at all businesses. The key is to follow his purpose into a field that cultivates his purpose through tapping into his passions, potential, and profits. Only then can a person make money pursuing what he loves, a true recipe for quality of life.

10. Be a Blessing to Others

The tenth principle is, once a person becomes wealthy, he should remember to be a blessing to others. A person should give to causes, charities, and organizations that he believes in, providing others who are less fortunate the opportunity to move ahead. Since a person cannot take his money with him, he should use wealth to bless others in need. Hoarding wealth is not the goal but developing a giving spirit is. Remember, it's not a person's net worth but a person's net change that truly matters in the world. How has the world changed because the person lived and strived for excellence? Money is just a tool to help people invest in themselves and others, leading to change and growth. Instead of creating generational

189

RESOLVED

dependence, one should support charities that inspire change in people and lead to personal responsibility (hand ups, not handouts) and productive lives. No one can make someone a student against their will, but one can find the hungry students and launch them on their success journey. Many people suffer hardships in life, and one of the best things a human being can do for another is to breathe confidence into the other person to help him overcome his obstacles. It has been said that man can live for forty days without food, four days without water, four minutes without air, but not four seconds without hope. Leaders are responsible for providing hope to others, first, by setting examples and, second, by blessing others when they are blessed.

The satisfaction felt when a person earns his keep by serving others endures. The following humorous story teaches the importance of working, earning, and saving.

His father had built a large multimillion-dollar business from the ground up. As this father approached retirement, he brought his son into his office and told him that he wanted him to take over his company. The son was excited to take over his father's multimillion-dollar empire and asked, "When are you going to give it to me?"

The father replied, "I am not going to give you anything. You must earn it."

The son replied, "How am I supposed to do that?"

The father answered, "First, you must earn $10,000 to purchase a small portion of ownership in the company. When this is accomplished, you will get your next instruction."

As the son left the house to begin his quest, his mother grabbed him and thrust $10,000 into his hand and told him to give the money to his father. Thrilled by his good fortune, he ran to find his father. His dad was sitting by the fireplace reading a book. The son approached his father and said, "Dad, Dad, here's $10,000 for the business."

Without even looking up, the father grabbed the $10,000 and tossed it into the fire and watched it burn. The son stood, frozen in amazement. As the money burned, the father said, "Come back when you have earned the money!"

As the son left the room, his mother once again thrust $10,000 into his hand. This time, she instructed him that he needed to be more convincing in selling his father on the idea that he had actually worked for the money. So the boy scuffed himself up a little, jogged around the block a few times, and then went to find his father again. His father

FINANCE MANAGEMENT

was again sitting in front of the fireplace reading a book. The boy approached his father and said, "It sure is tough earning money. Here's the $10,000. I really do want to own the business." Once again, the father took the $10,000 and, without even looking up, tossed the money into the fireplace. As the money burned, the son asked, "How did you know I didn't earn the money?"

The father replied, "It is easy to lose or spend money that is not your own."

At this point, the son realized he wasn't going to get the business unless he actually earned the $10,000. He wanted the business, so when his mother offered him money again, he declined her offer. He went out and picked up some odd jobs. His jobs required him to get up early and stay up late, but he worked and worked until he finally earned $10,000. Proudly, he walked to his father and presented him the money. Like before, his father was sitting by the fire reading a book. Again, the father took the money and threw it into the fire. As the money hit the flames, the son dove to the floor and, risking burns and pain, stuck his hands into the fire and pulled out the $10,000. The father looked his son in the eyes and said, "I see you really did earn the money this time."

When a person earns his money, he is more likely to treat it with respect. Conversely, a fool and his money are soon parted. The good news is that anyone can develop wisdom in financial matters by learning to apply the right principles at the right time. Financial success indicates a person owns everything free and clear, and no matter what happens to the economy, the bobber of his finances will not likely be pulled under. Eventually, he is living today on money made years before. This is financial freedom and the peace of mind that comes with it. He can now invest time with his loved ones, charities, and completing his legacy. In the end, people will not remember a person's net worth, but they will remember his investments in others. Building financial security allows a person to free himself from the mundane money-making tasks so that he can focus on his significant assignments. Don't worship things, for it's a poor substitute for an almighty God, but do develop financial literacy because personal freedom leads to the time to build a life of significance.

Ben Franklin: Financial Management – Money and Time

Over three hundred years ago, in the British colony port town of Boston, Massachusetts, Ben Franklin was born. In this baby's future, he was to be recognized as "the first great American," and this boggles the imagination. Indeed, Franklin achieved superhuman exploits in business, science, politics, and diplomacy and helped build a nation with his fellow Founding Fathers. While much has been written and rewritten on his impressive achievements, surprisingly little has been written on the economic engine that freed Franklin's time to apply his polymathic genius towards the challenges of his era. Franklin's life, in brief, progressed through three stages: apprenticeship, journeyman, and mastership, with each step vital in Franklin's pursuit of mastery.

Arguably, Franklin's greatest personal discovery occurred when, as a journeyman, he created a franchising model for the printing business. This innovation provided the financial means to allow Franklin to retire from day-to-day printing operations. This freed up his leisure time that led to his other famous exploits. Needless to say, if Franklin had not created a financial engine to free his life from everyday toil, today, he would be remembered as little more than a top-rate colonial printer.

Franklin's rise in business began as a sixteen-year-old. When tired of his elder brothers, he ran away from his hometown of Boston. Traveling to Philadelphia with little money and no connections, he started working as an apprentice in another print shop. In less than three years, he built his reputation not only as a diligent worker, but also as a man with a witty pen—a man on the rise. Franklin saved as much as possible, noting, "A man may, if he knows not how to save as he gets, keep his nose all his life to the grindstone, and die not worth a groat at last." He was prudent with money because he knew without capital he would never own his own business. To be sure, most apprentices never end up owning a print shop because the costs of the equipment, but Franklin was not the average apprentice.

Despite setbacks (his dad refused to loan him any money to start his own print shop, citing he was too young to han-

FINANCE MANAGEMENT

dle the responsibility), he merely worked and saved more. Franklin observed, "Think of saving as well as of getting: the Indies have not made Spain rich because her outgoes are greater than her incomes." Eventually, with his own savings and loans from friends, he launched his own printing business, his first step in his march to immortality. He had discovered the philosopher's stone, turning a leaden life into a golden one by hard work and saving capital. Franklin explains, "Get what you can, and what you get hold; 'Tis the stone that will turn all your lead into gold." His apprentice days behind him, he began his years as a journeyman printer with high expectations.

Franklin modeled one of his most popular sayings—"Early to bed and early to rise makes a man healthy, wealthy, and wise." He arrived to work early, diligently pursuing his profession, while his reputation expanded with his growing business. Not surprisingly, he was offered a position as the official printer of public records in South Carolina, but he was hesitant to leave Philadelphia. Instead of rejecting the offer outright, however, Franklin, in a true win-win spirit, proposed an alternative plan. He suggested South Carolina officials hire one of his journeymen, Thomas Whitmarsh, with Franklin funding Whitmarsh's new business. Franklin would sponsor his former apprentice and provide the equipment, fonts, and funds, while Whitmarsh would move to Charleston, South Carolina to run the day-to-day operations. All parties profited from this unique arrangement as South Carolina received a top-notch journeyman, trained under the tutelage of Franklin; Whitmarsh received capital and mentorship, both factors in short supply in the colonies, allowing him to start his own business; and lastly, Franklin received one-third of the profits for six years, after which Whitmarsh had the option to buy out Franklin's ownership position or continue with the status quo. Franklin's business acumen created it all. He realized he had capital with little time, while the typical journeyman had time with little capital. Naturally, this business arrangement benefitted both parties, for each side provided what the one lacked. This was win-win at its best. Furthermore, Franklin's frugality launched it all by permitting him to leverage capital to buy back time. He knew that time was life, as he had written, "Dost thou love life,

RESOLVED

then do not squander time, for that's the stuff life is made of." Franklin, like all true entrepreneurs, invested money to secure time whereas most people leverage their time to secure money. Of course, once Franklin realized the power of franchising, he expanded the concept across Colonial America, looking for hungry journeyman who wished to partner with him. These journeymen were Franklin's long distance proxies who ran sister newspapers under the leadership of his Pennsylvania Gazette masthead. In time, Franklin's expansive printing empire reached all the way from Hartford in the north to as far south as Antigua, with Lancaster, New York, and New Haven, Connecticut, to mention just a couple, in between. Those are not bad results for a young man whose father would not even invest in him. In fact, by 1755, eight of the fifteen newspapers printed in Colonial America were tied into Franklin's powerful conglomerate. Although not every partnership was profitable, most of them prospered under his leadership. He forged business relationships that produced residual income streams for over fifty years, leaving him free to pursue his purpose because profits were no longer a concern.

Thanks to his franchise model, Franklin was financially free at forty-two years of age. He used his free time to shift his focus from making money to leaving a legacy by pursuing his many areas of interest. These included science, politics, and issues in his local community. He described his philosophy in a letter to his mother: "I would rather have it said, 'He lived usefully,' than 'He died rich.'" Nevertheless, he ended up wealthy and useful because his business franchises continued to produce residual income streams. Not shockingly, however, he never used his liberty as an excuse for laziness; instead, he used it to build his legacy by making a difference. For making a difference was more important than merely making money. Franklin's franchises allowed him to use money to accumulate time rather than use time to accumulate money. He seemed to understand that money was a tool to free up his time. Put differently, he spent money to make time, while others spend time to make money. He wrote, "Money never made a man happy yet, nor will it. The more a man has, the more he wants. Instead of filling a vacuum, it makes one."

FINANCE MANAGEMENT

Reviewing Franklin's accomplishments is awe-inspiring, especially when one considers the number of unique fields he provided original insights into. Here is a partial list:

He set up the world's first franchise-type model, freeing himself from the day-to-day work routine.

He invented the famed Franklin stove, improving the heat efficiency of wood fires.

He created America's first volunteer fire department, recruiting others into the bucket brigade.

He founded an academy of learning in Philadelphia, which later became the University of Pennsylvania.

He founded America's first public library.

He discovered electricity and studied its nature through countless experiments, leading to the publication of his findings and international fame.

He invented the bifocal lens.

He was the first man to chart and study the temperatures of the Gulf Stream.

He published the best-selling Poor Richard's Almanac yearly.

He wrote one of the best-selling autobiographies of all time, a classic of English literature.

He revolutionized the mail service delivery of the colonies as the postmaster general by implementing home delivery and one-day service.

He played an active part in the creation of nearly every major American document, including the Declaration of Independence, the Constitution, the war alliance with France, and the peace treaty with England. In fact, he was the only Founding Father to sign all four documents.

These achievements alone would be enough to occupy the lives of a dozen energetic men. It's practically inconceivable that one person could have accomplished all of this, but Franklin, beginning with no funding, friends, or connections, in the backwaters of the British Empire, did just this. Indeed, he achieved this and more through disciplined time management, a relentless pursuit of knowledge, and the financial freedom obtained by franchising his printing business. He learned early in life the multiplying effect of good leadership, driving himself in a rigorous program of self-development, even, for a period of time, becoming a vegetarian in order to save more money to buy books. He focused on feeding his brain more than his belly. After all, he is the one who wrote, "If a man empties his purse into his head, no man can take it away from him. An investment in knowledge always pays the best interest." Still he didn't stop there; he studied the greatest influencers of history, seeking to develop the right mix of charm, posture, and tact to go along with his unquestioned character, in a quest to become a leader of leaders. Above all, he developed one of the first personal development programs, freely sharing his success principles in his autobiography and in his yearly Poor Richard's Almanac, a pamphlet loaded with witty sayings, pearls of financial wisdom, and solid leadership thoughts. In sum, he was a hungry student, studying the principles of character, task, and relationships to improve his leadership. He wrote, "Not a tenth part of wisdom was my own." His leadership training proved the most significant since all of his various achievements, including his business franchising, were supported by Franklin's impressive ability to influence others by disciplining self.

Ralph Frasca, the author of the groundbreaking book *Ben Franklin's Printing Network*, suggested that Franklin's motivation for setting up his printing empire had more to do with moral improvements than with monetary gains:

> *Franklin utilized the Pennsylvania Gazette in the same educational manner, recalling, "I considered my newspapers also as another means of communicating instruction and in that view frequently reprinted in it extracts from the Spectator and other moral writers, and sometimes published little pieces of my own," which he had first auditioned for the Junto, a group of intelligent young Philadelphia men dedicated to self-improvement. Throughout his life, Franklin viewed these published moral lessons as a service to humanity, and therefore to God. Citing the Book of Matthew Chapter 25, Franklin commented in a 1738 letter to his parents that he wished to serve God through his virtuous deeds. "Scripture assures me, that at the last Day, we shall not be examined by what we thought, but what we did; and our recommendation will not be*

FINANCE MANAGEMENT

that we said Lord, Lord, but that we did GOOD to our fellow creatures.

Nine years later, Franklin advised readers of his almanac: "What is serving God? 'Tis doing good to man." He believed that by inculcating virtue, he was improving man and culture, fulfilling his life's mission, a mission that he set as a teenager reading Plutarch, Mather, and others morally uplifting authors. Frasca described Franklin's purpose: "Thus Franklin viewed it as one of his life's duties to teach people the 'art' of virtuous conduct and show them how to practice it daily. To accomplish this task, he used the existing organs of mass communication. In addition to his Autobiography and pamphlets, Franklin employed his annual Poor Richard's Almanac and newspapers—both his own, the weekly Pennsylvania Gazette, and those published by others—to convey his ideology of virtue to the masses."

Interestingly, many times the moral and monetary reasons intertwine. For Franklin's printing consortium not only made a ton of money but it also taught early Americans personal responsibility, the ethics of savings, and the importance of service to others. Because Franklin was conservative with food, drink, and clothing, he had funds to invest liberally in businesses that generated money and improved morals, utilizing the power of leverage to duplicate his time and energy.

Finally, near the end of his life, Franklin's will and testament provided one more lesson on the importance of compound interest to financial health. He left a £1,000 (around $6,000 in today's money) trust to both the city of Boston and Philadelphia with the condition that the money couldn't be touched for two hundred years. The original £2,000 ($12,000) invested in the two trusts grew in two hundred years to over $7 million, an impressive return on investment for the cities, thanks to the financial mastery of Franklin.

Franklin's life reminds the world that incremental gains over time become great advances. As he had shared many years earlier, "Human felicity [happiness or fortune] is produced not as much by great pieces of good fortune that seldom happen as by little advantages that occur every day." Financial mastery is a process of learning how small investments, compounded over time, become large enough amounts

RESOLVED

to free people from endless toil and free up leisure time in which to pursue their destinies. He wrote, "Your net worth to the world is usually determined by what remains after your bad habits are subtracted from your good ones." This is a fitting description of his life, which, although not perfect, his net worth tallied certainly tallied near the top when his bad habits were subtracted from his good ones.

Whereas most people spend their lifetime in apprenticeship mode and only a minority ever reach journeyman status, only a few—the hungry and driven few—reach the level of mastership. Mastery level frees them from financial concern and allows them to invest into the lives of others. Through Franklin's business acumen, he was able to grow his business conglomerate and serve the world. He was an American original, a creative genius, and through his efforts, Franklin unleashed himself upon the world stage. This is the priceless lesson we can learn from his life.

CHAPTER 9

LEADERSHIP
Resolved: To Develop the Art and Science of Leadership

I know that everything rises and falls based on the leadership culture created in my community.
—Orrin Woodward

The resolutions have progressed from private achievements (inside victories) to public achievements (outside victories) and now onward to the leadership achievements (team victories).

Average leaders raise the bar on themselves; good leaders raise the bar for others; great leaders inspire others to raise their own bar. What is it about leadership? It seems the more it's studied, the harder it is to define. It is a topic that resists quantification, escaping our airtight definitions, no matter how many hours we spend on the subject. Although not sure how to define it, everyone knows when leadership is present and when it's not. Further, leadership does not exist at a constant quantity in an organization; rather, the level of leadership ebbs and flows, depending on the character and competence of the top leaders planning and directing the efforts.

The highest level of leadership is rarely achieved. The reason is because it's tough enough to perform, and even tougher to perform while encouraging others to do similarly. The championship teams, however, are created when leaders surround themselves with other leaders, raising the bar of excellence throughout their organization.

Michael Jordan is a great example of someone who grew into a great leader. After he returned to basketball from his eighteen-month minor league baseball sojourn, Jordan became a great leader because he finally understood weaknesses in others by experiencing it in himself in the game of baseball. In basketball, he had worked so hard for so long that he practically had no limits.

RESOLVED

Upon his return, however, his newfound empathy for his teammates catapulted him from a good leader to a great leader because leadership at the highest level demands a lifetime of service to others. This service involves empathy for others' strengths and weaknesses and sharing all recognition with the goal of building leaders throughout the organization. Dynasties like Michael Jordan's Chicago Bulls are created when teammates learn to complement each other's strengths and protect each other's weaknesses.

Sports Leaders and Business Leaders

Leaders in sports win by consistently developing and executing game plans to fulfill the an organization's purpose. The coach has clearly defined rules on how to play and win the game. The winning coach is the one who executes the game plan better and scores more points than his competitors. He cannot change the rules of the game, but he can develop and implement a plan that is better than that of his competitors and, thereby, win more games. If his team doesn't put enough points on the scoreboard, he will suffer a loss, which leads to PDCA adjustments in an effort to execute more effectively and score more points the next time.

Business leadership is similar to sports leadership with one significant difference. In a free-enterprise environment, a business leader doesn't just execute the game plan; he must first create a game out of his business. This includes setting the ground rules for how the game is played and won to satisfy customers. In business, in other words, the game isn't predefined. Instead, the game is developed by the organization's leaders through studying the customers' needs and competitors' strategies. Moreover, competitors can, at any time, change the rules of the game, making the competitive advantage of the former winner now obsolete in the new game. A business leader, therefore, even if he is winning, must beware of any technology shift that can make the rules of the old game no longer valid. Business leaders, in a word, must not only execute effectively on the existing game, but also change the rules before one's competitors do. This is a crucial difference between sports coaches and business leaders—one that magnifies the risk and rewards of the business world beyond those of the sports world.

Without a clearly defined game, one that satisfies current customers when played correctly, a team will flounder because it does not have an objective on which to focus. For without a game, there isn't a scoreboard. Without a scoreboard, there isn't an objective way to determine who is winning and losing. And without a win or a loss, no one can determine who is accomplishing the compa-

LEADERSHIP

ny's purpose. When an organization doesn't utilize a scoreboard, political maneuvering for personal advancement becomes the new default mode. The gameless organization focuses less on serving customers and more on serving self. Indeed, only the game and the scoreboard keeps leaders honest about their team's performances, ensuring that the game plan doesn't degenerate into self-centered political tactics designed to advance personal careers at the expense of the customers' satisfaction and organizational health.

Business, Scoreboards, and Game Plans

Interestingly, many times, it's an outsider (someone who isn't an industry expert) who redefines the game, leaving the former game and its strategies on the scrap heap of business history. Because an outsider isn't a prisoner of the current operating paradigms, he doesn't feel beholden to the old rules. Furthermore, if, by keeping score, one discovers that the old strategies no longer satisfy the customers, then most likely, someone has changed the rules of the game. For instance, Henry Ford changed the rules of the transportation game when he created his Model T automobile. No matter how good a manufacturer was at building horse carriages, he was left in the dust, forced to either play by the new rules or leave the industry.

A modern example of an upstart changing the rules is Amazon. com, which is in rivalry with Barnes & Noble. Jeff Bezos, founder of Amazon, changed the rules of the game, offering books online for the ease of making purchases from home. Furthermore, with the advent of digital books, shopping for books is going through another major transformation. Amazon is now selling more digital books than paper books every month. Imagine the competitive pressures the new game is placing on the traditional bookstores, with huge dollar amounts in inventory and store space, which must attempt to compete with digitally-based Internet companies with little inventory or overhead. The book business will never be the same again, thanks to an outsider (Bezos) who refused to play by the old rules. The myopic businesses who hold on to the glory of yesterday's game suffer an embarrassment similar to that of the fabled emperor. The emperors of business, ignoring the savvy entrepreneurs who stripped them of their glory, parade around naked in front of their customers, who are leaving them to join the new prince of business, who has developed a more effective game to satisfy the emperor's former customers. Every savvy business leader must break his business before his competitors do. Remember, the only constant in the game of business is satisfied customers; the

201

only way to achieve this is through continual and never-ending improvement both in the rules and in the game plan.

Business as a Game

When the game is defined properly, communities are attracted to the competition inherent in the game. Michael Gerber wrote, "People—your people—do not simply want to work for exciting people. They want to work for people who have created a clearly defined structure for acting in the world—a structure through which they can test themselves and be tested. Such a structure is called a game. And there is nothing more exciting than a well-conceived game." Just as every game has well-defined "rules of engagement" detailing how to score points and win the game, so must a business define its game properly.

Remember Collins's Hedgehog Concept? Another way of thinking about the game is to define the game plan through a company's hedgehog. By clearly defining and then updating the three circles as conditions change to determine the intersection point of passion (What are we passionate about?), potential (What can we be the best at?), and profits (What drives our economic engine?), the game plan is built around the Hedgehog Concept in order to win. Imagine two successful football teams that have different game plans based on how they answer the hedgehog questions. One team relies on a bruising ground game, while the other uses a lightning-quick passing game. Both win games following the same football rules, but each team uses specific strategies based on its own core strengths.

A business leader develops, defines, and sells the game to everyone in his community. Gerber elaborated, "The degree to which your people 'do what you want' is the degree to which they buy into your game. And the degree to which they buy into your game doesn't depend upon them but upon how well you communicate the game to them—at the outset of your relationship, not after it's begun." To define the game, a leader must decide which criteria are essential to satisfy the customers. Then, he turns the criteria into a game, helping everyone buy into winning the game to satisfy the customers. After this, it's time to reward the leaders and the team who execute the plays effectively. When the game is defined in this manner, it helps each team keep score by applying the PDCA process for continuous improvement.

Playing a worthwhile business game brings meaning and purpose into one's life, forming communities that play the game to

LEADERSHIP

win. Gerber explained, "Part of what's missing is a game worth playing...What most people need, then, is a place of community that has purpose, order, and meaning. A place in which being human is a prerequisite, but acting human is essential." The game creates a sense of community, a team, as people focus together on achieving worthwhile results that produce meaning in their lives and satisfaction for the customers. Since true competition creates cooperation, the more a team competes with other enterprises, the more it unites together as a community, achieving victory in the game. Military units, championship sports teams, and elite business teams all unify around common objectives, building relationships that last a lifetime. Competition creates cooperation because winning the game becomes more important than protecting an individual's perks. The only word of caution, as mentioned previously, is to stay alert to the changing rules of the business game. A company can become very efficient at a game that no longer serves customers. Businesses that endure must sacrifice their sacred cows because as Spencer Johnson said, "When the cheese has been moved, it's best to go find where it moved."

There are six steps for developing the business game and scoreboard in every field.

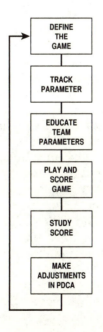

Aligning Culture to Create Current

Now that the game is defined, the leader must create a culture to win the game. Organizational theorist Edgar Schein has defined culture as "a pattern of shared basic assumptions that the group learned as it solved its problems that has worked well enough to be considered valid and is passed on to new members as the correct way to perceive, think, and feel in relation to those problems." The 13 resolutions are principles of life that, when learned and implemented, help solve problems personally and professionally. They can be taught in communities to create a culture around the 13 resolutions. As noted earlier, Emerson's statement, "Every great institution is the lengthened shadow of a single man. His character determines the character of the organization," conveys the same message. An entrepreneur's beliefs become the cultural principles of the institution. Great cultures, then, demand great character-based leaders. By making his business a game and adding the 13 resolutions, a person creates a character-centered, leadership-oriented culture that loves to compete and win the game. The culture determines how a group responds and solves problems in order to score points to win the game and satisfy customers. Culture is the current created in a swimming pool. Leaders jump into the pool and the community follows in the same direction, creating the cultural current that produces the company's results.

There is nothing more important, its proper implementation determining the destiny of nations, companies, charities, and families, than the creation of culture. Culture cannot be seen, but it influences every behavior within the community. Interestingly, despite nearly every leader expressing the need for right culture to produce right results, few seem to build culture with specific intent. This, I believe, is one of the biggest leadership mistakes.

In other words, every community must get intentional about culture or suffer the grave consequences. In a conversation with Chris Brady, he boiled down influence within a company to the 3 R's—require, recognize, or reward it. Although we weren't specifically talking culture at the time, it didn't take me long for me to realize Brady had just summed up the different methods one can create culture within a community. Ever since, I have thought deeply on how to create a culture that requires, recognizes, and rewards the right behaviors.

Needless to say, this is much more difficult to do than it sounds, for most companies suffer from cognitive dissonance—a malady in which the organization promotes one thing while rewarding another. Cognitive dissonance is perhaps the biggest failure-mode for

LEADERSHIP

most communities because it involves a misalignment between the culture and the long-term vision. This misalignment creates cultural inertia that, left to itself, will divide the community and blur the vision. Dissonance, in a word, destroys unity.

Accordingly, great leaders must identify a community's purpose and vision; then develop the culture of requiring, recognizing, and rewarding to ensure the proper behaviors are performed to accomplish the vision. Moreover, if the leader realizes the 3 R's currently instituted will not achieve the stated purpose and vision, he must have the courage to make the needed adjustments. In fact, this is what makes the leader the leader; namely, the courage to create the culture in order to achieve the community's purpose. Any leader not willing to do this is not truly a leader, for he merely follows the current culture rather than building the proper culture.

In essence, leaders are responsible for eliminating cognitive dissonance out of the culture to ensure the actions of the organization move it towards its purpose and vision. After all, nothing validates the leader's value so much as his/her ability to move the cultural current in the proper direction. It doesn't matter if it's easy; it doesn't matter if it's convenient; it doesn't even matter if it's popular. What does matters is whether the community can accomplish its reason for existing with the current culture. Thus, if there is cognitive dissonance, the culture must change.

When an organization is suffering in the throes of cognitive dissonance, the leader's responsibility is to charge to the front lines and resist the improper cultural current, converting the dissonance into resonance by aligning the 3 R's to the purpose and vision. Indeed, when the cultural current is flowing smoothly, the requirements, recognition, and rewards align the people win personally and professionally when the company wins purposefully. Proper leadership, therefore, creates the culture and the culture creates the results.

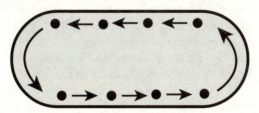

Cognitive Dissonance: Free Vision-Oriented Cultures

An aligned purpose, vision, and core principles help create a cognitive dissonance-free culture so that leaders run in the same direction in the pool, carrying new people along in the current until they learn to run with it. Needless to say, the goal is to teach as many people as possible in the community to run in the same direction in the pool. Proper vision-led culture drives a community's behavior better than a bureaucratically controlled culture ever will. Gary Hamel described the difference:

> *When it comes to mobilizing human capability, communities outperform bureaucracies...In a bureaucracy, the basis for exchange is contractual—you get paid for doing what is assigned to you. In a community, exchange is voluntary— you give your labor for the chance to make a difference, or exercise your talents. In a bureaucracy, you are a factor of production. In a community, you are a partner in a cause. In a bureaucracy, "loyalty" is a product of economic dependency. In a community, dedication and commitment are based on one's affiliation with the group's aims and goals.*

Leaders deny the urge to control others, realizing that other leaders don't need to be controlled but rather unleashed towards common goals and visions. Leaders buy into the great leader; then they buy into the leader's vision for the future, aligning themselves personally and professionally to achieve greatness together. Championship teams are created when communities buy into a common vision formed around purposes and principles to accomplish that vision, surrendering their personal egos and replacing them with a team ego to accomplish the team's vision.

Expecting and Inspecting

Leaders create a culture of expecting and inspecting great results. The best leaders understand that their individual results pale when compared to the overall community. Therefore, even though they may be highly competent, they must be effective delegators to accomplish massive community results. This is why inspecting what one expects is so vital. Since the leaders create culture and the culture creates results, the culture must include not just expecting but also leaders inspecting the team's results. When the results do not match expectations, then an opportunity to teach is present for the leader and an opportunity to learn is available for

LEADERSHIP

the student. The use of "teachable moments" separates good from great organizations. Just as failure is a learning opportunity for personal achievement, so too are leadership failures opportunities to teach and learn in communities. The culture of expecting, inspecting, and then either producing the expected results or learning from the experience is a practically unbeatable one because the team is either producing results or learning how to in the future. This culture of execution demands excellence from each individual. It compels others to raise their game, not by force, but by the positive peer pressure to fulfill the vision, proving themselves competent and teachable to leaders who have earned their trust.

Delegation is essential for large-scale results; however, many new leaders make the mistake of delegating both the assignment and the inspection of the scoreboard. This is a recipe for failure; if the leader delegates the scoreboard inspection, he shouldn't be surprised when an underling gives his interpretation of the facts rather than the reality of the. "Teachable moments" only occur when reality is confronted and it's very difficult for top leaders to confront reality, let alone expect the whole team to do so. This is why leaders must expect results to teach people how to confront reality and PDCA as they have learned. Few people, in essence, if given a choice, will confront their inadequate performance personally let alone admit it to their supervisor. Instead, they will give an exaggerated report to the supervisor and no "teachable moment" occurs. This is a sure-fire way to develop a culture of mediocrity. Without a doubt, improper delegation has caused as much damage as proper delegation has caused good, which is why great leaders delegate expect, but not inspect until they have produced another great leader. The toughest part of delegation is teaching a subordinate how to accurately study his scoreboard to spin the data, and the leader refuses to delegate the inspection until the subordinate consistently produces the right results, proving his competence and character. When this leadership culture is present, the birth of a new dynasty is in progress.

Culture of Execution—Runners, Bobbers, and Obstructionists

If every organization has a culture, why do so many fail to execute effectively in serving customers? Companies can play the right game and still lose by executing poorly, creating the wrong current in the pool. A company's cognitive dissonance can be viewed as the corporate version of an individual's civil war. For just as the

RESOLVED

personal civil war indicates the ant and elephant minds are not aligned, cognitive dissonance indicates the culture of rewards, recognition, and requirements are not aligned. Not surprisingly, this is why turnaround leadership is so highly valued, namely, because it's so rare. It demands guts, tenacity, and persistence to stay in the pool, even when the current is moving in the wrong direction. Turnaround leaders must determine which people are just bobbing and not actually running in the pool. Worse yet, they have to determine what is creating the cognitive dissonance in the current and get rid of it to kill the obstructionist, people who are running the wrong way for personal benefit and corporate harm. Without disciplined people to identify and fix the cognitive dissonance while running against the negative cultural current, no turnaround is possible. Collins wrote, "Discipline by itself will not produce great results...No, the point is to first get self-disciplined people who engage in very rigorous thinking, who then take disciplined action within the framework of a consistent system designed around the Hedgehog Concept." The Hedgehog Concept, in this case, ensures the culture is aligned and the current is flowing in the proper direction without cognitive dissonance. The leader, naturally, must attract others to help him do this while keeping the company afloat in the meantime.

Attracting and Developing Leaders

Leaders surround themselves with other high-achievers, disciplined people who buy into the cultural current and run. They learn the principles taught by the leader and emulate them through their individual personalities. No coach, not even the best ones, can win without talent, but the bad ones can lose even when they have talent by creating a bad culture. A leader must surround himself with the right people, or he is doomed to mediocrity. The more runners in a pool with an aligned culture, the more effective it is, however, the more bobbers, people who just float with current instead of helping create it, the less responsive to change the culture is. After all, the best jockey in the world will lose the Kentucky Derby if he races on a donkey. Covey emphasized this point: "I am convinced that although training and development is important, recruiting and selection are much more important." Align the culture to ensure there is no cognitive dissonance, then seek out thoroughbreds because they make leadership enjoy-

> **A leader must surround himself with the right people, or he is doomed to mediocrity.**

LEADERSHIP

able. Personally, I look for people who buy into the 13 resolutions, for all they need is to learn the game, and then run in the pool to produce results for themselves and the company. Everything the thoroughbred needs to learn he will through applying hunger to the 13 Resolutions.

Leadership Cultures and Freedom

Leadership cultures need freedom for leaders to blossom and grow. Ironically, Collins wrote, "Most companies build their bureaucratic rules to manage the small percentage of wrong people on the bus, which in turn drives away the right people on the bus, which then increases the percentage of wrong people on the bus, which increases the need for more bureaucracy to compensate for incompetence and lack of discipline, which then further drives the right people away, and so forth." This is the-chicken-or-the-egg scenario. Is it ineffective leaders that lead to bureaucratic rules, or is it the bureaucratic rules that drive out the good leaders, leaving only the less capable to remain? Either way, the companies who provide people the freedom to pursue points in the defined game will attract more leaders, while weeding out non-leaders. In today's competitive environment, companies that force people to follow oppressive rules and regulations will lose leaders to companies that give them the freedom to play the game and to win.

Sam Walton loved giving people freedom, but that freedom came with responsibility. Indeed, he had two objectives in developing the culture of his teams through the scoreboard: praise and teaching. He wrote, "All of us like praise. So what we try to practice in our company is to look for things to praise. Look for things that are going right. We want to let our folks know when they are doing something outstanding, and let them know they are important to us." On the one hand, Walton praised people who used their freedom to move the company ahead. On the other hand, what happens if someone isn't producing results? How does a person praise someone who isn't achieving the desired outcomes? Walton explained, "You can't praise something that's not done well. You can't be insincere. You have to follow up on things that aren't done well. There is no substitute for being honest with someone and letting them know they didn't do a good job. All of us profit from being corrected if we're corrected in a positive way." The goal, then, isn't to blast a person when he misses the mark but to instruct him through "teachable moments" so he can improve as a leader.

Trilateral Leadership Ledger and Sturgeon's Law

In our New York Times best-seller *Launching a Leadership Revolution*, Chris Brady and I taught people how to become more effective leaders through using the Trilateral Leadership Ledger (TLL). Every leader must grow in his character, tasks, and relationships to become a great leader. The TLL measures each of these three areas on a scale of 0 to 10; then one multiplies all three of these scores to obtain the total score. For example, if someone rated himself 2 on character, 1 on task, and 2 on relationships, then the total score is 4 ($2 \times 1 \times 2 = 4$). The lowest score, one that many—including the author—score when they start their leadership journey, is zero because any area that is a zero leads to the total score being zero. The highest score, one that no reader will ever obtain, is 1,000 ($10 \times 10 \times 10 = 1,000$). Perfection, although strived for daily, will never be achieved since no one reading this book is perfect, but the TLL has helped tens of thousands of people evaluate their current leadership scores and identify areas that need improvement.

Theodore Sturgeon, a science fiction writer, knew perfection would never be reached. In fact, he refuted many of the critics of the science fiction genre at the 1953 World Science Fiction Convention when he said:

> *I repeat Sturgeon's Revelation, which was wrung out of me after twenty years of wearying defense of science fiction against attacks of people who used the worst examples of the field for ammunition, and whose conclusion was that 90% of science fiction is crud. Using the same standards that categorize 90% of science fiction as trash, crud, or crap, it can be argued that 90% of film, literature, consumer goods, etc. are crap. In other words, the claim (or fact) that 90% of science fiction is crap is ultimately uninformative, because science fiction conforms to the same trends of quality as all other art forms.*

Sturgeon's Law is evident when studying the mass-participation Internet sites today. For example, if a person were to review every YouTube video, he would discover the majority (90%) were crud, not worth the time to watch them; however, the remaining 10% are not bad and the best of them are downright impressive. The free online encyclopedia, Wikipedia, displays the same trends, for less than 10% of the content authors provide around 90%of the useful content. Another example is the American Idol television

LEADERSHIP

show, in which numerous contestants audition for the opportunity to showcase their talents. Can one imagine having to listen to every person who auditions for the show? Tens of thousands audition, but only a select few are viewed by the TV audiences. It isn't shocking that 90% of the contestants are subpar because American Idol is a human endeavor, and thus, subject to Sturgeon's law. The remaining 10% have talent and go further, until it eventually filters down to the select group appearing on TV. American Idol isn't criticized because 90% of those who audition lack excellence since, because of Sturgeon's Law, it couldn't be otherwise.

Leaders aren't depressed by Sturgeon's Law; rather, they learn to work with it. Anyone can be a leader if they are willing to PDCA in each of the three areas (each is a resolution) needed to be a leader—character, tasks, and relationship. The reason, as a result, that more people aren't leaders is not talent but instead tenacity. Unlike many leadership experts, I strongly believe leaders can grow beyond their current limitations (and have helped many do so) through the mastery of the 13 resolutions into their lives. By studying Sturgeon's Law further, one realizes it represents the art side of leadership—the idea that anyone can lead, but few will because leadership takes focus, discipline, and persistence. This doesn't mean the rest of the people are crud, but only that they have not applied themselves to master the area of leadership. This is not different than my inability to play the piano does not indicate I am forever incapable, but merely that I have not applied myself to take lessons and invest the thousands of hours necessary to get good.

The TLL reveals how one can grow as a leader by growing into the elite top 10% in the three key attributes. When applied to the TLL, Sturgeon's Law reveals that only 10% of people will excel in any one of these attributes, but a top leader must excel in all three. Therefore, to calculate who will be in the top 10% in all three areas, it is 10% × 10% × 10%, which indicates a true leader develops about once every thousand people. Interestingly, this number, one out of a thousand, has been shared around the leadership circles for years, even though most leadership gurus haven't even heard of Sturgeon's Law, or for that matter, the Trilateral Leadership Ledger. For instance, Gladwell reported that a performer can build and maintain a community of around 100–150 people, but about one in a thousand will develop into a true leader, a person leading the performers. In any community, a thousand people doesn't just assemble; instead, gathering a community requires an elite leader who attracts, serves, and leads performers who build 100-

150 people communities. The elite leaders, in effect, are those who break through Sturgeon's Law in all three TLL attributes, building communities of thousands of people whom they serve.

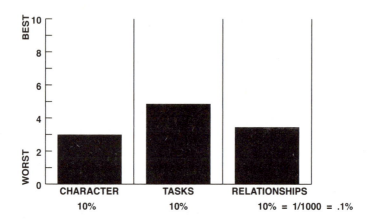

Study each of the three attributes of leadership in the TLL. The common tendency is for a person to overrate himself when tabulating his TLL score. A simple reality check for scoring is to compare one's results with the number of his following. If a person has around 100 people in his community, then his TLL score is around 50 points; but by developing three performers who can lead 100 people each, his TLL grows to 150 points. Top leaders with over 1,000 people in multiple communities can score over 300 points on their TLL evaluations. By knowing the total score based on his numbers, a person can estimate his individual scores in character, tasks, and relationships and ensure that he isn't suffering from self-delusion. Every leader has room to grow because no one has achieved perfection (1,000 points); nonetheless, a few have reached 500 points in their leadership journey. This leads to Woodward's law—a corollary law to Sturgeon's—which states that "90% of leaders are convinced they are part of Sturgeon's 10%." Strikingly, although only 10% of the people ever achieve the upper echelons in any category, the biggest reason most leaders do not continue growing is

It's only when a leader grows throughout his life that he attracts other elite leaders into his community, changing the lifetime leader's role from a leader of followers to a servant of leaders.

212

LEADERSHIP

they feel they are already there. Good truly is the enemy of great. Mentorship and the scoreboard are the essential ingredients to keep a leader hungry to grow his TLL score and not settle for good when great is available. As the leader grows, he attracts other elite leaders into his orbit, changing the lifetime leader's role from a leader of followers to the servant of leaders. Leaders of this ilk won't work for bureaucrats, dictators, or micromanagers but love to assume responsibility and feed on visionary leadership. Imagine developing one's TLL score to become a servant leader who attracts other top leaders into his community, thus creating a team of leaders who drive change in any field they set their minds to. Leadership isn't a nice add-on feature but an essential part of every world changer. As John Maxwell stated, "Everything rises and falls on leadership."

RESOLVED

Sam Walton: Leadership Excellence

Sam Walton's business results make him one of the greatest leaders of the century. By studying his leadership style and culture, a person can improve their leadership through modeling the secrets of Walton's legendary success. Author Richard S. Tedlow commented on Walton's leadership: "First he learned all the rules. Then he broke all the rules which did not make sense to him which meant almost all of them. Sam Walton did not become a billionaire because he was a genius (although he was without question smart, shrewd, and astute). The real reason for his success was that he had the courage of his convictions." Not surprisingly, this common sense approach to business did not befriend him to the bureaucratic Butler Brothers, the owners of Ben Franklin's five and dime stores.

Indeed, Butler Brothers' tight controls clashed with Walton's ability to serve change processes to serve his customers. Naturally, this caused Walton to work around the rules, rules the Butler Brothers considered sacred, a collision in leadership cultures that could not coexist. Walton's was on a constant search for lower priced suppliers and ignored most of the higher marked up items the Butler Brothers suggested.

Nonetheless, although the Butler Brothers were unhappy with Walton's freewheeling methods, the company tolerated his independent streak for years because he led in overall sales and sales increased year after year. For instance, sales increased over 45% during Walton's first year, moving up another 33% the next year, and then expanding another 25% the following year! These impressive numbers caught the Butler Brothers off guard, for they thought they were selling a slowly fading franchise to a greenhorn naïve enough to buy it; instead, Walton changed the perpetual loser into one of the franchise's elite stores, a store that broke nearly every record in Ben Franklin's storied history. While this might have surprised the Butler Brothers, Walton was hungry for even more. He reminisced, "I was the sucker the Butler Brothers sent to save him [the former owner]." By his fifth year, Wal-

LEADERSHIP

ton had a compounded annual growth rate of 28%, growth that made him the leading variety store owner in the state of Arkansas.

Unfortunately, Walton's fairy book story didn't last. Like many elite leaders, the road to the top is littered with setbacks. This particular one would have proved fatal to many lesser men's dream. Walton did not properly secure the lease he originally signed back in 1945. The young and impetuous Walton did not invest the time to have a lawyer read through the lease agreement to ensure it included the standard renewal clause. This oversight left Walton subject to the whims of the builder's owner to continue the lease or force Walton out despite his superb results. Dismally, the rental owner, seeing an opportunity to advance his son's interest at Walton's expense, refused to renew the lease contract and forced Walton, with few options available to him, to sell his store inventory and fixtures to the owner's son for bargain basement prices. In a flash, Walton's storybook rise, a rise that catapulted him from an unknown to the number one franchisee in the Franklin fold, a rise driven by relentless dreaming, planning, and doing, was now a storybook collapse. He received a mere $50,000 for his five years of tireless work, a bitter pill to swallow for the Walton family. He recalled:

> *It was the low point of my life. I felt sick to my stomach. I couldn't believe it was happening to me. It was really like a nightmare. I had built the best variety store in the whole region and worked hard in the community—done everything right—and now I was being kicked out of the town. It didn't seem fair. I blamed myself for getting suckered into such an awful lease, and I was furious with the landlord. Helen, just settling in with a brand-new family of four, was heartsick at the prospect of leaving Newport. But that's what we were going to do.*

Walton's reward for excellence was to be driven from Newport, a dismal end to an otherwise stellar performance. This is where champions are made, for Walton had the choice

RESOLVED

to get bitter or better. Thankfully, he chose better. Through his embarrassing setback, Walton learned several valuable lessons. First, he built a trusted legal team to review all future contracts to ensure everyone's roles and responsibilities would be clearly spelled out. With the help of his son and father-in-law, both lawyers, he protected himself from his overly trusting nature. Second, Walton refused to pass the buck, accepting full responsibility for signing the document without proper legal inspection. Perhaps this trait, more than anything else, is what separates leadership producers from pretenders.

Third, he turned rejection into energy, the rejection fueling his fire rather than quenching it. Walton used this setback as motivation to bounce back and win, unlike others, who simply turn rejection into excuses for losing.

The Walton family promptly moved to Bentonville, Arkansas and opened Walton's five-and-ten, changing the store name despite still being under the Butler Brothers umbrella, and began an uphill battle to succeed again. Bentonville, however, was only half the size of Newport and there were already three variety stores competing for its small market. As a result, his new store averaged less than half the volume of his old Newport store, but he was not deterred. Walton noted, "It didn't matter that much because I had big plans." He immediately invested $55,000 ($5,000 more than he had received in the sale of his Newport store), banking on his ability to produce even bigger results. And, in less than six months, his new store had tripled its sales, sales that proved Walton's culture worked wherever it was implemented regardless of the obstacles. Indeed, from 1950 to 1962, he expanded operations across the Southwest, building the largest independent variety store in the United States while receiving little fanfare or publicity. He recalled, "That whole period—which scarcely gets any attention from people studying us—was really successful." Needless to say, it was the years before Wal-Mart, years spent perfecting his leadership culture, when hardly anyone knew who Sam Walton was, when he developed his winning skills. Although plying his craft in near

LEADERSHIP

anonymity, he relentlessly invested over ten thousand hours in a quest for leadership mastery—a quest that rewarded him greatly.Walton, after a decade of being Butler Brothers' top performer, began to chafe under their rigid bureaucracy and mismanagement. Perhaps because the Butler Brothers made such huge profits with its existing business model, it seemed incapable of recognizing the competitive threat discount stores posed to its variety store chain model. Walton, on the other hand, not suffering from money myopia, saw the challenge immediately, telling the Butler Brothers they must adapt or die. Naturally, the Butler Brothers didn't appreciate the upstart's honesty. After all, the Butler Brothers were billionaires and who was Sam Walton to lecture them? Consequently, the billionaire Butler Brothers, in a hubris-induced coma, played it safe and erased themselves from history to secure higher margins temporarily. Of course, their business model eventually collapsed from not responding to the "creative destruction" inherent in the free-enterprise system.

Walton, in contrast, anticipated the future, a future in which high margins would follow the dinosaur into extinction, and realized he must migrate to the discount stores' more competitively priced business model. Giving the Butler Brothers one more opportunity to do the right thing, he flew to the Butler Brothers office in Chicago and proposed a partnership with them to launch a discount model. He wasn't too far into his presentation when he noted margins would have to be cut from the typical 25% to or 12.5% or less. Needless to say, this didn't go over well. In fact, the meeting was terminated, along with the relationship with Walton. Walton recalled, "They blew up," not willing to risk their easy profits, choosing instead to ride out the variety store model into business oblivion. Exasperated, Walton tried to explain that the profits would be made up in higher volume. Moreover, the high margins were going away in any event, but the Butler Brothers, blinded by the past, refused to see the future.

Not easily dismayed, Walton flew to Texas, hoping to become a franchisee of Herb Gibson, a highly successful discounter at the time. Gibson, however, rejected Walton outright, seeing him "as a bush-league variety-store merchant who possessed neither the finances nor the experience necessary to succeed in the Gibson chain." Predictably, the revolutionary leaders with the largest visions for the future must endure the criticisms from those who profited in the past. After all, they stand to lose the most when the future is fulfilled. Having been rejected at every possible avenue, a rejection that had to hurt, Walton did what all revolutionary leaders do—he proceeded with the plan anyway. Indeed, 95% of the money used for the start-up of the original Wal-Mart came from Walton himself, for the simple reason that no one else believed enough in his vision of the future to invest with him.

Walton's key philosophy, the one that drove every other action, was the desire to build loyal customers by building a leadership culture that would offer high-quality merchandise at the lowest price. Walton's years of retailing experience had created one unshakeable conviction: he believed that by keeping the over-head costs down, piling the merchandise high, and selling the products at a low price, the customers would beat a trail to his stores. His unwavering belief would not disappoint even his superhuman expectations. Walton, from the beginning, kept everyone focused on this simple formula of success, a formula that narrowed the focus of his employees, to give the customer the best price every day. He knew if he ever took his eye off this, he would lose his ability to compete with his bigger rivals. Walton's genius, as well as his gift to the world, was to build his entire leadership culture around giving his customers the best value proposition, period.

Another key was Walton's personal humility was driven into the culture of each Wal-Mart store. He didn't need to be "the guy," threatened by other leaders' ideas; instead, Walton leveraged their unique gifts for the benefit of his company and customers. He explained his reasoning: "I needed somebody to run my new store, and I didn't have much money, so I did something I would do for the rest of my run in the retail business without any shame or embarrassment whatsoever: nose around other people's stores searching for good talent." He understood the best coach would lose without tal-

LEADERSHIP

ent and this is why Walton constantly searched for hungry talent. Still, talent was not enough; he also expected each successful individual to buy into the company's culture of "team" over "I". Walton explained, "I hate to see rivalry develop within our company when it becomes a personal thing and our folks aren't working together and supporting one another. Philosophically, we have always said, 'Submerge your own ambitions and help whoever you can in the company. Work together as a team.' By working as a team, any lessons learned in one section of the company were quickly shared across regions." Walton further shared, "Communicate, communicate, communicate....We do it in so many ways, from the Saturday morning meeting to the very simple phone call, to our satellite system. The necessity for good communication in a big company like this is so vital it can't be overstated." By developing a world-class team that worked incredibly hard, merged individual egos into a team ego, and communicated any lesson learned across the company, Walton created the foundation of a culture that refused to lose. It's hard to compete with a talented group of individuals who are playing the game as a team. Walton commented, "This is a highly competitive business, and an even more competitive company.... Ever since my peewee football days, I've believed almost any kind of competition is great."

RESOLVED

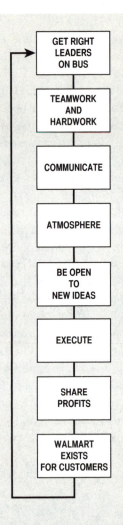

Walton's personal desire to learn was modeled in his leadership culture, a leadership culture in which everyone sought to learn something new every day to better serve their customers. Interestingly, some seem to believe that Wal-Mart's success was simply a matter of having a good information and technology system, but Walton emphasized, "A computer is not—and will never be—a substitute for getting out in your stores and learning what's going on. In other words, a computer can tell you down to the dime what you've sold. But it can never tell you how much you could have sold." The com-

220

LEADERSHIP

puters merely communicated the satisfaction, or lack thereof, of Wal-Mart customers. It was the leaders who made the day-to-day adjustments that ensured the computers displayed positive results for Wal-Mart shareholders and customers. Walton believed that the customer was king, and every move he made was geared toward satisfying him. He wrote, "Everything we've done since we started Wal-Mart has been devoted to this idea that the customer is our boss. The controversies it has led us into have surprised me, but they've been easy to live with because we have never doubted our philosophy that the customer comes ahead of everything else." That common sense statement is much easier to say than it is to implement, but this is what the leadership culture Walton created did consistently.

Walton believed customers wanted low prices, good quality, and courteous service; and in order to satisfy his customers, he provided just that. The sales resulting from his simple formula provide irrefutable evidence that he was right. He learned from everybody. In fact, he probably visited more competitors during his career than any other retailer did. Charlie Cate, one of his store managers, recalled, "I remember him saying over and over again: go in and check our competition. Check everyone who is our competition. And don't look for bad. Look for good. If you get one good idea, that's one more than you went into the store with, and we must try to incorporate it into our company." It was this continuous learning culture, a result of Walton's huger and humility, that drove further improvement and more customers to Wal-Mart.

Above all, however, what held Wal-Mart's culture together, even after Walton's early death, was his path-breaking profit sharing plan, a plan that allowed each of his partners to profit from Wal-Mart's growth. He commented, "The more you share profits with your associates—whether it's in salaries or incentives or bonuses or stock discounts—the more profit will accrue to the company. Why? Because the way management treats the associates is exactly how the associates will then treat the customers." His leadership culture followed the tried and true Golden Rule: "Do unto others as you would have them do unto you." He set the target to serve the customer, period; he created the scoreboard to mea-

RESOLVED

sure the results; and he rewarded the entire team when they achieved success.

Many companies with more money, more resources, and better connections started in the discounting profession the same time as Wal-Mart. In fact, in 1962, four companies with bright futures started discounting models: Kmart from the Kresge business, Woolco from the Woolworth business, and Target from the Dayton-Hudson business all formed discounting models along with a small variety retailer from Bentonville, Arkansas. Within five years, Kmart had 250 stores and $800 million in revenue, compared to the small Arkansas firm of 19 stores and $9 million in revenue; but by creating a leadership culture, David beat Goliath in the long run. Walton reminisced, "Here's what makes me laugh today: it would have been absolutely impossible to convince anybody back then that in thirty years most all of the early discounters would be gone, that three of the four new chains would be the biggest, best-run operators in the business, that the one to fold up would be Woolco, and that the biggest, most profitable one would be the one down in Arkansas. Sometimes even I have trouble believing it."

CHAPTER 10

CONFLICT RESOLUTION
Resolved: To Develop the Art and Science of Conflict Resolution

I know that relationship bombs and unresolved conflicts destroy a community's unity and growth.
—Orrin Woodward

After a person has built a following through his character and competence, he needs to learn the art of conflict resolution in order to nurture trust. Indeed, one of the most important arts of leadership, and also one of the least understood, is the art of conflict resolution. Whether one is leading a business, church, or charitable organization, the ability to resolve conflict is essential.

> **Whether one is leading a business, a church or a charitable organization, the ability to resolve conflict is essential.**

If one studies a beautiful city, he will discover that these cities have developed processes to purge the garbage that is created in the community. The process starts with the collection and transportation of the garbage out of the city to be processed at an incinerator or landfill. In a similar fashion, leaders must develop processes to purge conflict within the community to ensure conflict does not build up and cause damage. Issues will arise—it's part of human nature—but resolving conflicts is part of leadership; strengthen relationships through seeking each other out to resolve conflict and affirm the relationship. This is one of the key skills of for effective leadership. Gus Lee emphasized the destructiveness of not addressing conflict, writing, "Conflict aversion is the organizational bubonic plague of our times. It is cowardice wearing a smart, politically-correct hat. The hat allows it entry into all human organizations, where it befuddles, ensnarls, and twists communication. It turns dialogue from a leadership tool into a virus to which only a precious few are immune." Cowardice in organizations must be eradicated, root and branch.

Conflict, like fire, is easier to snuff out when it's small but can become nearly impossible to handle when allowed to spread unchecked. Imagine, just before going to bed, a person glances in a corner and notices a small flame flickering; hopefully, he wouldn't choose to ignore it until the next morning because surely his house would be burned down by then. Likewise, ignoring conflict is foolish, as a person might lose the relationships because he delayed in addressing the issue. Small issues, unaddressed, can become big issues, so do not avoid them. Conflict is a given, but resolution requires leadership and love. For every relationship needs nurturing to maintain the bond of friendship. There simply aren't any no-maintenance relationships. How a person treats his key relationships by building, encouraging, and resolving through critical conversations determines a leader's speed of trust. When a person doesn't resolve conflict when issues are small, they usually turn into bigger fires that can damage themselves and innocent bystanders caught in the fall out. These cowards avoid conflict, choosing to sacrifice innocent bystanders rather than resolve uncomfortable conflict. Leaders, in contrast, address conflict, for they know that unresolved conflict breaks trust and destroys communities built upon trust.

Imperfect People Have Imperfect Relationships

Even when leaders are operating with character, conflicts will still arise. Human beings are capable of doing so much good but remain imperfect, impetuous, and sometimes unreasonable. Emotions can get the best of anyone and when this happens, apologies are in order. The bond that holds communities together during times of disappointment and hurt is love. After all, love leads people to courageously restore damaged relationships while lack of love leads cowardice and shattered relationships. The longer issues aren't addressed, the less courage remains and the more cowardice increases. Disgracefully, as a person dwells on his hurts, running them like instant replays in his mind, he justifies himself while condemning the other. This bitterness and resentment builds inside a person until, like drinking poison and expecting someone else to die, it kills the person's love and attitude. No wonder conflict must be addressed as quickly as possible. Refuse to get bitter

CONFLICT RESOLUTION

and instead get braver—brave enough to sit down with the person you are in conflict with and seek to understand why both of your expectations were not fulfilled. What makes conflict resolution so fearful to so many? Lee explains, "We fear looking bad, even in our own minds. We fear hurt pride, repercussions from genuine discussions, being wrong, looking out of step, seeming awkward, being isolated. Not big things. Small ones. This stops us from acting courageously and therefore wisely." How sad for both parties, not to mention the community, who suffers from the residual damage associated with the improper actions of one or both parties. These improper actions must be understood and avoided to ensure relationship bombs are not thrown into the volatile situation.

Relationship Bombs

Relationship bombs are violations of the principles needed to resolve conflict, and when dropped into relationships they make simple conflict resolutions more complex because further conflict is created. Similar to how bombs expand war's destruction to nonparticipants, so too do relationship bombs expand the damage to parties not originally involved in the conflict. The two major types of relationship bombs are silence and violence. The first occurs when either one or both parties in the conflict dwell on hurts without addressing them to the other party. Silence simply refuses to talk about the hurt and attempts to pretend nothing is wrong. Naturally, this causes stilted, artificial and even hypocritical interaction amongst the parties as the bitterness and resentment builds in one or both parties. The second relationship bomb is created when one or both parties gossip to others about their unresolved conflict. This second bomb is usually a result of the first one because harboring bitterness is difficult; eventually, the "poison" spills out into gossip. Silence poisons the person who refuses to talk to the only person who can help resolved the conflict, which leads to violence when the infected person shoots poisoned darts of gossip at the other party's character. Not surprisingly, both bombs build when conflict is not addressed. Relationship bombs are not healthy, productive, or principle-centered. When a community tolerates relationship bombing, restoration becomes more difficult, the speed of trust is damaged, and the residual drama lingers on even if resolution is eventually achieved. Leaders must learn the factors that leads to these relationship bombs and cut them off at their roots.

225

Silence

The first factor leading to silence is fearing confrontation (even the principle-centered kind) more than fearing the damaging results from the ongoing conflict. This is another ego or excellence situation where a person can protect their ego by blaming the other person entirely, or he can be excellent by seeking to learn what part he played in the conflict. The leader makes it a rule that if he thinks about a received hurt more than once, feeling he is unable to forgive the other party without seeking to understand more, then he addresses the issue promptly and professionally in an understanding, non-attacking spirit. Too often, it seems that the "offended" party plays God, assigning malicious motives to the other person's actions without giving him the benefit of the doubt. It's hard enough to determine one's own motives, let alone omnisciently know others' motives. Refuse to play a Godlike role; instead, be a friend to others and seek to understand when conflict arises. By assuming the good intentions of the other party, a person will not build bitterness. Instead, he will have a conciliatory spirit, reflecting less on current hurts and more on previous joys with the other party.

> **Everyone should make it a rule that if a person thinks about a hurt more than once, feeling unable to forgive the other party, he should address the issue promptly.**

The second factor that leads to silence is the practically unlimited ability for people to self-deceive themselves. As noted in the character and PDCA chapters, self-deception is telling comfortable lies to oneself to avoid uncomfortable growth and change. Indeed, self-deception allows a person to place all the blame, all the responsibility, and all the need for apologies on the other party, leaving oneself only with all the hurt. Although this sounds absurd, after twenty plus years of conciliating resolutions, this is where many parties start the process. The less lies a person tells himself, the faster resolution can occur. Everyone contributes to conflict and everyone can learn from it. Why avoid a "teachable moment" by being silent when growth happens when discussion and learning begin. To combat self-deception, pause before judging, pray before becoming bitter, and think about one's role from the other person's vantage point. Perhaps after doing this, one will find the part in conflict he is at fault and can seek reconciliation in a humble spirit.

CONFLICT RESOLUTION

Empathy, the ability to view the situation from another person's perspective, is essential in combating self-deceit. It frees a person, helping him let go of offenses by understanding the conflict from another person's viewpoint, replacing a judgmental spirit with a graceful, forgiving one. He thinks through the chain of events and asks himself, "What could I have done differently?" By making each conflict a "teachable moment," one learns many valuable lessons to apply in the future. The bigger the heart of the leader, the quicker he takes responsibility and seeks resolution for the benefit of the entire community. Remember, a leader always apologizes first, focuses on another person's position, and addresses issues, not with a vindictive punishing spirit, but with a loving truthful one.

The third factor hindering relationship restoration is holding onto hurts to justify quitting on responsibilities or communities. Many times, a person is afraid to address changes needed on the inside, so he seeks offense on the outside to justify quitting rather than changing. He has no intention of seeking resolution because he is seeking justification for quitting instead. In other words, unresolved internal conflict embitters him into maintaining silent offenses used to break off relationships. Usually, this process starts at the subconscious level, and the person creates conflict to justify quitting, replacing the real reason for quitting (like lack of courage) with a scapegoat reason. This is his silent conflict with others that as the bitterness grows leads to him quitting. Predictably, he refuses to sit down and address the conflict for fear that if it gets resolved, he will lose his justification for quitting. People looking for an excuse to exit a group will avoid conflict resolution at all costs, or else their humpty-dumpty justifications for quitting fall apart, never to be put back together again. Leaders who understand this phenomenon resolve to love people where they are at, doing everything in their power to not be the reason someone else justifies quitting. Remember, hurting people hurts other people. However, instead of responding to their unjust remarks and providing them a reason for breaking off fellowship, seek instead to apply grace and love. Perhaps, by empathizing with their fears of inadequacy, they will stick around long enough to grow and change.

Violence

The second relationship bomb—violence—is endemic in today's drama-filled modern culture. People can attack others physically, but most practice the

> **When conflict is not resolved, it doesn't go away; it only goes underground.**

227

RESOLVED

more cowardly version: assassinating others' reputations through gossip. The Bible teaches that character assassinations are just one level removed from an actual assassination. This is another reason why conflict should be resolved promptly, for unresolved conflict doesn't go away, but merely goes underground. Conflict will be discussed either way; the only question is will it be discussed with proper parties to resolve it or discussed with improper parties to expand it. If a person's actions are just, then he has nothing to fear or hide from resolving conflict. If one's actions are unjust, then he has a character choice to make—either sit down and admit one's mistake (the right choice), or avoid resolution and go seek to win people to one's unjust side by exaggerating his side for good and the other's side for bad (the wrong choice). Dismally, more people choose to gossip about others than improve themselves and maintain character. Regretfully, communities that have a culture that condones gossip usually don't last long, for gossip divides friends, breaks trust, and makes future resolution more difficult. A popular story portrays the disastrous effects of gossip:

> *The story is told of a peasant with a troubled conscience who went to a monk for advice. He said he had circulated a vile story about a friend, only to find out the story was not true. "If you want to make peace with your conscience," said the monk, "you must fill a bag with chicken down, go to every dooryard in the village, and drop in each one of them one fluffy feather."*
>
> *The peasant did as he was told. Then, he came back to the monk and announced he had done penance for his folly. "Not yet," replied the monk. "Take your bag to the rounds again and gather up every feather that you have dropped."*
>
> *"But the wind must have blown them all away," said the peasant.*
>
> *"Yes, my son," said the monk, "and so it is with gossip. Words are easily dropped, but no matter how hard you try, you can never get them back again."*

Gossip spreads a wide net, which is why proper conflict resolution is so vital for healthy communities. Effectively, gossip is like dumping garbage on someone's front lawn. Therefore, when a person attempts to "dump garbage" by casting aspersion on another person's character, a leader's role isn't to take sides but to become a facilitator in getting the parties together for resolution. A leadership culture drives reconciliation, not rumor, hearsay, and gossip.

CONFLICT RESOLUTION

Stephen Covey explained, "One of the most important ways to manifest integrity is to be loyal to those who are not present. In doing so, we build the trust of those who are present. When you defend those who are absent, you retain the trust of those present." If someone gossips about another person, ask him, "Can I quote you on this?" Only a few, it seems, desire to be quoted. Mediation takes time and effort, but when a leader is drawn into the circle of gossip, he is loyal to those who aren't present and drives the process of conflict resolution by telling the person who brought up the conflict, "Either go to the person you are in conflict with and address it alone, or both of us can go to address it." Either way, a leader must follow through to ensure the process is followed for the sake of the particular relationship and the rest of the community. These are the only two options since leaders refuses to gossip or take sides and instead seek to resolve conflict.

Communication Triangulation

When dealing with a conflict, don't fall victim to communication triangulation, a sad state in which people are drawn into others' unresolved conflict through gossip. As Joseph Stowell wrote, "The 'juicy morsels' stay with us, permanently staining our perceptions of and appreciation for those about whom we are hearing. The vicious chain of gossip continues until it finally comes up against someone willing to stop spreading information about feuding factions and start praying. Only then will the fire die down." Why would anyone help assassinate the character of his friends by listening to gossip about them? Unless a person is asking an individual to help mediate a conflict and achieve a resolution, in which case the mediator hears both sides of the story when all together, he is simply gossiping, no matter what his claimed intentions are. Instead of falling victim to this disease, follow the process described by Kibbie Ruth and Karen McClintock, keeping the focus on resolving conflict, not on furthering gossip or taking sides:

> While people often suggest that venting is good for the soul, it is actually not very productive. Venting to someone about a third person is simply an avoidance technique that creates what is known in counseling theory as a relationship triangle, or triangulation. Triangulation is talking about feelings, opinions, or personal issues regarding some person or group with a third party instead of with the person or group actually concerned. Relationship triangles usually involve three people who each take one of three roles:

victim, persecutor, and rescuer. Once in a triangle, people change places among its three points. The only way to stop the triangulation is for each person to communicate his or her feelings, concerns, or opinions directly to the other.

Of course, the best communication strategy is to avoid being recruited into a triangle in the first place. However, so often, well-intentioned leaders and congregants listen to a person's concerns, feelings, or opinions and then realize they have inadvertently let themselves be co-opted, becoming involved and sometimes even taking sides. Once an individual is in a triangle, escaping may require some courage and clarity, but it must be done. A triangulated person can redirect a concerned person straight to the appropriate individual or committee—the one who is actually involved in the issues or the one who can address the concern or mend the relationship. A three-way conversation sometimes helps, but only if the third party facilitates without taking sides or having an agenda, without speaking for any of the parties, and without adding to the emotional drama.

In the proper culture, the gossiper quickly learns that communication triangulation isn't accepted in the community. Further, if he refuses to speak directly to the person he has gossiped about. Then he will be called out those he attempted to gossip to and end up sitting down anyway. This does two key things for the third party. First, it let's everyone know that he isn't a gossiper. Second, by protecting the party not present, he builds trust throughout the organization, as others realize he will do the same for them when someone gossips about them. Through these actions, a person displays his impatience for gossip and his refusal to be drawn into the communication triangulation game. Only by addressing a conflict directly can the merry-go-round of gossip and half-truths end.

Five Steps for Conflict Resolution

Now that we have avoided the "relationship bombs" that can blow up even long-term relationships, let's discuss how to confront a situation and resolve it. The goal, of course, is to improve the strength of the relationships, from better understanding on all sides, making it stronger than beforehand. This isn't just a pipedream and I have facilitated many resolutions in which this was the outcome. Through reading many books and studying great leaders, I have developed a five-step pattern for resolving conflict. I know of no other process to maintain healthy and productive communities as important as the proper implementation of the conflict

CONFLICT RESOLUTION

resolution process. On the other hand, I know of nothing that will destroy communities quicker than conflict avoidance. The five-step process works when both parties want to resolve the conflict, valuing truth over ego. If both parties are not sold out to resolution, then no amount of effort from one party will resolve it. It takes two or more to get into a conflict, and it requires the same group to resolve it. Relationships can bring so much joy and, conversely, a damaged relationship can bring so much pain. This is why mastering the ability to resolve a conflict quickly is vital for a person's leadership influence. To resolve conflict, the best plan is for an in-person sit down face-to-face meeting. This is major because in resolving conflict, one cannot pick up on the unspoken cues of body language over the phone, through email or even on video conference to the same level as in person. If one of the parties is not willing to meet in person, then this is not a good sign as part of the process is to convey to the other side that one values them; hence, not taking the time to sit down in person to listen is communicating the wrong message. If the people are ready, however, these five steps work amazingly to restore relationships and build unity within the community.

> **It takes two or more to get into a conflict, and it requires the same parties to resolve it.**

1. Affirm the relationship.
2. Seek to understand.
3. Seek to be understood.
4. Own responsibility by apologizing.
5. Seek agreement.

Affirm the Relationship

The first step is to affirm the relationship before diving into the conflict details. An example opening statement in starting the process of resolution is, "I am here, even though it's uncomfortable, because I value our relationship and would rather be uncomfortable while resolving our misunderstanding than comfortable with misunderstandings not resolved." The fact that two people invested the time to sit down displays each of them values the relationship. Let the other party know how important the relationship is. If acceptable, a prayer before initiating the five steps sets the right tone and invokes God's blessing. The goal of the affirmations is for both parties to validate each other as human beings before

231

RESOLVED

discussing the particular hurts. This helps when the hurtful issues are addressed later, since both sides understand the goal isn't to attack the person but address behaviors and underlying issues. People are affirmed, issues are addressed, and behaviors adjusted to restore, if not strengthen, the relationship. In the book *Crucial Conversations*, the authors discussed creating a safe environment in which true communication flourishes by pouring all thoughts into a shared pool of meaning:

> *When two or more of us enter crucial conversations, by definition we don't share the same pool. Our opinions differ. I believe one thing, you another. I have one history, you another.*
>
> *People who are skilled at dialogue do their best to make it safe for everyone to add their meaning to the shared pool— even if the ideas, at first glance, appear controversial, wrong, or at odds with their own beliefs.*

Seek To Understand

The second step of the process is to seek to understand the other person's thinking and viewpoints. This is a critical step. The objective should be to listen intently, seeing the conflict from the other person's perspective, not attempting to justify one's own position. He should let the other party know that he is there to listen and understand his thoughts and views. By providing the freedom for the other party to share his feelings, hurts, and perspectives, a person can expand his insight into how the conflict started and how to improve the conduct in the future. One has to allow the other party to unburden himself, not taking the words personally, but professionally, always remembering that hurting people can hurt other people. By doing this, hopefully, the other party can get any bitterness out of his system and start focusing on resolution. In a word, be curious, not furious with what the other side says. Only after listening to the other party, asking questions to clarify and understand, should one consider moving to the next step. A person shouldn't seek to defend his actions here but rather simply get a clear understanding of the other party's position, expressing empathy over the pain caused. Even though hurting others may not have been one's intention, this is usually the result; therefore, an empathetic spirit communicates one understands his

One should be curious, not furious

232

CONFLICT RESOLUTION

perspective of the issues. Many times, the hurt comes from an expectation not met by one or both parties. Better communication reduces false expectations and the subsequent pain associated with it. After listening, one should repeat back to the other person the concerns addressed, summarizing and affirming his views. Genuinely listening to another person is one of the most affirming things that a person can do for another human being, communicating respect towards him which helps in the resolution process.

Seek to Be Understood

The third step in the process is to seek to be understood. By this time, a person has invested time to sit down with the other, affirmed the value of the relationship, and listened to the other's viewpoint. Only after these steps have been patiently accomplished is a person ready to respectfully share the issues from his perspective. Hopefully, by being affirmed and having received deposits in his love/respect tank, the other party will listen intently to one's thoughts and feelings. The goal isn't to blast the other person but simply to address the issues, sharing where things could have been handled differently to ensure hurt feelings don't occur in the future. Remember, resolution, not justification, is the object. This requires both sides to be honest about the parts they played in the conflict, as it always "takes two to tango." Moreover, when discussing the issues, be careful not to assign motives to the other party. For example, a person might state that the other person neglected to call him, but when he states the person intentionally didn't call him, he is leaving facts and entering into opinions and feelings. Only God knows a person's motives; all the person can say is what happened and his perspective on what happened. After all, it's hard enough to discern one's own motives, let alone claim to know the motives of others. Share the tough issues without being dogmatic ("you always" or "you never"). Give the other party as much benefit of the doubt as possible. The Bible states, "love covers a multitude of sins" (I Peter 4:8). In most cases, if the other party has been affirmed, respected, and heard, his willingness to accept some of the responsibility increases greatly, making resolution possible. If a person focuses on incorrect behaviors and actions, rather than on bad people and motives, resolution becomes highly likely.

Own Responsibility and Apologize

The fourth step is to own as much of the conflict as possible while still being truthful. Leaders search for "teachable moments", the areas they can improve in, in every conflict resolution. The objective for both parties is to see where their actions caused pain

233

to the other person, leading to an apologetic spirit and a restored relationship. Unfortunately, so many people struggle with apologizing to others. Even though they know they aren't perfect, many seem unwilling to admit their imperfections by apologizing; therefore, their pride leaves a trail of broken relationships where a genuine apology would have made all the difference. Needless to say, leaders learn that genuine apologies create more good will than a thousand justifications ever will.

A great example demonstrating the power of an apology was illustrated *in Crucial Conversations*. An Executive VP asked a local supervisor for a tour to learn about a new manufacturing process. Six hourly workers volunteered to work late and prepare for the anticipated tour. The supervisor, upon discovering the VP wanted to implement ideas that would harm the quality of the operations, made a leadership decision to skip the tour and use the time to address his concerns and help the VP see his concerns. Although he changed the VP's mind, saving the jobs of his employees, he forgot to inform his team, leaving them wondering why the VP didn't do the tour. As the supervisor was escorting the VP to his car, he ran into his six disappointed employees. *Crucial Conversations* described what happened next:

"We pulled an all-nighter, and you didn't even bother to come by! That's the last time we are busting our hump for you!"

Time stands still. The conversation has just turned crucial. The employees who had worked so hard are obviously upset. They feel disrespected.

But you miss the point. Why? Because now you feel disrespected. They've attacked you. So you stay stuck in the content of the conversation—thinking this has something to do with the factory tour.

"I had to choose between the future of the company and the plant tour. I chose our future, and I'd do it again if I had to."

Both sides, interestingly, are fighting for respect and are not truly communicating with each other. Instead of defending his violated respect, a person should attempt to see the other's actions in the context of violating their trust and restore the trust by apologizing. *Crucial Conversations* shared the proper response: "I'm sorry I didn't give you a call when I learned that we wouldn't be coming by. You worked all night, it would have been a wonderful chance to showcase your improvements, and I didn't even explain what happened. I apologize." Since we all know we aren't perfect, revealing this fact to others by apologizing isn't a monumental revelation, but the respect to other the apology displays is monumental. Indeed,

CONFLICT RESOLUTION

the higher a person climbs the leadership ladder, the more he has to apologize to others simply because, as a leader, he juggles many things at the same time, causing hurt feelings without any intention of doing so. When the supervisor apologized, he restored trust in the relationship, and then was able to explain what happened without the need to defend himself. Alexander Pope, the great English writer, declared, "To err is human, to forgive divine." Leaders will err, and then must sincerely apologize. Leaders will also be hurt, but this drives them into conflict resolution to understand what happened and maintain the unity of the relationships. If two people genuinely value their relationship and willingly follow the five-step process for resolution, then their conflict will be resolved.

Seek Agreement

The fifth and final step in the process is to seek agreement on the future roles and responsibilities for both parties. Now that everyone has been affirmed, heard, and apologies made where needed, the parties are ready to seek agreement. This is designed to unite and strengthen the relationship. Flushing the negativity out of the relationship leaves only the bonds of love, unity, and trust remaining. Seeking agreement conveys the strengths of both parties in accomplishing their community's objectives and reaffirms the value of the relationship in working together for the common purpose. The vision of their community aligns the task of each person, creating unity in the team and producing better results by the interdependence among the leaders. Agreement between two leaders is a form of a "buy in," making both leaders desire unity to accomplish the mission bigger than their individual missions. The conflict is now over and the restored unity is better than before because there is the shared experience of understanding each other at a deeper level. The unity in the community is what creates progress while disunity creates regress. Leaders understand that conflict is a given, but resolution is a choice.

I have been personally blessed with many long-term relationships, including my relationship with Laurie, my wife since 1992, as well as my relationships with my great friend and business partner for over twenty years, the CEO of LIFE, Chris Brady. In addition, George Guzzardo, Claude Hamilton, Bill Lewis, and Dan Hawkins each have been great friends and business partners for a decade or longer. Conflicts have certainly arisen, but by practicing the methods of conflict resolution discussed above, not only did we resolve issues, but we strengthened the relationships in the process. Trust is maintained among friends when both sides know

235

RESOLVED

that the relationship is based upon light and truth and nothing will separate it unless one side refuses to deal in truth and moves into darkness. In fact, the reason conflict resolution is one of the 13 Resolutions is because it is the best way for a person to see his own blind spots, by hearing them from a friend who one knows loves him. The hungry leader recognizes if he is hearing the same truth from multiple conflict resolutions and chooses to change. Why run away from conflict resolution when it is one of the best learning experiences available anywhere? Only when pride gets out of control and people value their egos more than truth do they slide down the slippery slope of character assassination and conflict procrastination. Communities that choose to follow the five steps of conflict resolution will enjoy the power of unity, which will propel them to extraordinary results.

> **Why should one run from conflict resolution when it is one of the best learning experiences around?**

CONFLICT RESOLUTION

Lewis and Tolkien: Lost Friends

What happens when two of the most prolific writers and friends allow small slights and misunderstandings to go unaddressed? Moreover, how could it be that two men, who did so much to advance the cause of good in this world, fail to maintain the close personal bond that produced these impressive results? The answer, dismally, is similar to the answer G. K. Chesterton once gave to the essay question, "What's wrong with the world?" Chesterton's response was short and poignant: "Dear Sirs, I am. Sincerely yours, G. K. Chesterton." Indeed, no matter how close a personal friendship, without both parties practicing the principles of conflict resolution, the pesky problem of self not conquered in either or both parties can torch the relationship of even the closest of friendships.

C. S. Lewis and J. R. R. Tolkien were close friends for over a decade. Indeed, the two shared a unique friendship built on three key principles, which sharpened the iron of both: common interests, consistent encouragement, and permission to speak truthfully in love. One can see all three principles at work in the story of their friendship. It was the synergy in this friendship that permitted both authors to become better writers than either one of them would have been on his own.

Author Colin Duriez, in an interview about Lewis and Tolkien, was asked, "You have said that Lewis and Tolkien shared three interrelated commitments—to 'romanticism, reason, and Christianity.' Can you elaborate?" He answered:

The two friends were interested in the literature of the Romantic period because many of the poems and stories attempted to convey the supernatural, the "otherworldly"—and thus provided a window into spiritual things. Lewis explored romantic themes like joy and longing, and Tolkien emphasized the nature of people as storytelling beings who by telling stories reflect the creative powers of God. But they both rejected an "instinctive" approach to the imagination. Many Romantic writers were interested in a kind of nature

237

mysticism. They looked within themselves and at the world around them and sought flashes of insight into "the nature of things"—illuminations of truth that could not be explained, reasoned, or systematized. But Lewis and Tolkien insisted that the reason and the imagination must be integrated. In any understanding of truth, the whole person must be involved.

In 1929, when Tolkien gave Lewis the poetic version of Beren and Lúthien called *The Lay of Leithian*, it was already apparent that Lewis was Tolkien's greatest encourager. Lewis wrote to Tolkien after reading it: "I can quite honestly say that it is ages since I have had an evening of such delight: and the personal interest of reading a friend's work had very little to do with it....The two things that come out clearly are the sense of reality in the background and the mythical value: the essence of a myth being that it should have no taint of allegory to the maker yet it should suggest incipient allegories to the reader."

Lewis was careful not to offend the delicate ego of Tolkien, having learned to speak truth with love to his friend. Lewis knew that Tolkien's response to criticism was either to ignore the criticism, along with the author of it, or to start over with a complete rewrite. Lewis commented, "His standard of self-criticism was high and the mere suggestion of publication usually set him upon a revision in the course of which so many new ideas occurred to him that where his friends had hoped for the final text of an old work they actually got the first draft of a new one." Lewis learned to offer suggestions to his friend by indirect methods, desiring to help Tolkien's work without hurting his friend. After reading *The Lay of Leithian* and praising it profusely, Lewis waited nearly a year before writing fourteen pages of mock academic commentary, presented as make-believe German critics, sharing profound suggestions for Tolkien's poem in a non-offensive manner. Many of the suggestions were implemented by Tolkien, who appreciated the feedback given as a spoof, learning through the humor without feeling attacked personally.

CONFLICT RESOLUTION

It was their common interest that brought them together, and it was the love for truth that deepened their relationship. But it was the respect and encouragement given to each other that made them the best of friends. Friendships that have these qualities are rare and should be cultivated with tender loving care, as they have a value that's beyond any price. Ethan Gilsdorf studied extensively the unique friendship between these two authors and wrote:

Intellectually, they craved each other's companionship. But their relationship had emotional depth as well. They bonded over their harrowing experiences in the trenches of World War I. They shared the loss of their parents, which they had both endured as children. Sorrow over their pasts and their retreat from modernity gave them nowhere to go but their imaginations. They lost themselves in anachronistic tales and created make-believe places—engaging in what today we might disparagingly call "escapism." Of course, the realms of Lewis' Narnia and Tolkien's Middle-Earth are fraught with troubles, wars, and imperfections, at least as much as our so-called real world.

The two authors made each other better, maintaining a close relationship for well over a decade despite major differences in temperaments. Lewis was socially extroverted, outgoing, and voluble, developing friends across the world with his professional achievements in books and broadcasting, which reached the pinnacle of worldly success in 1947 when he graced the cover of Time magazine.

Tolkien, on the other hand, was socially introverted—reserved and soft-spoken. Despite his professional competence, writing groundbreaking essays on *Beowulf* and translating many early Anglo-Saxon works, he did not achieve the same level of professional fame in his lifetime as his younger cohort. Compounding this frustration was the fact that Tolkien's peers, his professorial colleagues at Oxford, were unable or unwilling to recognize the genius of his Middle-Earth creation; they ridiculed his second life of wizards, dragons, and

RESOLVED

rings and denigrated him and his work by asking, "How is your hobbit?"

Lewis's second life, on the other hand, was readily accepted, opening doors for Lewis wherever he turned. His Christian sermons were entertaining, informative, and thought-provoking, not to mention highly popular. In fact, by the 1940s, between his BBC broadcasts and his best-selling *The Screwtape Letters*, Lewis was a bona fide international figure. His first *The Chronicles of Narnia* book was released in 1950, which fueled his fame even further. Lewis easily eclipsed, at least at that time, the success of his friend Tolkien.

Lewis's schedule, along with Tolkien's unspoken but strongly felt desire for quality time, led to several unaddressed issues that began to chill their once-warm friendship. The first issue was Lewis's meteoric rise to success, which forced him to divide his time among his many interests and reduced the quality and quantity of time he could spend with Tolkien. The second issue, Tolkien's twinge of jealousy, arose when he compared his monumental efforts and moderate successes with his friend's seemingly moderate efforts and monumental successes. Sadly, their rift grew bigger, although with a little more understanding and communication on Lewis's part and a willingness on Tolkien's to discuss his hurts openly, the friendship could have, and should have, thrived through the changing seasons of life.

Unfortunately, when issues are not discussed, envy and jealousy rear their ugly heads. What makes the poison of unaddressed jealousy so damaging to friendships is that its acids are poured directly into the roots of the relationship. Tolkien, by nature, was not a jealous man; but he valued Lewis's fellowship so greatly that when fame pulled on his friend's time, a silent, subtle, but all-pervasive hurt corroded the bonds that united them. Tolkien, the introvert, was troubled because he no longer had Lewis's undivided attention. Lewis, the extrovert, on the other hand, was overjoyed with his new celebrity status, making new friends everywhere he went. By the time Lewis had departed from Oxford, accepting a chair of literature at Cambridge, the two friends were

CONFLICT RESOLUTION

speaking less regularly than probably either preferred. Time and distance, plus the unspoken hurts, had tempered their fruitful collaborations. Their differences in beliefs, personalities, and opinions could not cause a crack in their relationship; but Lewis's move to Cambridge, his new friends, and his subsequent marriage did. All these ripped apart the unity that had made them the best of friends. Fueling the stress, and further dividing the friendship, was Lewis's prodigious book-writing exploits. He literally completed the seven-book *Narnia* series in seven years—a torrid pace, writing a book every year!

Tolkien, in contrast, toiled for over seventeen years on *The Lord of the Rings*, rewriting it numerous times in the pursuit of perfection. He worked tirelessly with no applause before releasing it. Eventually, the world would learn of his remarkable gifts, just as it had learned of Lewis's previously; but sadly, it was too late to repair the frayed friendship.

The Lord of the Rings became the fourth best-selling book series of all time, topping Lewis's *The Chronicles of Narnia*, the fifth best-selling series. Lewis would not have been surprised, having predicted his friend's success many years before. In 1954, he wrote, "This book is like lightning from a clear sky. It represents 'the conquest of new territory.'" In a letter written to a friend, Lewis shared that the book "would inaugurate a new age."

Tolkien, however, having swallowed the poison of his own pain, began to believe that Lewis didn't like his work, writing in 1967, four years after his friend's death, "To tell the truth, [Lewis] never really liked hobbits very much." Tolkien had grossly misread his friend, as nothing could have been farther from the facts. Lewis was enthralled by *The Lord of the Rings* series, believing in Tolkien and his fantasy fiction years before anyone else had even heard of Middle-Earth. Lewis, as a matter of fact, was one of the first people to recognize Tolkien's genius.

In his book, Duriez discussed a 1964 letter in which Tolkien described the fraying of his friendship with Lewis: "We saw less and less of one another after he came under the dominant influence of Charles Williams"—a writer whom Tolkien

241

perceived as a wedge between himself and Lewis—"and still less after his very strange marriage." That marriage was to Joy Gresham, which was unacceptable to Tolkien because she was divorced and an American. Although Tolkien later called Lewis "his closest friend from about 1927 to 1940," by the early 1950s, their friendship had soured.

For fourteen years, the two men were best friends, leading to two of the most prolific and productive series of works in the written history of mankind. When Lewis accepted the Chair in Medieval and Renaissance Literature at Cambridge in 1954, a position that Tolkien ironically helped him obtain, the fire of their friendship died down due to lack of oxygen, although the remaining embers smoldered for the rest of their lives. Lewis leaving Oxford was similar to Frodo leaving the Shire, choosing the adventure of the unknown in the Undying Lands rather than the peace and security of the comfortable Shire:

"But I thought you were going to enjoy the Shire too for years and years, after all you have done," said Sam, choking on his tears.

Frodo, looking at Sam, resolutely replied, "So I thought too, once. But I have been too deeply hurt, Sam."

Like Frodo, both Lewis and Tolkien were hurt and carried their unresolved pains to their graves, apparently missing each other dearly but unwilling to resolve their issues. When Tolkien heard of Lewis's passing in 1963, he wrote to his daughter that it felt "like an axe-blow near the roots."

Reflecting on their lives, I believe there are few, if any, friendships in recorded history that have had as great an impact on both friends as Lewis and Tolkien's did. The two Oxford professors created a lasting legacy by loving, respecting, and encouraging one another and utilizing the gifts given to them by the Author of all gifts. As a result, they accomplished what they set out to achieve and fulfilled their God-given purposes. The bad, however, is an equally "teachable moment." When two friends who love each other dearly do not communicate, petty jealousies and enviousness, which can poison the hearts of one or both of them, are bound to develop. There is no such thing as a no-maintenance relation-

CONFLICT RESOLUTION

ship; therefore, it is wise to constantly nurture one's friendships through words, thoughts, and deeds. In addition, when misunderstandings arise, a person must deal with them immediately and not stew on them for months. Imagine if Tolkien, when he thought about Lewis's neglect of their friendship for the second time, had sat down with Lewis in person, spoken from his heart, and resolved the conflict while it was still small. Who knows what this collaboration of geniuses would have produced!

Lewis and Tolkien may have drifted apart, but the world is still a better place today because on a spring day in 1926, two professors met and became inseparable friends. This friendship provided the oxygen for the fire within each of them that set the world aflame with stories of faith, hope, and redemption, a flame that still lights their eternal legacy.

CHAPTER 11

SYSTEMS
Resolved: To Develop Systems Thinking

I know that by viewing life as interconnected patterns rather than isolated events, I improve my leverage.
—Orrin Woodward

What Is a System?

Systems are everywhere. Indeed, both nature and organizations operate within innumerable systems. Nature has ecosystems involving air, water, plants, animals, and more in organized patterns to sustain life, while organizational systems consist of people, structures, and processes that interact to produce results. One can take something as basic as filling a glass of water and see that it is a simple system because there is a systematic way to achieve a specific result. Filling the glass with water follows an ongoing water regulation system, which includes a PDCA between the person's mind, the faucet, and the glass.

First, a person creates a plan to fill a specific glass with water from a chosen faucet. Second, he initiates action by placing the glass under the faucet and turning the faucet on. Third, he checks the gap between desired water level in the glass and the current level. Fourth, as the water fills the glass, he adjusts the faucet until it is turned completely off when the desired water level is reached. If something as remedial as filling a glass with water is a system, imagine how many systems have been misidentified by leaders, who, in their attempt to improve a situation, only made it worse for their lack of a systematic mind-set. Regretfully, the more specialized our world becomes, the less systematic most people think.

Professor, Peter Senge, gave the following description:

> *Systems thinking is a discipline for seeing wholes. It is a framework for seeing interrelationships rather than things, for seeing patterns of change rather than static "snapshots."...*
>
> *Today, systems thinking is needed more than ever because we are becoming overwhelmed by complexity. Perhaps for the first time in history, humankind has the capacity to create far more information than anyone can absorb, to foster far greater interdependency than anyone can manage, and to accelerate change far faster than anyone's ability to keep pace...*

Systems thinking is the antidote to this sense of helplessness that many feel as we enter the "age of interdependence." Systems thinking is a discipline for seeing the "structures" that underlie complex situations, and for discerning high from low leverage change. This is why systems thinking is so invaluable to a leader. In order to think systematically, though, one must learn to recognize the system and its parts, or put another way, the forest and the trees.

Parts or Whole?

Detailed knowledge about specialized fields has helped man improve his quality of life by dividing the workload into manageable tasks, but it also has a downside. The fractionalization of knowledge caused by specialization has taught many to be experts in one tree, while remaining clueless on the forest that one lives in. The story of the blind men and the elephant displays the effects of fractionalized knowledge, revealing how snapshots of individual truths must be connected together to receive a larger view of truth:

246

SYSTEMS

Once upon a time, there lived six blind men in a village. One day, the villagers told them, "Hey, there is an elephant in the village today."

The blind men had no idea what an elephant was. They decided, "Even though we would not be able to see it, let us go and feel it anyway." All of them were guided to the elephant, and every one of them touched it.

"Hey, the elephant is a pillar," said the first man, who touched the leg.

"Oh, no! It is like a rope," said the second man, who touched the tail.

"Oh, no! It is like a thick branch of a tree," said the third man, who touched the trunk of the elephant.

"It is like a big hand fan," said the fourth man, who touched the ear of the elephant.

"It is like a huge wall," said the fifth man, who touched the belly of the elephant.

"It is like a solid pipe," said the sixth man, who touched the tusk of the elephant.

They began to argue about the elephant, and every one of them insisted that he was right. It looked like they were getting agitated, each blind man wondering how the others could be so stupid and each believing he had the truth since he felt it with his own hands.

A wise man was passing by, and he saw this. He stopped and asked them, "What is the matter?"

They said, "We cannot agree to what the elephant is like." Each one of them told what he thought the elephant was like.

The wise man calmly explained to them, "All of you are right and all of you are wrong. The reason each of you is telling it differently is because each one of you touched a different part of the elephant. Each of you has a partial truth. The elephant has all the features that each of you described, but isn't fully what you described unless you combine all of your answers."

Each of the blind men had touched on a truth about the elephant, but none of them had the whole truth. How many issues in life stem from people arguing from their specific experiences, insisting on their version of truth when actually, in many cases, the whole truth cannot be understood without a systematic mind-set? Many partial truths are parts of a system that must be pieced together to get closer to the whole truth and a more accurate perspec-

247

RESOLVED

tive of the invisible systems archetype, where all the parts combine to form the whole truth.

Learning to "See" Systems

Imagine a team of five mountain climbers scaling a one-thousand-foot cliff. A person can recognize the systematic interdependence of the climbers by viewing the ropes and pulleys attached to each of the climbers. The five climbers are an interconnected system, and an action by one of them affects the actions of the others. No climber can climb to the top if another one chooses to rest because one cannot move too far without the others. The role of the leader, accordingly, is to direct all the climbers towards the common objective—the mountaintop. If one is tired, then they must all rest, as their efforts will be in vain, leading to fatigue and frustration instead of the intended results. A leader who moves too fast, leaving the other climbers in the dust, will only exhaust himself on the systematic constraints applied by the rope. The leader in this system must balance the goals and needs of the climbers. If he allows one or more to slack, expecting the other climbers to make up the difference, he hurts the team's performance and morale. He must encourage and remind each climber in the system of the personal responsibility they have to the team to ensure the objective is achieved in a timely fashion.

In the same way, all organizations require personal and team responsibilities to achieve their goals. The ropes that connect the climbers are a visual representation of the interconnectedness of all teammates in communities. Whether mountain climbers or any other profession, communities are interconnected and must work together to achieve the team's goals. Each person within the interdependent community must understand how his actions affect others by developing a systematic mind-set. Moreover, the leader, like the cliff-climbing leader, must know how to think and see systematically, understanding how individual parts influence one another within the entity as a whole, to lead his team to its full potential. Senge described the importance of leaders seeing and thinking systematically: "Structures of which we are unaware hold us prisoner. Conversely, learning to see the structures within which we operate begins a process of freeing ourselves from previously unseen forces and ultimately mastering the ability to work with them and change them."

Auto stereograms are an example of hidden structures, because a person's mind is held hostage to his two-dimensional (2-D) paradigm until he trains his mind to recognize the third di-

248

SYSTEMS

mension. Indeed, a single-image stereogram (SIS) is designed to create the visual illusion of a three-dimensional (3-D) picture in the mind from studying a 2-D image on paper. The brain must be trained to see the 3-D view in the 2-D picture by overcoming the brain's automatic coordination between focusing and vergence (movement of the eyes in opposite directions). Magic Eye produces books filled with random-dot auto stereograms that one can study for hours at a time. At first, the attempts to see the 3-D picture can be a frustrating experience; but with enough practice, one can develop the skills to routinely see past the 2-D surface into the 3-D picture within. Similarly, one's mind can be trained to recognize the 3-D systematic order hidden beneath the apparent 2-D cause-and-effect data. Naturally, the mind defaults to the simple cause-and-effect linear 2-D thinking; but once the world's systematic architecture, 3-D, is understood, one will never view problems the same way again. Systems are all around us, and training the brain to see them opens a new world of patterns and potential solutions to leaders. Organizational theorist Charles Kiefer described the mental training necessary to recognize systems: "When this switch is thrown subconsciously, you become a systems thinker ever thereafter. Reality is automatically seen systematically as well as linearly (there are still lots of problems for which a linear perspective is perfectly adequate). Alternatives that are impossible to see linearly are surfaced by the subconscious as proposed solutions. Solutions that were outside of our 'feasible set' become part of our feasible set. 'Systemic' becomes a way of thinking (almost a way of being) and not just a problem solving methodology."

Solving Challenges Systematically

Stephen Covey shared an excellent story on thinking in systems. A fisherman went to the river to enjoy a day of fishing. Just minutes after getting there, he sees a young boy flailing his arms in the middle of the river, screaming for help. The fisherman jumps into the water and saves the young boy and although disheveled, the boy is fine. The fisherman resumes his fishing again, but fifteen minutes later, a young girl is flailing her arms and yelling for help in the middle of the river. The fisherman saves her and she is fine also. At this point, he wonders what the odds are that two children would need help on the same day in the same river. Fifteen minutes later, when a third child needs to be rescued, he is certain that there is more to the picture (system) than the isolated events he is experiencing. He starts asking questions, no longer believing that the children needing to be rescued are isolated cause-

249

RESOLVED

and-effect events and begins walking upstream to see what's up. Eventually, he discovers a children's camp on the riverside. The fisherman also determines the root cause when he notices some distressed kids and a bully tossing them in the river every fifteen minutes everyone's lunch money is surrendered. The fisherman, a true problem solver, takes the bully by the ear and walks him into the camp's office. This solves the challenge at its roots rather than just trimming leaves that come back. Now, he is able to enjoy his remaining fishing time uninterrupted.

Although a simple example, how many times are issues "solved" by saving "drowning kids" instead of addressing what's causing the kids to be in the river in the first place? Stop trimming leaves, in other words, and start pulling roots. Unfortunately, most people are professional leaf trimmers, running from one emergency to another, without ever stopping to think if the emergencies are interconnected. Covey's story describes a simple system, which included the boys and girls, the bully, the river, and the fisherman downstream. The fisherman would have been busy all day had he not sought to discover the root cause. In the same way, one can stay busy dealing with isolated events instead of recognizing the systematic cause and killing it at its roots. After all, unless problems are solved at the root cause level, nothing of long-term consequence is accomplished. The same problems will reappear; it's just a matter of time. Think about how much better life would be if people stopped diving into rivers daily and instead sought to determine the underlying system creating the floating kids in the river. This is the power of systems thinking. Business leaders must recognize systems to learn how to eliminate customer challenges at the roots rather than just engaging in a never-ending trimming of the leaves.

> **Most people run from emergency to emergency in life, never stopping to think if the emergencies have an underlying systematic cause.**

Building Business Systems

The best businesses design systematic solutions to their business's and customers' needs. Building a successful business requires building a system that can produce consistent results for the customer without the need for superhuman performers. Systems guru Michael Gerber noted, "It is literally impossible to produce a consistent result in a business that is created around the need for extraordinary people; you will be forced to ask the difficult

250

SYSTEMS

questions about how to produce a result without the extraordinary ones." Gerber explained, "You will be forced to find a system that leverages ordinary people to the point where they can produce extraordinary results. To find innovative solutions to the people problems that have plagued business owners since the beginning of time. To build a business that works. You will be forced to do the work of business development, not as a replacement for people development but as its necessary correlate." The question to be asked and answered is: How does one create a "super-systems-dependent," not a "superstar-dependent," process for customer satisfaction? Gerber expressed, "How can I give my customer the results he wants systematically, rather than personally?"

The business equivalent of the biblical saying, "As [a man] thinks in his heart, so is he" (Proverbs 23:7) is "As a business man thinks, so is his business." Thomas Watson, the founder of IBM, understood systems and created a business model that produced results long after he retired:

> *I realized that for IBM to become a great company, it would have to act like a great company long before it ever became one. From the very outset, IBM was fashioned after the template of my vision. And each and every day, we attempted to model the company after that template. At the end of each day, we asked ourselves how well we did, discovered the disparity between where we were and where we had committed ourselves to be, and, at the start of the following day, set out to make up for the difference. Every day at IBM was a day devoted to business development, not doing business. We didn't do business at IBM, we built one.*

Business systems make extraordinary results an ordinary occurrence. The secret is to learn where the leverage points lie within the system. As Senge explained, "The bottom line of systems thinking is leverage—seeing, where actions and changes in structures can lead to significant, enduring improvements. Often, leverage follows the principle of economy of means: where the best results come not from large-scale efforts but from small well-focused actions." Few disagree with the principle of leverage, but the difficulty is in determining where energy needs to be focused to produce the biggest leveraged results. The leader, in other words, must understand the system to orchestrate duplicable results through the power of leverage.

251

RESOLVED

Systems Thinking to Satisfy Customers

Theodore Levitt said, "Discretion is the enemy of order, standardization, and quality." Put in simpler terms, discretion is the enemy of duplication. Duplication is the goal for the best systematic process to be used across all similar operations, reducing learning curves and increasing output. The way to create a system that guards against operating discretion is to discover what works consistently and teach those best practices to everyone performing similar processes.

> **For people to duplicate, leaders must orchestrate the best practices through culture, recognition, and rewards.**

For people to duplicate, leaders must orchestrate the best practices through creating a culture, based upon requirements, recognition, and rewards. Gerber explained: "Orchestration is based on the absolutely quantifiable certainty that people will do only one thing predictably—be unpredictable. For your business to be predictable, your people must be. But if people aren't predictable, then what? The system must provide the predictability. To do what? To give your customer what he wants every single time. Why? Because unless your customer gets everything he wants every single time, he'll go someplace else to get it!"

In fact, if an organization is not duplicating, a person knows that the leaders are not orchestrating the "best practices" across their communities. The plan is simple: Develop the patterns and systems to satisfy the customer, teach the patterns and systems to the employees, and reap the harvest of satisfied customers through a duplicable business system. Gerber explained, "The system becomes a tool your people use to increase their productivity to get the job done. It's your job to develop that tool and to teach your people how to use it. It's their job to use the tool you've developed and to recommend improvements based on their experience with it."

Even duplication, however, can be taken too far. If it denigrates into "just do it this way and stop thinking," then a team has lost the creativity needed to continuously improve. Leaders work on the system, and the team works within the system, but both must be constantly engaged in looking for ways to improve. A great idea to improve the system can come from anyone, and many times, it comes from the person directly responsible for a certain step in the process, since he spends the most time doing it.

SYSTEMS

The Japanese became famous for their system of Kaizen, recognizing and rewarding good ideas from anyone in the company who could help improve their systems. Ray Stata, former CEO of Analog Devices, said, "In the traditional hierarchical organization, the top thinks and the local acts. In a learning organization, you have to merge thinking and acting in every individual." As Lao-Tzu said, "A leader is best when people barely know he exists, when his work is done, his aim fulfilled, they will say: we did it ourselves." Finding the right balance between duplication, creativity, and discretion is essential for long-term systematic results. In today's competitive environment, if the system isn't broken, then a person must break it anyway to improve it before his competitors do this and put him out of business.

> **Finding the right balance between duplication, creativity, and discretion is essential for long-term systematic results.**

Scoreboard and PDCA

When a person applies systems thinking to his life, many times, a seemingly small change can have a huge effect, as Professor Donella Meadows illustrated:

> *Near Amsterdam, there is a suburb of single-family houses all built at the same time, all alike. Well, nearly alike. For unknown reasons it happened that some of the houses were built with the electric meter down in the basement. In other houses, the electric meter was installed in the front hall.*
>
> *These were the sort of electric meters that have a glass bubble with a small horizontal metal wheel inside. As the household uses more electricity, the wheel turns faster and a dial adds up the accumulated kilowatt-hours.*
>
> *During the embargo and energy crisis of the early 1970's, the Dutch began to pay close attention to their energy use. It was discovered that some of the houses in this subdivision used one-third less electricity than the other houses. No one could explain this. All houses were charged the same price for electricity, all contained similar families.*

The difference, it turned out, was in the position of the electric meter. The families with high electricity use were the ones with the meter in the basement, where people rarely saw it. The ones with low use had the meter in the front hall where people passed the little wheel turning around, adding up the monthly electricity bill many times a day.

The Dutch families unconsciously used the PDCA process to improve their results, thanks to an ever-present scoreboard: the electric meter. By changing the location of the electric meters, or scoreboards, their electric bills were reduced by one-third. In studying this example through the lens of the PDCA process, one can see that the scoreboard is part of the feedback loop within the system. Notice how a small change in location produced leveraged consequences. The meter, then, becomes the check step in the process. When the families noticed the wheel in the meter turning faster, they were able to check and therefore make adjustments in their electricity use, ultimately reducing their electrical loads. Because the scoreboard was visible, adjustments were made quickly, leading to decreased electrical usages, thus conserving energy and money.

Butterfly Effect

The Butterfly Effect, a part of the chaos theory, confirms the massive results that slight changes can have when applied to a leverage point in a system. The Butterfly Effect posits that a butterfly flapping its wings has the capacity to change the initial atmospheric conditions enough to trigger a series of changes that compound into a hurricane on the other side of the world. The same effect applies to human affairs in that subtle adjustments to initial conditions can create profound differences in results. According to the University of Bath, it was by studying weather patterns that the Butterfly Effect was first expounded:

> *In 1960 a meteorologist named Edward Lorenz was researching into the possibilities of long-term weather prediction. He created a basic computer program using mathematical equations which could theoretically predict what the weather might be. One day he wanted to run a particular sequence again, and to save time, he started it from the middle of the sequence. After letting the sequence run, he returned to find that the sequence had evolved completely differently from the original. At first he couldn't comprehend such different results but then realized that he had started the sequence with his recorded results to three decimal places, whereas the computer had recorded them to six decimal places. As this program was theoretically deterministic, we would expect a sequence very close to the original;*

SYSTEMS

however, this tiny difference in initial conditions had given him completely different results.

Lorenz's findings teach that slight changes running through complex systems compound over time, creating significant differences in results. For leaders who understand systems, a little extra "flapping of the wings" at key points of leverage can multiply over time, creating major changes in the long-term outcomes. Although no one can predict the results in complex systems omnisciently (as in weather forecasting), leaders know that small variances in initial conditions can produce big differences in the finished products. History is filled with examples of how little incidents impacted the destiny of civilizations. The Great Courses series, taught by historian J. Rufus Fears, dramatized this point:

> *January 10, 49 B.C.: Julius Caesar crosses the Rubicon River into Rome, igniting a civil war that leads to the birth of the world's greatest ancient civilization.*
>
> *October 12, 1492: The Spanish explorer Christopher Columbus, weary after months at sea, finally drops anchor at the island of San Salvador and takes Europe's first steps into the New World.*
>
> *September 11, 2001: On a calm Tuesday morning, a series of terrorist attacks on the United States of America ignites a global war on terrorism that continues to this day.*

History is made and defined by landmark events such as these—moments that irrevocably changed the course of human civilization. While many believe anonymous social, political, and economic forces are the driving factors behind events of the past, acclaimed historian and award-winning Professor J. Rufus Fears believes that it's individuals, acting alone or together, who alter the course of history. These events have given us:

- Spiritual and political ideas;
- Catastrophic battles and wars;
- Scientific and technological advances;
- World leaders both influential and monstrous; and
- Cultural works of unparalleled beauty.

Without them, human history as we know it today would be shockingly unfamiliar. It's because of these events that our world will never be the same again.

255

RESOLVED

Systems Thinking to Change the World

History is one of the most complex of social systems, but it's still true that individual actions, just like a butterfly flapping its wings, can cause impactful historical changes for good or for bad. By studying systems thinking, a leader can learn the leverage points where he can create huge changes through small seemingly insignificant adjustments. As Senge described, "Tackling a difficult problem is often a matter of seeing where the high leverage lies, a change which—with minimum effort—would lead to lasting, significant improvement."

Creating change on a world-sized scale requires leadership and leverage. A person cannot lift ten thousand pounds by himself, but with the right system, a fulcrum, and a long-enough lever, the same task is easier, just as Archimedes exclaimed: "Give me a lever long enough and a fulcrum on which to place it, and I shall move the world." What is believed impossible by a non–systems thinker is known to be achievable to a leader who thinks systematically.

One of the systems gurus of the twentieth century is a man named Buckminster Fuller. When Fuller was a young man, he initially felt he had wasted his life. When he was thirty-two, his only daughter died, and he became severely depressed. Soon afterward, alone at an ocean beach, Fuller waded farther and farther from shore, contemplating ending his life. But at the point of surrender, he realized he hadn't really given life a chance. On the brink of suicide, he resolved to spend all of his energy discovering what a single human life could achieve. In a 1972 interview, Fuller explained the power a single human life had to change the direction of the world:

> *Something hit me very hard once, thinking about what one little man could do. Think of the Queen Mary—the whole ship goes by and then comes the rudder. And there's a tiny thing at the edge of the rudder called a trim tab. It's a miniature rudder. Just moving the little trim tab builds a low pressure that pulls the rudder around. Takes almost no effort at all. So I said that the little individual can be a trim tab. Society thinks it's going right by you, that it's left you altogether. But if you're doing dynamic things mentally, the fact is that you can just put your foot out like that and the whole big ship of state is going to go. So I said, call me Trim Tab.*

SYSTEMS

A trim tab is a small tab placed on the main rudder that turns the rudder, which ultimately turns the big ship. The trim tab's function is to make it easier to turn the ship by helping to turn the rudder. The larger the ship, the more important the trim tab becomes because it's progressively more difficult to turn the rudder as the size of the ship increases. Senge explained why the trim tab is so appropriate for leverage in a system:

> *What makes the trim tab such a marvelous metaphor for leverage is not just its effectiveness, but its non-obviousness. If you knew absolutely nothing about hydrodynamics and you saw a large oil tanker plowing through the high seas, where would you push if you wanted the tanker to turn left? You would probably go to the bow [front] and try to push left. Do you have any idea how much force it requires to turn an oil tanker going fifteen knots by pushing on its bow? The leverage lies in going to the stern and pushing the tail end of the tanker to the right, in order to turn the front to the left. This, of course, is the job of the rudder. But in what direction does the rudder turn in order to get the ship's stern to turn to the right? Why to the left, of course....*
>
> *The trim tab—this very small device that has an enormous effect on the huge ship—does the same for the rudder. When it is turned to one side or the other, it compresses the water flowing around the rudder and creates a small pressure differential that "sucks the rudder" in the desired direction. But, if you want the rudder to turn to the left, what direction do you turn the trim tab?—to the right, naturally. The entire system—the ship, the rudder, and the trim tab—is marvelously engineered through the principle of leverage. Yet, its functioning is totally non-obvious if you do not understand the force of hydrodynamics.*

So, too, are the high-leverage changes in human systems non-obvious until we understand the forces at play in those systems.

One can quickly see that although purpose, vision, and work ethic are all crucial, the resolutions are not complete without the holistic understanding gained through systems thinking. Senge described the disastrous consequences of visionary leadership without a systematic mind-set:

257

RESOLVED

Such 'visionary crisis managers' often become tragic figures. Their tragedy stems from the depth and genuineness of their vision. They often are truly committed to noble aspirations. But noble aspirations are not enough to overcome systemic forces contrary to the vision. As the ecologists say, 'Nature bats last.' Systemic forces will win out over the most noble vision if we do not learn how to recognize, work with, and gently mold those forces.

A person must learn to see the "trim tabs" in his organization. Further, he must learn to see the interconnectedness of the world around him and learn to think in systems. In doing so, he will learn how to lead his organization toward its destiny, to fulfill the purpose for which it was created.

SYSTEMS

Ray Kroc and McDonald's

Early in 1954, a fifty-two-year-old salesman whose multi-mixer sales business was plummeting traveled to California, where he discovered his destiny. The salesman was none other than Ray Kroc, and his destiny was McDonald's.

Kroc needed a breakthrough; he had already cut all extraneous expenses and laid off two of his employees, but his multi-mixer business continued to stumble backwards. He was fighting for his business life. Then an order came in for an unprecedented tenth mixer from an unknown San Bernardino–based fast-food restaurant called McDonald's. Intrigued, he decided to pay one of his best customers a visit. What happened on Kroc's California boondoggle changed the course of franchising history.

In California, Kroc experienced the future of fast-food service when touring the McDonald's facility; he decided that he wanted in on the action. Krox explained, "This had to be the most amazing merchandising operation I had ever seen!" His thirty years of extensive business effort, despite never getting his big break, had created a hunger, an unquenchable thirst for an opportunity to do something big. This is why he was a man on a mission when he discovered McDonald's. He knew in his gut that he was just the man needed, having the skills and the leadership, to take this McDonald's store and build it into something special.

Kroc flew back to Chicago, but he couldn't get McDonald's out of his mind. A week later, he called the owners, the McDonald brothers. Author John Love shared the story:

He called Dick McDonald. "Have you found a franchising agent yet?" he inquired.

"No, Ray, not yet," was McDonald's response. "Well then," asked Kroc, "what about me?" Ray realized that he could sell McDonald's franchises, saying, "This will go anyplace. Anyplace!"

Neal Baker, a fast-food competitor in California, said, "Ray Kroc was always traveling, and when he thought of McDonald's, he thought big. He had seen cities all over the country, and he could just picture a McDonald's in every one of them."

Kroc recognized he had found the best fast-food system, a system designed to improve profitability and decrease complexity, birthed in the late 1940s by Dick and Maurice McDonald. By pulling the sales receipts from their last three years of business and studying the data, the McDonald brothers realized that 80% of their business was hamburgers, not the complex barbecue items originally on the drive through menu. This new understanding led the brothers to a revolutionary conclusion: create the first mass production assembly line process for food.

Requisitioning their tennis court, the brothers drew out a prototype assembly line for hamburger production, just as Henry Ford did for automobiles. The brothers learned to place the equipment most efficiently by studying the employees assembling the various foods, an idea they borrowed from management guru Federik Taylor. They eliminated the carhop and used a self-service counter instead. Following the data, the brothers eliminated the barbecue pit completely and reduced their twenty-five-item menu down to just eleven: hamburgers, cheeseburgers, French fries, three soft drink flavors, milk shakes, milk, coffee, potato chips, and pie.

With a fully reengineered stainless-steel kitchen, capitalizing on the advantages of speed and quality in the mass production process, the McDonald brothers slashed the price of their hamburger from a competitive thirty cents to an unbelievably low price of fifteen cents. This was no longer a redesign of their old restaurant; instead they had created the future of fast food. The changes made to the restaurant nearly doubled the sales from a healthy $200,000 to over $350,000! Love observed: "The brothers refused to let even the choice of condiments impede their fast food format. All hamburgers were prepared with ketchup, mustard, onions and two pickles. Any order deviating from that was penalized by a delay in service. That not only allowed the McDonald brothers to streamline their production techniques, but it also opened the way for preparing food in advance of the order. That was a major break from conventional food service practices, but

SYSTEMS

the brothers believed it was vital to their concept of volume through speed. 'If we gave people a choice,' explained McDonald, 'there would be chaos.' The McDonald brothers, with a twelve-man crew, had revolutionized the fast-food industry.

The McDonald brothers might have created the system, but it took a leader of Ray Kroc's ability to visualize and fulfill McDonald's potential. He knew that the McDonald's system was a winner, a franchising system he could sell across the world. However, in order to do this, he understood he was selling more than just cheap hamburgers. Indeed, what he was offering franchisees was a complete franchising system that produced results when followed. According to Michael Gerber, "Ray Kroc created much more than just a fantastically successful business. He created the model upon which an entire generation of entrepreneurs have since built their fortunes: the franchise phenomenon. But the genius of McDonald's isn't franchising itself. The franchise has been around for more than a hundred years. The true genius of Ray Kroc's McDonald's is the Business Format Franchise." The Business Format Franchise provided the franchisees with a turnkey system for doing business that worked for anyone who worked it.

McDonald's broke the mold for franchising because, unlike traditional franchises that sold their names and product offerings, expecting the franchisees to develop a business system to sell the merchandise, Kroc understood that his first customer, the one he needed to sell, was the franchisee. In fact, if the franchisee didn't believe the McDonald's system could produce profitable results, no one would purchase the franchise, thus no hamburgers would be sold. Kroc, then, realized that he must become a salesman for the McDonald's business system, not just hamburgers. Ultimately, his success or failure would depend on convincing hungry entrepreneurs that the McDonald's business system produced results. Gerber wrote:

> At that point, Ray Kroc began to look at his business as the product, and at the franchisee as his first, last, and most important customer. For the franchisee wasn't interested in hamburgers or French fries or

261

milkshakes; he was interested in the business. Driven by the desire to buy a business, the franchisee only wanted to know one thing:

'Does it work?'" Kroc believed the McDonald brothers had cracked the code for high-speed but low-cost fast-food service; he would complete the package by providing visionary leadership and salesmanship to make his dream a reality. He was energized for the challenge, having been in sales all his life, so he knew a winner when he saw one. Gerber concluded, "If McDonald's was to fulfill the dream he (Kroc) had for it, the franchisee would have to be willing to buy it....He wasn't competing with other hamburger businesses. He was competing with every other business opportunity.

In April of 1955, Kroc made his first move, opening the first prototype store in Des Plaines, Illinois. The prototype gave Kroc a place to test and improve his operating system. His vision drove him to create cookie-cutter concepts where anyone who followed the system could produce profitable stores. Gerber described Kroc's system: "Forced to create a business that worked in order to sell it, he also created a business that would work once it was sold—no matter who bought it. Armed with that realization, he set about the task of creating a foolproof, predictable business." Kroc's emphasis on developing a successful business format franchise was fiscally sound since his agreement with the McDonald brothers allowed for only a $950 franchising fee and a mere 1.9%revenue sharing, 0.5% of which went to the McDonald brothers. Indeed, unless the franchisees were profitable quickly, Kroc could end up bankrupt due to his aggressive expansion plans. The Des Plaines store was crucial in the development of a duplicable system. In Gerber's words, "How could the components of the prototype have to be constructed so that the resulting business system could be replicated over and over again?...The business-as-a-product would only sell if it worked. And the only way to make certain it would work in the hands of a franchisee anywhere in the world would be to build it out of perfectly predictable components that could

SYSTEMS

be tested in a prototype long before ever going into mass production."

Kroc's system had perfectly predictable component parts, leading to uniform best practices across McDonald's; however, this didn't mean he was against creativity. After all, Kroc constantly inspired his people to improve his system, leveraging his community of like-minded franchise entrepreneurs.

Love elaborated:

The real secret to McDonald's successful operating system is not found in its regimen but in the way it enforces uniform procedures without stifling the entrepreneurship of franchisees....Without the freedom of franchisees and suppliers to exercise their entrepreneurial instincts, to test their own ideas on new products and procedures, and even to challenge the corporation head-on, McDonald's might still have attained its celebrated uniformity, but at a terrible price. It would lose the grassroots creativity that diverse franchisees and suppliers provide. It would, in short, lose touch with the marketplace.

Fred Turner, former CEO and the brains behind McDonald's system, said, "It's one of the superficial notions about McDonald's that no one has put into perspective. The independent-mindedness of our operators prevents regimentation. While they stick to the basics of the system, they zig and zag by making refinements and changes, and everyone benefits from their willingness to zig and zag. The system deals with setting uniform standards, but regimentation? No way!" In other words, through Kroc's leadership, McDonald's achieved the benefits of systems and the creativity of the community—a rare combination in the days of command and control management.

McDonald's unique blend of uniform systems and creativity energized the entire community, becoming one of Kroc's original contributions and his competitive advantage. The corporate-like rules were needed to maintain quality standards, while the creativity manifested itself through the leadership teams' encouragement of innovative ideas. These

RESOLVED

two seemingly conflicting principles were the backbone of McDonald's growth. Indeed, what other franchise has created so many top sellers, such as the Big Mac, Egg McMuffin, and Filet-O-Fish, that were not ideas from the corporate staff, but from the franchisee leaders?

Love shared, "Decisions at McDonald's have always been the product of individual initiative. Ideas are never homogenized by committees. New directions are the result of a continuous trial-and-error process, and new ideas spring from all corners of the system. The key ingredient in Kroc's management formula is a willingness to risk failure and to admit mistakes." McDonald's wasn't the typical top-down decision-making corporation. Instead, Kroc searched, listened, and asked for ideas from everyone, intuitively understanding that the whole team was better than any individual on the team. His leadership style encouraged people to make suggestions and test ideas.

James Kuhn, former McDonald's vice president, explained McDonald's corporate culture: "We have a public image of being slick, professional, and knowledgeable marketers who also happen to be plastic and shallow. In fact, we are a bunch of motivated people who shoot off a lot of cannons, and they don't all land on target. We've made a lot of mistakes, but it is the mistakes that make our success, because we have learned from them. We are impulsive, we try to move faster than we can, but we are also masters at cleaning up our messes."

Kroc created a win-win system, where each participant had common economic incentives and a common standard of quality, service, and cleanliness, and nearly everything else was up for discussion.

By leasing the restaurant site to the franchisee and only approving store expansion one at a time, Kroc had the necessary influence to keep maverick franchisees in line for the good of the entire store system. By late 1957, Turner was producing training films for franchisees, teaching best practices and procedures, but he soon realized this would not be enough. In 1961, McDonald's was the first fast-food franchise to launch a full-time training facility, which they called Hamburger University. Kroc said, "Our aim, of course, was to en-

SYSTEMS

sure repeat business based on the system's reputation rather than on the quality of a single store or operator. This would require a continuing program of educating and assisting operators and a constant review of their performance."

Nancy Fraser, a Life magazine reporter, visited Hamburger U., intending to write a tongue-in-cheek article on the hamburger zealots. But after attending the class, she changed her mind, saying, "I realized how dedicated you all are to Hamburger University. It didn't deserve to be put down."

All future franchisees attended the university giving McDonald's a leg up on the competition. Eventually, seeing McDonald's incredible results, every fast-food franchise created its own training facility as well.

Kroc's vision and drive helped him see and build something big; his salesmanship helped him assemble a winning team of franchisees, corporate managers, and suppliers; his leadership helped him unite the team in a win-win fashion; and his Hamburger University assured that he captured the best principles, processes, and procedures, creating a competitive advantage for his McDonald's franchising system.

Kroc's leadership produced a business that, at his death, had grown from humble beginnings to over eight thousand stores producing nearly $9 billion in sales. These figures are dwarfed by the over thirty-two thousand outlets today, which generate nearly $24 billion in sales. Results like this are a testament to the business and organizational systems Kroc created. McDonald's was built to last by a founder who knew how to inspire others with his compelling vision and competitive drive.

Love concluded, "The history of the McDonald's System is the story of an organization that learned how to harness the power of entrepreneurs—not several but hundreds of them. It is run by decisions and policies considered to be for the common good. But the definition of common good is not set by a chief executive or by a management committee. Rather, it is the product of the interaction between all the players....In essence, the history of McDonald's is a case study on managing the entrepreneurs in a corporate setting."

265

RESOLVED

Leaders can learn from Kroc's example and begin to unleash the latent creativity locked within a community's entrepreneurial-minded people. Systems thinking in no way requires one to sacrifice originality. The two are not mutually exclusive. In fact, the two go very well together. Ray Kroc proved how successful one can become by using systems thinking to recognize a brilliant business model and leverage the predictability of that model as well as the ingenuity of the franchisees in order to continuously improve upon the model and boost sales and customer satisfaction.

CHAPTER 12

ADVERSITY QUOTIENT (AQ)
Resolved: To Develop Adversity Quotient

*I know that AQ leads to perseverance in
overcoming obstacles and setbacks.*
—Orrin Woodward

Everyone gets knocked down, but winners get back up and learn from it while the rest just stay down. Adversity quotient (AQ) is a combination of mental and emotional intelligence that helps a person step back up to the plate and take another swing after striking out. People with high AQ refuse to compromise personal and professional excellence no matter how difficult or how long it takes to overcome the obstacles. Author Paul Stoltz elaborated, "Your success in life is largely determined by your AQ:

1. AQ tells you how well you withstand adversity and your ability to surmount it.
2. AQ predicts who will overcome adversity and who will be crushed.
3. AQ predicts who will exceed expectations of their performance and potential and who will fall short.
4. AQ predicts who gives up and who prevails."

Not surprisingly, AQ is one of the biggest factors people lack in their success journey today. For today's purposeless generation, the ability to apply AQ to persevere through one's challenges is becoming a lost art. Nonetheless, perseverance is one of the essential traits that all consistently successful people have because there are moments on everyone's success journey where he has given it his all and the results have not come. At this point, a person must rely on the faith he has in his purpose to drive him to further action without any visible results. This is the role of Adversity Quotient.

RESOLVED

Without a strong faith in his purpose, a person will too often make shortsighted decisions that compromise his long-term dreams for short-term comfort. High AQ helps a person continue to climb the mountain even when the scoreboard is providing little evidence of future success. As a matter of fact, it's these gloomy periods, when everything in a person wants to quit, that AQ is revealed. Needless to say, a person can implement all the other resolutions, but if he lacks AQ, he will fail when the "chicken hits the fan" because he will not endure the mental pain of delayed achievement. Great leaders, in contrast, went through their desert experiences, where everything looked lost, yet somehow mustered the strength to carry on anyway, "faithing" it until making it.

The Formula AQ = IQ × EQ × WQ

The formula for adversity quotient is AQ = IQ (intelligence quotient) × EQ (emotional quotient) × WQ (will quotient). Just as IQ is intelligence for the mind, EQ is intelligence of the heart, and WQ is intelligence for the will. AQ, as a result, is only developed when a leader combines the mind, heart, and will together as discussed in the Introduction. Many people feel they are not smart enough to succeed, but usually the most successful people do not have the highest IQs. Remember, IQ alone is only one of the three attributes needed to create a strong AQ, the essential quality of all winners. For example, Henry Ford, the automobile tycoon, although scoring off the chart in AQ, had only an average IQ. Interestingly, in a lawsuit between Ford and the Chicago Tribune, he proved that IQ was not the secret to his success. Dr. David Schwarz explained, "The Tribune asked him scores of simple questions such as 'Who was Benedict Arnold?', 'When was the Revolutionary War fought?', and others, most of which Ford, who had little formal education, could not answer. Finally he became quite exasperated and said, 'I don't know the answers to those questions, but I could find a man in five minutes who does.' Henry Ford was never interested in miscellaneous information. He knew what every major executive knows: the ability to know how to get information is more important than using the mind as a garage for facts."

> Many people feel they are not smart enough to succeed, but typically, the most successful people are not the highest scorers on an IQ test.

The world is filled with educated derelicts, but even someone with below-average IQ, can become highly successful if he is will-

268

ADVERSITY QUOTIENT

ing to grow his EQ and WQ by focusing on his purpose and destiny. Every person has strengths and weaknesses and a high IQ with a weak EQ is just as damaging as the reverse. In reality, leaders surround themselves with teammates who are good at the areas where they are weak. The key is to magnify a person's strengths and protect his weaknesses within the community. In some ways, the person with average IQ is better off, for people with high IQs tend to overestimate their abilities, leading them into overconfidence, which is fatal to success, as Ford said:

> None of our men are "experts." We have, most unfortunately, found it necessary to get rid of a man as soon as he thinks himself an expert because no one ever considers himself an expert if he really knows his job. A man who knows a job sees so much more to be done than he has done, that he is always pressing forward and never gives up an instant of thought to how good and how efficient he is. Thinking always ahead, thinking always of trying to do more, brings a state of mind in which nothing is impossible. The moment one gets into the "expert" state of mind a great number of things become impossible.

Ford understood that it's high AQ, the hunger to press on regardless of current conditions, not high IQ, that is the secret behind every successful person. In contrast, experts no longer feel the need to learn, grow and change; therefore, they are as good as they will ever get, as author Henry Hazlitt once noted, "Nothing is more securely lodged than the ignorance of the experts."

EQ and Phineas Gage

The physical pathway the senses take to travel through the body move from the spinal cord, to the back of the brain, then to the center limbic system (where you feel), and finally move to the front rational system (where you think). Since all the senses go through the feeling limbic portion before reaching the rational brain, the challenge is to not respond emotionally before allowing time for the rational mind to think through the proper response.

Perhaps the most striking example of how the two minds work together is the story of Phineas Gage. A railroad supervisor, Gage was considered one of the best leaders, always punctual and reliable in his work. Tragically, however, in an on-the-job accident, a forty-three-inch-long tamping iron with a diameter of 1.25 inches rocketed through the frontal lobe of Gage's brain. Somehow, Gage

RESOLVED

survived the grisly accident! Although it was a miracle that he lived, others soon realized he was a changed man in more than just physical appearance. Instead of exhibiting his normally high EQ, Gage now lost his temper quickly and was emotionally unstable at the slightest provocation. When under stress, he would curse like a sailor, creating tension and chaos among his confused crew, who knew his previously calm and cool demeanor. Gage plummeted from the top supervisory position to unemployed because he could not mentally handle the stress of the job. In short, he had lost his EQ. Unlike most people, of course, Gage, had an excuse for his low EQ because he literally lost the use of his frontal lobe, where reasoning and emotions combine, making it impossible for Gage to think through his feelings. This is not an excuse that most EQ-impaired people can use.

People with high EQ trust the situation will work out best by applying both feelings and logic to how

> **All great victories in life begin with a victory over self.**

one responds. It is true the senses hit the "feeling" part of the brain first (elephant mind), but with discipline, one can train himself to combine feeling with the "reasoning" mind (ant), before responding. This allows a person to use his whole mind and live life with high-EQ. Leaders refuse to react on emotions, choosing instead to respond with a high level of EQ trust, allowing the mind to both feel and think. No one enjoys associating with low-EQ people because there is always tension from not knowing how he is going to react. In other words, his behavior is unpredictable and when behavior is unpredictable, people do not value the association because the low EQ person could hug them this time and hit them the next. Put simply, low-EQ people are not trusted.

People with low EQ haven't mastered their own emotions; therefore, they are not leading themselves. Naturally, a person not leading himself cannot lead others. EQ, as a result, is one of the highly developed traits of all great leaders. Before reacting emotionally to stress, a person should take a deep breath, forcing the mind to remain calm. Then, one can reflect rationally, responding to the situation rather than reacting to it. True, making this habitual takes practice, but the results are well worth the investment. When a person lifts his EQ, it reverses the Phineas Gage effect. Gage lost his EQ when he lost a portion of his previously active brain; a leader, on the other hand, gains EQ by using a portion of his previously inactive brain. It's almost like having brain surgery, adding a function to one's brain that was previously unused. Not

270

ADVERSITY QUOTIENT

surprisingly, EQ is one of the single biggest changes a person can make on his leadership journey, one that is quickly noticed by his associates.

Will Quotient (WQ)

There are two aspects of AQ that make perseverance possible. Both, in fact, are needed to endure the dark nights of the soul: trust (EQ) and obey (WQ). WQ is the ability to align the will to obey the laws of success, consistently doing what everyone else is merely discussing. For when all is said and done, much more is said then is ever done. If a person trusts but doesn't obey, success will not arrive. On the other hand, if a person obeys but doesn't trust, he can become disillusioned by the slow rate of growth in the success process. Results typically require longer time periods than expected, providing ample opportunity to apply AQ on one's success journey. A common saying among Christians is, "Work as if everything depends upon you, and pray as if everything depends upon God." This, in essence, describes the mix between faith and work (trusting and obeying) needed to achieve enduring success. The trust-and-obey process applies even when people do not believe in the Creator who developed the law, for Matthew 5:45 reads, "That you may be the children of your Father which is in heaven: for he makes his sun to rise on the evil and on the good, and sends rain on the just and on the unjust". Therefore, the process of reaping and sowing, just like gravity, works for believers and non-believers alike.

Consider the farmer as an example. He farms his fields on faith, trusting God to provide an increase. Still, no farmer has a right to expect an increase unless he has first obeyed the process by sowing the field. To say a person trusts when he hasn't obeyed is illogical, as John Locke once explained: "The best way to read a man's mind is through his actions." People who say they trust but do not obey are lying to themselves and, thus, to others. AQ leaders plan (IQ) their work, do (WQ) the work consistently, and trust (EQ) that if they do it long enough, they will succeed. Similarly, a farmer has no right to expect a harvest until he has planned and performed and trusted the work will produce the desired result. Trust is the highest EQ response to the stressful events in a person's life. While the preceding chapters have covered various aspects of obeying, even if all the resolutions are implemented, one must still trust the process, persevering through the tough times and poor results to achieve a great victory.

AQ is non-negotiable because real success isn't the destination, but the person one becomes while pursuing the destination. Dismally, when a person quits his success journey, he also quits the real success, namely, whom he could have become. Hell, it's been said, is when the person you are meets the person you could have become. Exercising AQ in moments of trials and tribulations is what separates the winners from the wannabes. Planning, obeying, and trusting are equivalent to IQ, WQ, and EQ, which combine together create the AQ Resolution. One can move ahead confidently when one knows that everything that can be done has been done, one has the AQ to endure disappointments, and one trusts the process to produce the desired results. It's always darkest before dawn, and many times, people give up just before dawn, inches away from the goal line, receiving heartache and disappointment as their lasting legacy instead of the elation of victory they deserve. When a person stops trusting the process, hope is lost, leading to lost perseverance and dreams. Regretfully, many talented people remain nameless because they lacked the AQ to persist when the going was tough. Author Paul Stoltz shared a sobering story about dreams and perseverance from when his friend Eric and several of his graduating class buddies attempted to relive a class tradition at their fifteenth-year reunion:

> *It is said that you can never go back. Likewise, their ritual could not be relived. That night, they drove the same roads they had fifteen years before—roads now populated with malls and fast-food franchises. Flagstaff was now a mountain-chic city of fifty-six thousand. The dirt clearing was now a fully-lit parking area patrolled by the National Forest Service. They were greeted by a huge trail sign, welcoming them and enumerating a long list of hiking dos and don'ts. Yes, they brought beer. But since they were more sensible now, no one dared drink an entire six-pack. Instead, three guys drank a couple of light beers, and another guy, a recovering alcoholic, responsibly chose an alcohol-free brand. After making a fairly weak display of downing the beverages, they started their hike. They started out singing, but this time the trail seemed steeper; the song gave way to the panting of these thirty-something-year-old hikers—the hike had become a climb. Eric, still in reasonably good shape, was dismayed by how soft his friends had become. Even Bucky, the ex–running back, was struggling. It seemed like yesterday that they had bounded up this hill, half-drunk, singing at the tops of their lungs. Now they gasped and panted, and the hill had become as formidable as Mount Everest.*

ADVERSITY QUOTIENT

Halfway up, three guys reluctantly called it quits, probably sparing themselves a coronary. The rest persevered. At the top, they lay on their backs, more exhausted than exhilarated, looking at the stars, except this time, there was pain in their voices as most of them reflected on their dreams for the first time in over a decade, and each rationalized the compromises he had made along the way. The entire group was strangely quiet on the way down. How had all the others aged so much? Eric wondered. What had happened to their spirits and strength? It struck Eric as odd, if not chilling, that had he told his friend Bucky fifteen years ago that he would someday be bald, overweight, divorced, and never travel beyond the West Coast, Bucky would have punched him in the face. Tonight, Bucky was matter-of-fact, if not resigned. Eric was stunned by the power of gradual change. Fifteen years ago, had he and his buddies awoke to the malls, concrete, government regulations, receding hairlines, and pot-bellies-in-the-making, they would have been immobilized with shock. Yet when these changes occur over time, they are accepted if not completely unnoticed.

Upon returning home, Eric walked by the bathroom mirror and paused. This time, for the first time, he saw the face his friends must have seen. Although healthy and strong, he too had aged. For a moment, he saw the passage of fifteen years.

Staring into the mirror, in a moment of introspection, Eric confronted the gap between his and his friends' former elephant-sized dreams and their current antlike aspirations. He realized that the significant compromises that each had made led to the growing disparity between their old dreams and the new reality. Without applying AQ daily, one's dreams, like Eric's and his friends', crumble into yesterday's fantasies through seemingly small, subtle compromises. AQ provides the faith for a person to persevere in his ideals, even when everything inside him is screaming to compromise for his convenience. Winners endure the pain of the process in order to achieve their dreams, while others skip the pain in the process by compromising. Although compromising temporarily alleviates the short term pain, it eventually leads to a much greater long-term pain: the pain

> **AQ provides the faith for a person to persevere in his ideals, even when everything inside him is screaming to compromise for his convenience.**

273

of regret. Eric and his friends experienced the gnawing pain of regret when their adolescent dreams collided with their adult realities. They became like the frog in water, which, when the water temperature is slowly raised, is unaware of the slow changes and is eventually cooked. What is it that seems to replace hope and optimism with despair and pessimism? If hope is based on the faith that one can overcome, then despair, conversely, is the belief that fate is destiny and nothing a person does can change it. What are these compromises that cause people to despair and, as Thoreau said, "lead lives of quiet desperation"?

Learned Helplessness

One such compromise was discovered by Dr. Martin E. P. Seligman in 1965, when he stumbled across what the American Psychological Association have called the landmark theory of the century— learned helplessness. Learned helplessness is a belief that what a person does cannot alter his outcomes, that somehow, life's cards are stacked against him. Seligman's research created a revolution in psychology, displacing Skinner's hopeless behaviorism (stimulus controls response). Pavlov's original study, in which he rang the bell and provided food, displaying dogs salivating at a ringing bell, seemed to prove humans only responded to the stimulus provided. From this experiment, Pavlov, and later Skinner, concluded that man lives by learned behaviors, leaving no room for thinking, responsibility, and change, and, therefore, no room for destiny. But Seligman's experiments altered the field of psychology forever with his hope-filled cognitive psychology revolution (thinking determines behavior). His experiments revealed, in other words, that what we do does matter.

Seligman tested three groups of dogs based on Pavlov's foundation, but with a key variation in the stimulus. Group A dogs were harnessed individually, hearing a bell tone and receiving a harmless electric shock afterward. Group A dogs could stop the shock by pressing a bar with their nose, which they quickly learned to do. Group B dogs, on the other hand, heard the bell tone and received the shock but had no ability to stop the electric shock. Lastly, Group C received no shocks at all; they merely heard the bell tone. The breakthrough occurred on the second day of testing when each of the dogs from the previous day was randomly placed in a shuttle box, a box with a low barrier down the middle. One at a time, the dogs were place in the shuttle box. Each dog heard the bell tone and received the shock, but the different responses of the three groups launched the cognitive revolution. Both groups A and

ADVERSITY QUOTIENT

C quickly jumped the middle barrier, eliminating the discomfort of the electric shock. Group B, contrary to expectations, did not attempt to jump over the barrier; instead, the dogs merely crouched down and whimpered. Stoltz described the breakthrough theory: "What Seligman and others discovered is that these dogs had learned to be helpless, a behavior that virtually destroyed their motivation to act. Scientists have discovered that cats, fish, dogs, rats, cockroaches, mice, and people all are capable of acquiring this trait. Learned helplessness is simply internalizing the belief that what you do does not matter, sapping one's sense of control."

When a person believes that he cannot change his situation, he won't even try, becoming hopeless because he believes he is helpless. On the other hand, people can change nearly anything when belief is combined with the right knowledge applied consistently and persistently. Learned helplessness, because it destroys hope for change, must be exposed as the lie it is. Leaders must rid themselves and their teams of the learned helplessness because it's fatal to personal growth. One must realize that practically any change is possible when a person believes it is.

Improper Response to Pain

Another compromise that leads to failure and despair is an improper response to the pain inherent in the process of growth. There are actually two types of pain: One comes from the inside due to the change process; the other comes from the outside due to criticisms from those unwilling to make the same changes. Hope is the only fuel capable of burning through both types of pain. Without hope, either of these two types of pain will trump one's willingness to endure, enticing one to choose to stop the pain by quitting the journey. Author Robert Grudin wrote, "One might reply that most people who surrender simply lack the ability to get very far. But it is more accurate to say that ability and intelligence, rightly understood, include a readiness to face pain, while those characteristics which we loosely term 'inadequacy' and 'ignorance' are typically associated with the avoidance of pain." When pain reaches a certain threshold, everything inside a person screams for relief, but champions, people with high AQ, persevere. Pain is overcome through continuous focus on one's purpose. Moreover, achieving greatness will require a faith that can move mountains and an AQ to endure the rising pain in the process. With perseverance, one

> **Pain is overcome through the continuous focus on one's purpose.**

275

RESOLVED

will eventually reach levels of success that more timid souls refuse to believe are possible.

Grudin elaborated on the outside pain given to achievers as an unjust reward for their quest for personal excellence:

> *Modern society has evolved an idiomatic defense of non-achievement so subtle and elegant that it almost makes failure attractive. We can equivocate with failure by saying that we could not stand "the pressure." We can inflate mediocrity by calling cow colleges universities, by naming herds of middle-level executives, vice presidents or partners, and by a thousand other sorts of venal hype. We can invert the moral standard by defending a fellow non-achiever as being too sensitive or even too good for the chosen arena. This double rejection of pain—a surrender sanctified by a euphemism—has in our time achieved institutional status. Because it includes its own anti-morality, it can be passed on with pride from generation to generation. Other ages may have been as full of non-achievers as ours, but no other age, I believe, has developed so comprehensive a rhetoric of failure. To conclude, then: those people in quest of intellectual dignity and independence in the late twentieth century must act in a cultural context that has done its best to annul or camouflage one of the key elements in the quest, the challenge of pain. For this reason such people currently labor under a double burden: they must face the pains inherent in their task, and they must do so in a culture that has little appreciation for their suffering.*

Today's achievers, then, handle not only the traditional pain associated with excellence but also the additional pain from the criticisms of the envious Internet age non-achievers. Champions, nonetheless, understand it's better to be mocked by non-achievers than to become one. AQ can be developed, but only by discarding excuses, rejecting compromises, and choosing to feed one's faith, not one's fears. To achieve dreams, people must be willing to surrender who they are to become who they dream to be. One cannot have his cake and eat it, too. AQ refuses to surrender personal responsibility (what one desires) to an impersonal environment (what is available now).

> **In order to achieve dreams, people must willingly surrender who they are to become who they dream to be.**

Best-selling author Chris Brady articulated   in his book *Rascal*

276

ADVERSITY QUOTIENT

what it takes to break free from the herd: "It takes character to be different. It takes character to stand apart from the masses for legitimate, purposeful reasons. It takes character to be who God called you to be without succumbing to the pressures of others and their ideas of who you should be and how you should live. For those who embody this concept and live a truly authentic life, we will assign the name of Rascal." People with AQ are Rascals, refusing to be lulled to sleep by comfort, choosing instead to follow their convictions over conveniences. Rascals pay the temporary price of pain for success, rather than the permanent price of regret for failure.

Washington, Franklin, and Edwards developed AQ and heroic virtues by consistently studying their resolutions, but where are the heroes of this type today? George Roche explained:

Heroes are a fading memory in our times, but we can still recall a little about them. We know at least what sets the hero apart is some extraordinary achievement. Whatever this feat, it is such as to be recognized at once by everyone as a good thing; and somehow, the achieving of it seems larger than life. Even by this sparse definition, the hero's deeds rebuke us. We have been struggling frantically merely to achieve the ordinary: that measure of happiness each of us is supposedly entitled to. The hero, in contrast, overcomes the ordinary and attains greatness by serving some great good. His example tells us that we fail, not by aiming too high in life, but by aiming far too low. Moreover, it tells us we are mistaken in supposing that happiness is a right or an end in itself. The hero seeks not happiness but goodness, and his fulfillment lies in achieving it. His satisfaction such as it may be is thus a result: a reward if you please for doing well. This path to happiness is open to all, not just heroes, and until modern times nobody believed there was any other. To pursue happiness for its own sake was believed to be the surest way to lose it.

Colonel Harland Sanders

Every so often, a person comes along and, through the strength of his resolves, shows an immeasurable AQ. Such a person breaks through the mass of mediocrity. Tony Robbins shared the story of Colonel Sanders, the founder of Kentucky Fried Chicken:

Have you ever heard of a guy named Colonel Sanders? Of course you have. How did Colonel Sanders become such an unbelievable success? Was it because he was born wealthy? Was his family rich? Did they send him to a top university like Harvard? Maybe he was successful because he started

RESOLVED

his business when he was really young. Are any of these true?

The answer is no. Colonel Sanders didn't begin to fulfill his dream until he was 65 years old! What drove him to finally take action? He was broke and alone. He got his first social security check for $105, and he got mad but instead of blaming society or just writing Congress a nasty note, he started asking himself, "What could I do that would be valuable for other people? What could I give back?" He started thinking about what he had that was valuable to others.

His first answer was, "Well, I have this chicken recipe everyone seems to love! What if I sold my chicken recipe to restaurants? Could I make money doing that?" Then he immediately thought, "That's ridiculous. Selling my recipe won't even pay the rent." And he got a new idea: "What if I not only sold them my recipe but also showed them how to cook the chicken properly? What if the chicken was so good that it increased their business? If more people come to see them and they make more chicken sales, maybe they will give me a percentage of those additional sales."

Many people have great ideas. But Colonel Sanders was different. He was a man who didn't just think of great things to do; he put them into action. He went and started knocking on doors, telling each restaurant owner his story: "I have a great chicken recipe, and I think if you use it, it'll increase your sales. And I'd like to get a percentage of that increase."

How many times do you think Colonel Sanders heard no before getting the answer he wanted? He was refused 1,009 times before he heard his first yes. He spent two years driving across America in his old, beat-up car, sleeping in the back seat in his rumpled white suit, getting up each day eager to share his idea with someone new. Often, the only food he had was a quick bite of the samples he was preparing for prospective buyers. How many people do you think would have gone for 1,009 no's—two years of no's!—and kept on going? Very few. That's why there is only one Colonel Sanders. I think most people wouldn't get past twenty no's, much less a hundred or a thousand! Yet this is sometimes what it takes to succeed.

Colonel Sanders, through his chart-breaking AQ, refused to surrender. He applied the PDCA process to his efforts over and

ADVERSITY QUOTIENT

over until he got it right. This eventually led to him founding one of the most successful franchises in the world. What if Sanders had given up after one hundred, five hundred, or even a thousand rejections? AQ is what keeps someone in the game when he is doing everything right but still hasn't achieved the success he deserves. If he compromises during this crucial period, success will not reveal its secrets to him. Sanders denied himself the comfort of compromising; instead, he relentlessly pursued his purpose with AQ, thus fulfilling his destiny by never surrendering. Romans 5:3–4 says, "And not only that, but we also glory in tribulations, knowing that tribulation produces perseverance; and perseverance, character; and character, hope" A person who desires to climb life's mountain must build AQ. He must overcome innumerable tribulations in developing his character, hope, and perseverance, proving nearly anything can be conquered so long as he refuses to surrender, no matter how difficult the current adversity. This is why AQ is the final leadership achievement, for it mixes with all the others to create the success recipe.

Billy Durant: Adversity Quotient

William "Billy" Durant is an adversity quotient (AQ) icon. If a person were looking for one person that epitomized the term, he would be hard-pressed to find someone better than Durant. He grew up in Flint, Michigan, and from his humble beginnings, he created the world's largest company. Strikingly, he founded Buick, GM, Chevrolet, and Durant Motors—all of them successful car companies. Durant was the quintessential serial entrepreneur, founding or purchasing numerous companies during his lifetime. His story represents the "can do" spirit of free enterprise because he had dreams, struggles, victories, and defeats along the way, Regardless of the magnitude of the failure, however, he had the AQ to get up and do it again. Personally, I have been inspired by his dreams, humbled by his setbacks, and educated by his entrepreneurship. His life story strengthens every entrepreneur's AQ.

Starting with nothing but vision and drive, Durant foresaw the coming of the worldwide automobile revolution. Unfortunately, despite founding many of today's most successful brands, few have ever heard of him. Perhaps this is because his story does not have a happy ending, for despite his world-changing achievements, he died practically penniless. Nevertheless, one can learn key principles of life from both great successes and great failures. As a matter of fact, many times the failures reveal the principles clearer than the successes.

Durant started in the horse carriage business but was one of the few to recognize the seismic shift occurring when automobiles were invented. He teamed up with David Buick to create one of the first successful automobile brands, selling more cars than any other manufacturer during this time. Buick, however, was only the beginning for Durant; he pursued his brainchild of forming a trust to combine numerous car manufacturers under one holding company, a holding company he called General Motors (GM). By offering stocks and cash, he purchased Pontiac, Oldsmobile, and Cadillac, to name just a few, and integrated them all into GM.

Unbelievably, on several different occasions, Durant nearly bought out Henry Ford! Durant and Ford agreed on the price, but Durant offered GM stocks in payment, but Ford demanded cash, not wanting the stocks. Indeed, not once but twice, the price at which Ford agreed to sell Ford Motors to GM had been set, but Durant missed the deadline because he could not raise the cash in time. Once, he missed the deadline by less than 24 hours! Imagine how different automotive history would be today had Durant purchased Ford Motor Company. Ford, of course, went on to build the historic Model-T and ascended into automobile fame and fortune. The king of the automobile industry, the true visionary that predicted the automobile's meteoric future, was not Henry Ford but instead Billy Durant. Regardless of the automobile history one has read, history written by the victors, Durant was the prime mover in the automobile revolution. It was his vision that changed transportation as we know it.

As is normally the case with huge leaders, Durant's drive surpassed his financing. At the beginning of the second decade of the twentieth century, during an economic downturn, the car market stalled, tightening cash flows throughout GM's divisions. Durant ran out of money, having used all of his and his friends' money reserves. This forced him to sell his GM stocks to a banking syndicate. The bankers, naturally, were happy to take GM from Durant at a bargain basement price. For the majority of people (those without AQ), a setback of this size would have knocked them out, but Durant's legendary AQ propelled him forward, undaunted by his "failure."

Moving quickly, he partnered with a successful racer and mechanic named Louis Chevrolet. With Durant's business savvy, and Chevrolet's design, the new car company zoomed to the top of its class. Chevrolet, in fact, outsold all the brands in the GM stable. GM's non-visionary bankers were running the company into the ground, so averse to risk-taking that little innovation occurred. The GM stock plummeted and Chevrolet's stock continued to grow. The bankers' money was simply no match for Durant's AQ and drive. Simply put, Durant wasn't afraid of failure, while the bankers were deathly afraid to lose any of their precious capital. Durant, however, was just getting started. Parlaying his success at Chevrolet, Durant started swapping single shares of his high-value Chevrolet stock for multiple shares of the low-value GM stock. He planned nothing less than the take-over of his old

RESOLVED

company by gaining a majority share of the GM stocks to wrest control of GM from the bankers.

Needless to say, in 1916, Durant achieved his goal. In a move few thought possible, he walked into the GM board meeting and announced he was officially the majority shareholder of GM stock. One can only imagine the shock and dismay on the bankers' faces when they realized that Durant had outwitted the money powers through his entrepreneurship and AQ. Durant announced to the board that he intended to merge GM and Chevrolet. In other words, it was Chevrolet that purchased GM, not the other way around. Durant's AQ is a testament to the power of an aligned ant and elephant vision, as he rebounded from a humiliating defeat to achieve an astounding victory. He had refused to stay down and surrender his vision for GM, regardless of the odds against him, thanks to one of the most amazing AQs in American business history.

In addition to his incredible AQ, Durant had an understanding that talented people were essential to the success of GM. With his magnetic vision, he drew strong leaders into the GM community. Nearly all the top automotive men of the time either worked for GM or, like Ford, nearly did. In fact, Walter Chrysler, later the founder of Chrysler Motors, worked for Durant for many years as the head man of Buick Motors, being paid over $100,000 per year to do so. Durant's strong AQ attracted other strong leaders into the automotive field, helping GM prosper. Charles Kettering and Alfred Sloan are a couple of the other top names who worked with Durant.

Durant's successful takeover of GM, however, did not go unnoticed by the Wall Street bankers. They weren't happy that an upstart businessman had outfoxed them for control of GM, and they waited patiently for an opportunity to settle the score. With his business booming, Durant needed to raise more money for expansion. Eventually, John Raskob and his DuPont family friends purchased large chunks of GM stocks, making them one of the largest investors behind Durant. But if selling millions of vehicles and expanding his company across the globe was Durant's major objective, the Eastern Establishment bankers and businesses had another goal in

ADVERSITY QUOTIENT

mind. Knowing Durant's loyalty to his business partners, the Eastern Establishment, the same partners who had helped him fund Chevrolet and the GM takeover, began a covert operation to reduce the GM stock price by selling shares. Even though GM was profitable, the stock price began to tumble as the market was manipulated against the GM shares. Durant, always loyal to his friends, purchased millions of dollars of GM stocks with his own money. He didn't need any more stocks, but out of loyalty to his friends, he invested his fortune in an effort to stabilize the stock price and protect his friends' life savings. The Wall Street crowd, knowing Durant's loyalty, calmly drove the stock price down until Durant ran out of personal funds. With over $10 million of his own money invested (a huge sum even in today's inflated dollars), Durant was on the brink of bankruptcy. Forced to concede defeat, he had no remaining options but to sell his business empire to the Wall Street crowd, this time to a syndicate consisting of J. P. Morgan, the DuPont family, and John Raskob, for nickels on the dollar. Durant, for the second time in his life, had lost his beloved GM. Durant's second business failure wasn't a failure of business strategies but a failure to conceive of the level of animosity against him; his AQ and intense desire to win generated jealousy and envy from the Eastern Establishment. At this point, most people would have surrendered their dreams, choosing to become bitter at the injustices suffered, but Durant, again, was not like most people.

Durant refused to wallow in misery or have a pity party; instead, he applied his legendary AQ to start his third automobile company from the ground up, namely, Durant Motors. This was his third successful brand in less than twenty-five years. But as fate would have it, the 1929 stock market crash cost him millions of dollars and led to America's Great Depression. Durant was now penniless and company-less (but not hopeless, thanks to his AQ) at an age when most people are planning their retirement.

Of course, Durant wasn't without fault here. An honest evaluation would conclude that Durant's AQ and vision would have benefited by partnering with a more conservative financial person to balance he wheeling and dealing style. For example, Bud Walton was the conservative influence for Sam Walton and had Durant a similar influence, Durant

283

would be a household name today. Alas, it wasn't to be. Nonetheless, even without this, no one can discount the strength of Durant's AQ, an AQ that led him to overcome practically every setback he faced. Perhaps he should have played it safe after going from millionaire to broke three times in his life, but that just wasn't the way he played the game.

In his late seventies, with his AQ still intact, Durant began working in two new fields. While America was in the middle of World War II, he saw a bright future for fast-food restaurants and bowling alleys. The automobile industry had changed the American landscape, creating thriving suburbs outside the cities. Durant believed that intersections and highways would be dotted with restaurants to feed the motorists. It's hard to comprehend the level of entrepreneurial spirit and AQ inside Durant, who recognized the upcoming fast-food revolution over a decade before Ray Kroc of McDonald's did. Indeed, it was only Durant's failing health and eventual death in the mid-1940s that overcame his inspiring AQ and prevented it from helping him succeed in his last comeback attempt.

There are many lessons to be learned from Durant's life. First, he didn't have the perfect upbringing; his dad left his mom when he was young, forcing his mom to raise him on a tight budget. Durant knew that if he was going to make his dreams a reality, it would be with his own leadership and AQ, not with gifts from a rich family. Not only was he up to the task, but the challenge fueled his AQ and enthusiasm, urging him to do something great. This drive led him to create the largest car company in the world for nearly a century. Durant also understood that it isn't where a person starts in life but how far he goes that counts. It didn't matter that he had to borrow money from a local Flint bank to get started in the horse carriage industry, it didn't matter that he had to ditch the horse carriage business when automobiles were invented, and it didn't matter that he failed as long as his AQ didn't fail him. It's AQ, not ease, that determines how far one goes in his quest for success. Billy Durant's life teaches a person that AQ is more important than his current resources in reaching for his dreams.

Second, Durant possessed keen foresight and saw a bright future for automobiles. His visionary mind saw it ear-

ADVERSITY QUOTIENT

lier than others did as he dropped his carriage business to put all his energies into cars. As early as 1910, long before most people had a car, he spoke of every household owning an automobile and espoused the vision of roads crisscrossing America. But the dream alone wasn't enough; it was his superhuman level of AQ that made his dream of superhighways connecting big cities become a reality, providing better travel for all Americans. Durant's is the story of a young man whose never-failing AQ helped him accomplish greatness, not once, not twice, but three separate times in his life. With his dream, struggle, victory stories, he symbolized the American Dream for an entire generation. In a superb tribute to Durant, Clarence Young wrote:

> *In the creation of the Mass Production Age, Durant was not only the presiding genius; he was, indeed, the Titan—and, as was the fate of the original Titans, he was destroyed by the Olympians whom he had created.*
>
> *It is almost poignant now to tell the beads of carping criticism reiterated against Durant: He lacked or ignored technical mastery....he was a good promoter, but no administrator....He had no organization....He could not delegate authority....He made poor choices of executives....He was a promoter, a gambler....He was wrong in believing in himself....*
>
> *It is completely true that W. C. Durant had a weakness: He was human. His humanity included love and trust of his associates—the not-always-correct assumption that they were as honorable as he. He gave a degree and quality of loyalty to "his people" beyond any measurement; he expected the same magnitude of loyalty from them.*
>
> *He surrendered the control of General Motors in 1910 to preserve the company for its investors. In 1920, his loyalty to his company and its stockholders drove him to spend more money than he had preserving the value of the company's name, reputation, and stock. As for his feckless choice of executives, he hired and developed Charles W. Nash, Charles F. Kettering, Alfred P. Sloan (also Walter Chrysler and almost Henry Ford), and a few thousand others.*

RESOLVED

What was Durant?...A small-town boy from a broken home who had no advantages at all except his own character. With a borrowed $2000 he built up the largest carriage company in the world. With a debt-ridden, faltering motor company, he created the world's largest corporation, providing millions of jobs all over the world in the past 65 years [over a 100 years now].

Although small in stature, W. C. Durant was larger than life in every aspect of his thought, spirit, and practice. He was, indeed, so much larger in concept that he made the lesser men who surrounded him uncomfortable—he was unpredictable as an elemental force of nature.

Durant was an original genius who escapes classification and definition. He had an almost-godlike presence. He had the creativity to translate his vision into reality, not only for himself but for his fellow men. He was compassionate, gentle, charming, delightful, considerate, brilliant, generous, ingenious, and infinitely loyal.

Mass production—the greatest servant ever tamed for mankind to use—was just an idea when Durant grasped it. He, more than any other man, implemented this great multiplier of goods for mankind. He was, indeed, what Dickens called the "Founder of the Feast"—and we are still eating at his bountiful table, although we have forgotten his name.

CHAPTER 13

LEGACY
Resolved: To Reverse the Current of Decline in My Field of Mastery

*I know that a true legacy leaves the world
a better place than I found it.*
—Orrin Woodward

The reader has now reached the last resolution, the one that ties all the others together, capping off the symphony of success by leaving a legacy for others. People will not remember a person for what he has, but they will remember him for what he did in other's lives. With society falling into decline, there has never been a time when leaving a leadership legacy can have a greater impact.

The Decline of Civilizations

Why do civilizations rise, decline, and fall? Civilizations as diverse as the Sumerians, Egyptians, Persians, Greeks, Romans, and Chinese all declined, eventually falling under their own weight. Is decline the natural condition of life, with growth being a temporary leadership anomaly in the march of history? Arnold Toynbee, an English historian, authored *A Study of History*, a multi-volume classic on the history of world civilizations, in which he detailed the rise and decline of twenty-three civilizations. Despite detecting uniform patterns of disintegration in each civilization, Toynbee insisted that leaders have a moral responsibility to end the cycle of decline. Schmandt and Ward explained:

Toynbee reserved the terms "challenge and response" for major threats and actions that impacted the well-being of the entire population. "Challenge" threatened the very survival of the existing system. "Response" would range from inaction to major change in the living conditions of individuals

RESOLVED

as well as the group. It could embody new technology, social organization, and economic activities, or a combination of various factors. "Response" was never predictable, and its outcome would only be known over time. This was the risk humans took—resulting in success or failure.

Toynbee's historical analysis focused on the spiritual, economic, and political challenges in civilizations, believing that leadership "creative minorities" responded to the challenges in order to sustain a civilization's progress. Conversely, however, a civilization declines when its leaders do not respond creatively to the challenges they face. Indeed, the growth or decline of civilizations, according to Toynbee, is not based on historical determinism but on leadership capabilities present in society. Unlike the deterministic Oswald Spengler who believed in civilizations as unalterable machines following predictable cycles of decline, Toynbee viewed them as networks of social relationships susceptible to leadership decisions, both wise and unwise, which determine their fates. When leaders in a civilization stop responding creatively, the civilization sinks under nationalism, militarism, and the tyranny of a despotic minority. After decades of research, Toynbee proclaimed, "Civilizations die from suicide, not by murder."

Why does it seem that life is a never-ending struggle against powerful forces conspiring to cause decline in every field? Indeed, it requires little effort for things to deteriorate but rigorous discipline for them to consistently improve. Leaders must overcome the degenerative tendencies inherent in all human communities, for decline is the natural state of any civilization, while growth is a leadership anomaly.

Still, even the most successful leadership examples will not last forever. Regardless of how strong a leadership team, an organization, or a civilization appears to be, in due time, it will fall. The goal of a leader is to create a culture (current) of progress that can extend the life of his organization for as long as possible. Eventually, when leadership is lacking for a few successive generations, all progress reverses itself. Even so, this is not intended to depress potential leaders; instead, it's intended to help leaders identify the forces working against all human progress in order to overcome them. These forces of decline can be conquered and have sometimes been overcome for centuries at a time.

What are these forces of decline, and how can one identify and overcome them? Imagine a pool with five water jets streaming below the surface in the same direction. Each jet has its own regres-

LEGACY

sive current, but when all five are working together, they form a current or system of decline. For leaders, this is not new, as one rarely comes to the poolside without the current already flowing toward a decline. In fact, it's the challenge of all leadership teams to align together and run against the current of decline. Countering the current of decline is a tough job; that is why leadership is so needed in every generation because it's up to the leaders to create progress.

As a former systems engineer, I have studied many leadership teams, organizations, and cultures searching for underlying patterns in the companies. Through extensive historical research, I began to recognize similar failure modes or laws of decline at work within different communities. With appreciation of thinkers as varied as Frédéric Bastiat, Albert Jay Nock, Theodore Sturgeon, and Isaac Newton, I developed a systems model that explains why civilizations, nations, and communities fail: the five laws of decline (FLD). The laws explain the patterns of disintegration observed repeatedly throughout mankind's history. Each of the above authors provided clues, helping me piece together the pool analogy and the five laws of decline. The laws systematically flow against progress, similar to gravity working against flying objects or entropy working from order to disorder. Leadership in organizations and communities is the only known way to reverse the decline, but in order for it to last long, it must be applied generationally, maintaining progress against the declining forces when the leadership baton is passed from one generation to the next. Identifying the systematic forces working against progress helps leaders design systems to overcome the regressive effects of the five laws.

The Five Laws of Decline

1. Sturgeon's Law

The first law was discussed previously in the Leadership Chapter. Theodore Sturgeon, in developing his law, stated, "90% of science fiction writing is crud, but then again, so is 90% of anything." This law applies to nearly everything, but its meaning to leadership is that 10% of any typical group are leaders and 90%are followers. Only 10% of the people who say they are running in the pool are actually running; most are simply bobbing in the water. The 90% are just along for the ride, coasting with the current, or worse yet, running in the wrong direction. The goal is to mentor the 10% to have the courage to run against the declining current and help reverse it. Leaders cannot beat Sturgeon's law, but they

289

can create a culture that attracts the 10% who choose to lead, rewarding performance, not politics. Communities explode when the 10% of leaders fill the leadership spots responsible for creating the current of progress. Alexander the Great understood this thousands of years ago when he declared, "An army of sheep led by a lion is better than an army of lions led by a sheep." Communities decline when the 90% sheep are given leadership spots since they are incapable of reversing the current of decline.

2. Bastiat's Law

Frédéric Bastiat, a French economist, taught the fatal tendency existing in man's heart to satisfy his wants with the least possible effort. This is Bastiat's Law: Since men are naturally inclined to avoid pain, which labor is itself, it follows that they will resort to plunder whenever it is easier than work. Much of history is a record of man's plundering of his fellow man. Bastiat wrote:

Man can live and satisfy his wants only by ceaseless labor; by the ceaseless application of his faculties to natural resources. This process is the origin of property. But it is also true that a man may live and satisfy his wants by seizing and consuming the products of the labor of others. This process is the origin of plunder. Now since man is naturally inclined to avoid pain—and since labor is pain in itself—it follows that men will resort to plunder whenever plunder is easier than work. History shows this quite clearly. And under these conditions, neither religion nor morality can stop it. When, then, does plunder stop? It stops when it becomes more painful and more dangerous than labor. It is evident, then, that the proper purpose of law is to use the power of its collective force to stop this fatal tendency to plunder instead of to work. All the measures of the law should protect property and punish plunder.

Every organization must ensure that people carry their own weight rather than riding off the backs of others' labors. This law is why creating a scoreboard to accurately identify performers from non-performers is essential for any thriving organization.

Sadly, bureaucratic companies and governments violate this law repeatedly because it's hard to separate performers from political exploiters in an environment with no quantifiable scoreboard.

Why would someone work hard when he is assured a job either way? Bastiat's Law is the fatal flaw in communistic theories, since

290

LEGACY

the 90% will do as little as possible if given an opportunity, while the 10% will be driven to despair because they aren't rewarded for their productive efforts. The only proven way to combat Bastiat's law is to develop, score, and reward performance.

3. Gresham's Law

Thomas Gresham, an English financier, developed his law originally to be applied to monetary policy. He stated, "that when government compulsorily overvalues one money and undervalues another, the undervalued money will leave the country or disappear into hoards, while the overvalued money will flood into circulation." For example, throughout history, when inflated paper money flows into the marketplace, real gold and silver coins are removed from the marketplace. No one willingly pays for goods and services with real money when paper is made a legal currency by government fiat. Real money remains out of circulation until the paper fraud runs its course. The same principle applies to other areas: bad education drives out good education, bad leadership drives out good leadership, and poor character drives out good character, to name just a few. It occurs in companies when political managers are promoted ahead of productive leaders. When the poor behaviors are rewarded, the company is quickly filled with others exhibiting the same nonproductive activities. Leaders, on the other hand, are driven out of the company, not willing to play the political games of a declining company. In other words, if the 10% leaders are not rewarded for running in the pool to create a winning current, they will quickly hop out of the pool, leaving only the 90% bobbers. Gresham's law points out that the bobbers drive out the leaders when bobbers seize control of the company. Getting the right people on the bus and in the right seats is the only way to ensure the 90% do not infiltrate and eventually take over the company. What is rewarded will increase; conversely, what isn't rewarded will decrease.

4. Law of Diminishing Returns (LDR)

This law, one of the more famous in economic history, is defined as "a law affirming that to continue after a certain level of performance has been reached will result in a decline in effectiveness." In other words, when a certain point of production is reached, the returns begin to decrease and continue to decrease as further production proceeds, assuming all other variables are held constant. For example, a garden produces tomatoes, and by adding a pound of fertilizer, production of tomatoes goes up. Adding another pound of fertilizer increases tomato production even further, but at some point, adding even more no longer increases tomato production and even decreases production as too much fertilizer burns the plants. The LDR affects the quality of anything when attempts are made to produce benefits on a large scale. Mass music, education, and tourism, for example, have decreased in quality with the corresponding increase in quantity. Author Wendy McElroy wrote, "Consider the everyday experience of vacationing at a location that has not yet been 'discovered' by floods of tourists. When tourists begin to flock to the location, the return to everyone abruptly decreases. Both the many and the few no longer receive real benefit. In accommodating popular demands, the vacation site (and all other experiences in life) fall prey to the law of diminishing returns." The LDR, according to Albert Jay Nock, explains America's educational disaster: "Socrates chatting with a single protagonist meant one thing, and well did he know it. Socrates lecturing to a class of fifty would mean something woefully different, so he organized no classes and did no lecturing. Jerusalem was a university town, and in a university every day is field-day for the law of diminishing returns. Jesus stayed away from Jerusalem, and talked with fishermen here and there, who seem to have pretty well got what he was driving at; some better than others, apparently, but on the whole pretty well. And so we have it that unorganized Christianity was one thing, while organized Christianity has consistently been another." In other words, the more people attempted to receive the benefits of education, and the bigger the educational system became, the less education actually took place.

5. Law of Inertia

Newton's First Law states: "Every body remains in a state of rest or uniform motion (constant velocity), unless it is acted upon by an external unbalanced force." In layman's terms, an object at rest tends to stay at rest, and an object in motion tends to stay in motion unless acted upon by another force. Inertia works in the pool when the current carries people in the direction of the flowing water. When a leader must reverse directions in the pool, he has to work not only to move in the new direction but also to overcome the inertia of the current still moving in the former direction. Likewise, the longer the current is allowed to flow in the declining direction, the more difficult it is to reverse because one must overcome the built-up inertia. Creating a current in a stagnant pool is tough enough, but it is even tougher to reverse a current of decline, which is what most leadership assignments demand. Think of leaders who have been in a culture of decline, who, even when they decide to turn around the unhealthy culture, must struggle against the poor habits, processes, and attitudes in the existing culture. Big company turnarounds are so rare because the task is so huge. Stopping the inertia of the old culture, which fights change, burns through the leader's energy.

A good way to illustrate this is to take a group of people and have them run in one direction in a pool. When the current is flowing briskly, have them change directions. The group will be carried by the current even though they are working hard to run in the opposite direction. Leaders must overcome cultural inertia if they plan on turning around an organization.

When a person studies the Five Laws of Decline (FLD), he quickly sees the system of decline working against all progress, revealing why all organizations and civilizations eventually fall. Regretfully, in due time, Sturgeon's Law will eventually place a "90% non-leader" into the top position. This person will allow the wrong people on the bus, initiating the process of decline as power, plunder, and politics work their destructive forces within the declining organization or civilization. In fact, if a "10% leader" doesn't appear quickly and reverse the culture before it's too late, the current will pick up speed and ultimately destroy the organization or civilization that had once prospered.

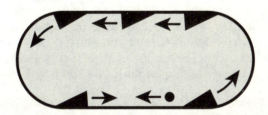

There is a solution, however. Leaders can overcome the FLD by implementing the 13 resolutions in their lives and organizations. The question is: How long can they maintain progress in the pool amid the jets flowing against them? Indeed, the progress will last only as long as leaders are forged in the discipline of study and will run with the current of progress, resisting the jets pushing for decline.

A Leadership Legacy

What, after all this, is a legacy? A person's legacy, one that will stand the test of time, is living the principles within the 13 resolutions and sharing them with the next generation. The objective is to provide an environment, a culture, for others to "school" themselves and build the leaders of tomorrow. Leaders who build the 13 resolutions into their lives are able to model the standard of excellence from which newer leaders can learn. This helps every leader gain strength and confidence for his life's mountain climb. Successful people, the legacy builders, refuse to place people on mountaintops; instead, they build bridges at every chasm on the mountain trail, helping the next generation advance. Legacy builders, through their tireless efforts to overcome the FLD, provide a positive current and teach how to maintain it by modeling the 13 resolutions to others. In reality, the biggest gift a generation can give to the next generation is a leadership legacy. A leader's example and teachable moments used in mentoring the next generation on how to maintain, if not increase, the positive growth current are more valuable than any of the temporary perks of money, fame, or power. A positive growth current is more valuable than money, fame, or power because all of these will dissipate over time in the streaming jets of the FLD. For instance, how much of Napoleon's wealth, fame, or power has truly endured? Money, fame, and power, in reality, hinder the process of personal growth by fooling people into believing they have already arrived at the destination when the truth is, they haven't even begun the journey. This explains, again, why success is the journey, not the destination. When leaders do not leave a legacy, the next generations of leaders suffer the most, struggling to maintain the positive current as the FLD gradually slows the positive current.

The leaders and thinkers of the past provided a legacy by providing liberty, allowing people the opportunity to develop themselves without coercion. This legacy must be passed forward by recreating the positive current before it's too late. If a person has learned financial principles and has made a difference in his life, then he should document how and share this with as many others as possible. Likewise, if a person has learned friendship principles that have helped him build long-term relationships, then he should capture and

> **Any area where one learns and applies truth, producing fruit in his life, is a platform for leaving a legacy to others.**

LEGACY

share them, imparting his legacy to others. Any area in which one learns and applies truth, producing fruit in his life, is a plat-form for a legacy to others. Further, since a legacy lasts longer than the person, the positive pool current provides time for tomorrow's leaders to learn, gaining needed experience before filling the gap left by the previous leaders. The goal of a legacy is to maintain or increase the forward progress of the battle entropy of the FLD. Legacies are lifetime gifts, offered with no strings attached, with the objective of making a difference in others' lives. A legacy, then, is like the passing of the baton, giving the resolutions to the next generation of leaders.

Three Types of Liberty

The Founding Fathers and Mothers were men and women of resolve, who lived the principles discussed in this book, making mistakes but learning from them in the process. Because they lived their resolutions, they freed themselves from the day-to-day grind of working in order to eat. They focused instead on their purpose, working to fulfill it and leaving in their wake a legacy of liberty for the future generations. Washington, Franklin, and Edwards responded to the challenges of their time by helping reverse the current of decline in their day. Each of them contributed greatly to the liberties that America and the West as a whole have enjoyed for two centuries.

However, the current has reversed again. Leadership, and thus liberty, is declining in the West. Where are today's Washington's, Franklin's, and Edwards's to answer the call of leadership? The three freedoms needed for society to be restored are:

1. Spiritual liberty
2. Political liberty
3. Economic liberty

It's not a coincidence that political and economic freedoms resulted from improved spiritual freedoms since they stand or fall together. Spiritual liberty was fought for and won in the West several hundred years ago, beginning with the Reformation. Spiritual autonomy means that no one can force a person to believe against his conscience. Each person must stand or fall based on his own beliefs and actions before the Almighty God. Free dialogue and discussion are encouraged, while tyranny and force are not part of freedom. Everyone has the responsibility to learn what spiritual

295

RESOLVED

freedom means in his life. *In other words, know why you believe what you believe.*

Since man is free before God, a corollary that follows is that man is free before his fellow man, bound only by the rule of law. The rule of law describes a society in which law is king; everyone, whether rich or poor, follows the laws of the land, which follow the laws of God and human nature. Where law rules, oppression and dictatorship cannot satisfy their every whim; but when tyrants rule, the rule of law is quickly destroyed. The United States Constitution was an attempt to bind the government to follow the rule of law, hindering governmental oppression and arbitrary violence against the citizens.

Lastly, liberty means economic freedom—the freedom to buy and sell without needless regulations and interventions from governments. The freest people in the world lived in Western Christendom from the end of the eighteenth century until the beginning of the twentieth century. For nearly 150 years, Western man was allowed the spiritual, political, and economic freedom to flourish. It's not surprising that the greatest increase in prosperity occurred during this era. However, liberty is waning, as leaders have stopped creating positive cultural currents and the ever-present Five Laws of Decline are reversing them. For liberty to reign again, a group of men and women must relearn the power of resolutions, applying them into their lives and reversing the currents of decline, not only for their own liberty, but also for the enhancement of the next generation's freedoms.

Autonomy is the liberty to choose responsible actions, while license is absolute freedom that leads to chaos because license isn't tempered with responsibility. Liberty, then, is not license. The rules of the road serve as an everyday-life example of the difference between liberty and license. Although people have the liberty to go anywhere they choose, they do not have the license to drive on any side of the road or to switch back and forth freely on a whim. The liberty-loving driver is responsible for following the rules of the road, regardless of whether a police officer is watching because he knows that his being responsible provides freedom for all to enjoy the roads. For without this responsibility, by demanding license rather than liberty, chaos will ensue. Cars would crash into one another since not everyone is following the rules of the road. The irony for those who demand freedom for license is that when it's granted, all people lose their liberty to drive the road, becoming too fearful of reckless drivers demanding license. In the same way, society must be designed under the rule of law, self-evident rules

296

LEGACY

of society that have worked for many millennia. Ordered freedom lifts a society upward, while disordered license destroys everyone's freedom, creating a situation in which force must be used to end chaos. Viktor Frankl described it thus: "Freedom is only part of the story and half the truth...That is why I recommend that the Statue of Liberty on the East Coast be supplanted by a Statue of Responsibility on the West Coast." For a society to be free, then, it must also be responsible for creating leaders—thus the need for the 13 resolutions.

By reviewing the pool analogy again, a person can see that the difference between leaders and followers in the pool is the responsibility accepted for the direction of the current. Followers, naturally, move with the current, regardless of whether the current is flowing in the proper direction for leadership growth. Leaders are different; they are Rascals (as Chris Brady says) and know that following a current of decline, no matter how easy, is just wrong. Leaders follow an inner compass, determining which direction the current should be flowing and making a stand against the current and the crowd if necessary (and, typically, it is necessary). Standing against the current is a brave act; moving against the current is the beginning

> **Standing against the current is a brave act; moving against the current is the beginning of leadership, and forming a team of people willing to move against the current is what top leaders do.**

of leadership, and forming a team of people willing to move against the current is what top leaders do. Only a few leadership teams run against the current and encourage others to do the same, literally reversing the current of decline and creating a current of progress. This is the pinnacle of leadership, which is reached by only a select few. As the old saying goes, "Any dead fish can float downstream, but it takes a live one to swim against the current." It takes leadership at the uppermost echelons to reverse the current of decline. Learning to reverse the current and sharing the leadership principles needed to do so with potential future leaders is the only way to continue to progress against the currents of generational decline. This is a true legacy worth leaving to posterity.

As we near the end of this book, I wish to share a few of my personal observations. First, leadership is not for the weak of heart because every leader must make decisions that will not endear himself to all parties. But decide he must if he plans on leading. Second, being a leader in today's selfish and cynical environment causes anyone who lives the 13 resolutions and hopes for a better tomorrow to be portrayed as out-of-touch at best and manipulative at worst. This is the tragic irony as the West denies the principles of character, honor, and purpose, yet it is dying for lack of them. C. S. Lewis concluded, "Such is the tragicomedy of our situation—we continue to clamor for those very qualities we are rendering impossible. You can hardly open a periodical without coming across the statement that what our civilization needs is more 'drive', or dynamism, or self-sacrifice, or 'creativity'. In a sort of ghastly simplicity we remove the organ and demand the function. We make men without chests and expect of them virtue and enterprise. We laugh at honor and are shocked to find traitors in our midst. We castrate and bid the geldings be fruitful." Leaders must arise to reverse the current in the pool and turn Lewis's tragicomedy into a drama between the forces producing progress and the forces producing decline within a society.

In his 1920 poem "The Second Coming," W. B. Yeats conveyed the hopelessness pervading the twentieth century, a hopelessness even more prevalent today:

> *Things fall apart; the centre cannot hold;*
> *Mere anarchy is loosed upon the world,*
> *The blood-dimmed tide is loosed, and everywhere*
> *The ceremony of innocence is drowned;*
> *The best lack all conviction, while the worst*
> *Are full of passionate intensity.*

Yeats's words describe the effects of the Five Laws of Decline unleashed upon a faithless, leaderless world. If, as Yeats wrote, "the best lack all convictions," then the worst are the only ones remaining in the pool willing to run. But the worst are running with the current of decline, making the West's defeat seemingly inevitable. Without "challenge and response" leadership, all civilizations will fall into decline. In fact, Edward Gibbon, in his classic *The Decline and Fall of the Roman Empire*, defined five attributes that marked the Roman Empire at the time of its fall over 1,500 years ago:

1. A mounting love of show and luxury (affluence)
2. A widening gap between the very rich and the very poor
3. An obsession with sex
4. Freakishness in the arts, masquerading as originality
5. An increased desire to live off the state

LEGACY

Even a perfunctory examination of the modern West would reveal it is suffering from a cultural decline similar to that of the Roman Empire. Indeed, a solid argument could be made that the modern West has surpassed Rome in many of its negative influences. The parallels are not coincidental since the degenerative effects of the Five Laws of Decline span across time and space, destroying the economic, political, and moral or spiritual foundations of any leaderless society. Confirming this assessment, Harvard historian Niall Ferguson, in his book *Civilization: The West and the Rest*, wrote, "For it is only by identifying the causes of Western ascendancy that we can hope to estimate with any degree of accuracy the imminence of our fall. My conclusion is that we are already living through the twilight of Western predominance...because we ourselves have lost faith in our own civilization." Sadly, when the West progressively rejected faith in God, it was only a matter of time before it lost its faith in everything.

Even with the dismal currents created from modern man's poisonous brew of beliefs, the current of decline can still be reversed. For the last eighteen years, I have communicated to millions of people across North America through a leadership and personal development training community now called LIFE. I have witnessed numerous downtrodden and depressed people turn around through the power of faith, hope, love, and leadership. In truth, there simply are no hopeless situations, only hopeless people in situations. As a Christian leader, I refuse to lose hope for the future, I refuse to succumb to the demonic despair around me, and lastly, I refuse to surrender my role in sharing the good news with others. If a leader's role is to "school his soul" and forge the 13 resolutions into his being, leaving a legacy and reversing the currents for the next generation, then what the West needs is a leadership revolution, creating thousands of leaders who will reverse the currents of decline. To borrow Toynbee's words, the challenge has been identified and the response has been proposed, but what the West lacks is morally courageous leaders who will stand in the gap. Indeed, the Western civilization hasn't been murdered; rather, having lost faith in her guiding principles, she is committing suicide. With the signs of decay, decline, and demoralization increasing daily, society has been sounding an ignored alarm for nearly a century. I have resolved to respond to the distress call, to reverse the current of decline. Will the reader help me?

Colonial New England Fiat Money

Murray Rothbard, the late dean of the Austrian School of economics, wrote a book titled *A History of Money and Banking in the United States*, an insightful read on government and money. In the book, there are many examples of monetary schemes that have failed over the years. Each of Rothbard's monetary examples displays a similar lack of systematic understanding on the part of society's political leaders. Author Henry Hazlitt explained:

> The art of economics consists in looking not merely at the immediate but at the longer effects of any act or policy; it consists in tracing the consequences of that policy not merely for one group but for all groups. Nine-tenths of the economic fallacies that are working such dreadful harm in the world today are the result of ignoring this lesson. These fallacies all stem from one of two central fallacies, or both: that of looking only at the immediate consequences of an act or proposal, and that of looking at the consequences only for a particular group to the neglect of other groups.

When governments attempt to solve society's problems by only looking at the short-term effects, instead of the long-term effects, the proposed fix becomes a tax imposed by those who are above on those who are below through the politicians' ignorance of economic laws. By studying systems thinking and the five laws of decline, a person can identify these improper measures, aiming to teach governmental leaders the corrosive effects of wrong policies on society.

It's not well-known, but apart from the medieval Chinese, Colonial Massachusetts was the first government to issue fiat paper money. Fiat money is money that is not backed by gold or any other valuable item. The paper magically transforms itself into something that has value simply because a government says so, by fiat. Indeed, the Colonial Americans were the reigning experts on fraudulent paper money issues backed by nothing more than the misplaced trust the colonists had in their state governments.

LEGACY

This dismal monetary history began with a failed plundering expedition in the French colony of Quebec. The Massachusetts government had grown accustomed to victorious raids in Quebec and typically paid the colonial recruits out of the proceeds lifted from the defeated French. But in 1690, the New England colonials were defeated, causing a small problem for Massachusetts and a huge problem for the West because of the poor precedent set by the decisions made that day.

The soldiers arrived back in Boston, ill-tempered and demanding their salaries regardless of the failed outcome of the raid. Hosting discontented soldiers, who had weapons and the will to use them, was not an enjoyable experience for the Boston citizens. After their attempt to raise the funds to pay the soldiers through local merchants were rejected, the government leaders struck upon an idea that still echoes today. The Massachusetts State government concluded that printing £7,000 of paper notes to pay the soldiers was safer than having unpaid solders within the city. Concerned that the public would not accept the paper, the government made several pledges in an attempt to alleviate the public's suspicion. It pledged, first, that it would redeem the paper notes with gold or silver from tax revenues collected over the next couple of years and, second, that no more notes would be issued. Not surprisingly, both pledges were disregarded as fast as government politicians could say, "Free money." It took less than four months for more notes to be issued, ignoring the pledge altogether because of the government's greed for free funds. By February of 1691, another £40,000 of unbacked paper notes was issued to make up for a shortage of government funds, and the politicians proclaimed boldly, and falsely, that this would be the last issue of notes.

The five laws of decline went unrestrained and started crushing progress, causing the negative flow to hinder growth in the colonies. The first law of decline that came into effect was Sturgeon's law. It was at work as most of the colonial politicians had no idea what a poor precedent they were setting in their attempt to satisfy the unhappy soldiers. Any time a vote is taken, the 90 percent looking for an easy way out regardless of the long-term consequences will vote for short-term ease over the long-term principles every time. In this case, they voted to print paper money backed by nothing to

301

RESOLVED

pay the soldiers and hoped the issue would go away. Additionally, Sturgeon's law led to Bastiat's law since people would do the least amount of work and effort to produce the results they desired. When politicians learned that they could access money simply by printing it without the pain of asking for more tax dollars or the pain of cutting back programs, a nirvana on earth was proclaimed by local politicians. Bastiat's law created the illusion that people could have their cake and eat it, too. Not surprisingly, the politicians, feeling the Midas touch, dipped into the well again and again, multiplying the fiat money nearly seven times in just one year.

Massachusetts had stumbled across the SFN (something for nothing) formula, and notwithstanding the number of their pledges to stop issuing notes, the local politicians were like kids running loose in a candy store. Government-induced fiat paper inflation was born and bred upon the shores of America. The increasing supply of paper money, along with the citizens' increasing lack of confidence in the local politicians' inflationary intentions, led to a 40 percent depreciation of the paper money when compared with gold and silver specie. Like all governments caught with their hands in the cookie jar, Massachusetts used force to make the "greedy," "traitorous" merchants take paper on par with specie. This simply caused Gresham's law to kick in, driving real money underground while everyone bought and sold using paper (just paper, like *Monopoly* money) in the New England economy. The citizens learned quickly: Why should anyone use real specie when paper money was worth 40 percent less and other citizens were forced, by law, to take it on par with gold and silver coins (specie)? The corresponding shortage of coins drove more of the immoral behavior, which caused the inflation in the first place. Over £240,000 of paper money had been issued by 1711, and by that same time, specie had all but disappeared. The shortage of gold and silver didn't cause the need for paper money; instead, the paper money enacted Gresham's law, which caused the predictable shortage of coinage from the bad money driving out the good.

The British Crown finally intervened to halt the mad rush into insolvency caused by the SFN paper-induced fever suffered by the local New England governmental leaders. However, before the British closed the money presses, the

LEGACY

money printed between 1744 and 1748 had already ballooned to a shocking amount! Paper money expanded from £300,000 to £2.5 million! The depreciation of Massachusetts' money was to such an extent that silver had risen to over sixty shillings an ounce, over ten times the price that it sold for before the paper mania. Gresham's law drove out not only the real money in silver and gold but also the honest politicians, who would have nothing to do with the immoral printing of fiat money. Bad politicians with dishonorable motives and ignorant politicians with a hunger for power drove out the good politicians with honorable motives.

Next, the law of diminishing returns kicked in, as the more fiat money the government produced, the less effect it seemed to have because citizens realized the fraud, forcing the paper money to be heavily discounted compared to gold and silver. Fiat money, like a drug continually used by an addict, requires larger and larger "doses" in order for its effect to be felt mainly because of the law of diminishing returns.

The final law, the law of inertia, made it nearly impossible to stop the fraud once it had begun in Massachusetts. Politicians knew they could resort to fiat money when emergencies arose and thought fiat money was more palatable politically than legitimate financial measures (taxation or reduced spending) in stemming the monetary decline. The five-laws-of-decline current flowed strongly in Colonial America, interrupted only by the intervention of the British Empire.

In the Revolutionary War, when the colonials squared off against the British, the colonials no longer had the restraining influence of the British, so the Continental Congress produced millions of dollars of fiat money, called Continentals. The five laws bankrupted the Continental Congress and Colonial America. Remember the famous saying "Not worth a Continental?" That phrase was the result of the Continental Congress's inflationary policies. Even though the colonials won the war, they could not service their debt, leading to the Constitutional Convention, which was in part an attempt to discover a way out of the financial morass.

One of the first items discussed and approved in the new United States Constitution was the barring of states and the federal government from ever printing fiat paper money again. (It didn't last, but that's another five-laws-of-decline

303

RESOLVED

story.) The vote for no paper money was unanimous. And it was said by many states that had this door not been shut, they would have left the Constitutional Convention, for so great were the painful lessons of fiat money and the colonials' resulting fear.

The founders of America stood against the five laws of decline. They built a culture that taught the value of character, work ethic, and freedom from government intervention to pursue happiness and chase one's dreams. The Constitution was designed to ensure that men and women could achieve based on their willingness to work and dream. The founding leaders built a community of like-minded people from all nations who were willing to stand against the currents of decline. The founders' legacy is measured through the generations that have lived free upon these shores.

In her poem "The New Colossus," which is displayed in the museum at the base of the Statue of Liberty, Emma Lazarus wrote:

> *Not like the brazen giant of Greek fame,*
> *With conquering limbs astride from land to land;*
> *Here at our sea-washed, sunset gates shall stand*
> *A mighty woman with a torch, whose flame*
> *Is the imprisoned lightning, and her name*
> *Mother of Exiles. From her beacon-hand*
> *Glows world-wide welcome; her mild eyes command*
> *The air-bridged harbor that twin cities frame,*
> *"Keep, ancient lands, your storied pomp!" cries she*
> *With silent lips. "Give me your tired, your poor,*
> *Your huddled masses yearning to breathe free,*
> *The wretched refuse of your teeming shore,*
> *Send these, the homeless, tempest-tossed to me,*
> *I lift my lamp beside the golden door!"*

The "tired...huddled masses" were people sick of running against the currents of decline, longing for an opportunity to reach for their dreams in a free environment. This is what the founders provided to men and women of all nationalities. Although their ideals were not lived out perfectly, the millions of people who immigrated to America hoping to enjoy

LEGACY

the freedom available in the land of opportunity, are a testament to the founders' work.

America's Founding Fathers reversed the current of decline that was forming through tyranny, mercantilism, and fiat money and provided a progressive current for the next generation. They ensured free trade across state borders, no personal income taxes, separation of powers, an independent judicial system, and the Bill of Rights to spiritual and economic freedoms needed to pursue one's dreams.

However, in America and the West today, many of these principles are being disregarded. Total taxation in most Western countries is now greater than the taxation load that was placed on the serfs in the Middle Ages. The current isn't progressing forward anymore; rather, it's declining faster every year. Sadly, many citizens, instead of demanding freedom, are seeking government protection, security, and even exploitation of others, selling their birthrights for a pot of porridge. What the West desperately needs is a group of leaders—similar to Washington, Franklin, and Edwards—who refuse to surrender their freedoms and are willing to stand in the pool against the current of decline. Once their feet are firmly planted, they must dare to run against the current until it reverses once again, bringing the Western nations back from the precipice of imminent destruction. This feat was accomplished in the past, and it must be attempted again. Reversing any current of decline is tough work against immeasurable odds that demands the disciplined application of the 13 resolutions, but when the fate of the West is at stake, courageous leaders cannot afford to play it safe. Action must be taken.

APPENDIX A

George Washington's Rules of Civility and Decent Behavior in Company and Conversation

1. Every action done in company ought to be with some sign of respect, to those that are present.
2. When in company, put not your hands to any part of the body not usually discovered.
3. Show nothing to your friend that may affright him.
4. In the presence of others, sing not to yourself with a humming noise, nor drum with your fingers or feet.
5. If you cough, sneeze, sigh, or yawn, do it not loud but privately; and speak not in your yawning, but put your handkerchief or hand before your face and turn aside.
6. Sleep not when others speak; sit not when others stand; speak not when you should hold your peace; walk not on when others stop.
7. Put not off your clothes in the presence of others, nor go out your chamber half dressed.
8. At play and at fire its good manners to give place to the last comer, and affect not to speak louder than ordinary.
9. Spit not in the fire, nor stoop low before it neither put your hands into the flames to warm them, nor set your feet upon the fire especially if there be meat before it.
10. When you sit down, keep your feet firm and even, without putting one on the other or crossing them.
11. Shift not yourself in the sight of others nor gnaw your nails.
12. Shake not the head, feet, or legs roll not the eyes lift not one eyebrow higher than the other wry not the mouth, and bedew no man's face with your spittle by approaching too near him when you speak.
13. Kill no vermin as fleas, lice, ticks &c in the sight of others; if you see any filth or thick spittle, put your foot dexterously upon it; if it be upon the clothes of your companions, put

RESOLVED

it off privately, and if it be upon your own clothes return thanks to him who puts it off.

14. Turn not your back to others especially in speaking; jog not the table or desk on which another reads or writes; lean not upon any one.

15. Keep your nails clean and short, also your hands and teeth clean yet without showing any great concern for them.

16. Do not puff up the cheeks, loll not out the tongue rub the hands, or beard, thrust out the lips, or bite them or keep the lips too open or too close.

17. Be no flatterer, neither play with any that delights not to be play'd withal.

18. Read no letters, books, or papers in company but when there is a necessity for the doing of it you must ask leave: come not near the books or writings of another so as to read them unless desired or give your opinion of them unasked also look not nigh when another is writing a letter.

19. Let your countenance be pleasant but in serious matters somewhat grave.

20. The gestures of the body must be suited to the discourse you are upon.

21. Reproach none for the infirmities of nature, nor delight to put them that have in mind thereof.

22. Show not yourself glad at the misfortune of another though he were your enemy.

23. When you see a crime punished, you may be inwardly pleased; but always show pity to the suffering offender.

24. Do not laugh too loud or too much at any public spectacle.

25. Superfluous complements and all affectation of ceremony are to be avoided, yet where due they are not to be neglected.

26. In pulling off your hat to persons of distinction, as noblemen, justices, churchmen &c make a reverence, bowing more or less according to the custom of the better bred, and quality of the person. Amongst your equals expect not always that they should begin with you first, but topull off the hat when there is no need is affectation, in the manner of saluting and resaluting in words keep to the most usual custom.

27. Tis ill manners to bid one more eminent than yourself be covered as well as not to do it to whom it's due; likewise he that makes too much haste to put on his hat does not well, yet he ought to put it on at the first, or at most the

APPENDIX A

second time of being asked; now what is herein spoken, of qualification in behavior in saluting, ought also to be observed in taking of place, and sitting down for ceremonies without bounds is troublesome.

28. If any one come to speak to you while you are sitting, stand up though he be your inferior, and when you present seats, let it be to every one according to his degree.

29. When you meet with one of greater quality than yourself, stop, and retire especially if it be at a door or any straight place to give way for him to pass.

30. In walking the highest place in most countries seems to be on the right hand; therefore, place yourself on the left of him whom you desire to honor: but if three walk together, the middest place is the most honorable; the wall is usually given to the most worthy if two walk together.

31. If any one far surpasses others, either in age, estate, or merit yet would give place to a meaner than himself in his own lodging or elsewhere, the one ought not to except it; so he on the other part should not use much earnestness nor offer it above once or twice.

32. To one that is your equal, or not much inferior, you are to give the chief place in your lodging, and he to who 'is offered ought at the first to refuse it but at the second to accept though not without acknowledging his own unworthiness.

33. They that are in dignity or in office have in all places precedency, but whilst they are young, they ought to respect those that are their equals in birth or other qualities, though they have no public charge.

34. It is good manners to prefer them to whom we speak before ourselves, especially if they be above us with whom in no sort we ought to begin.

35. Let your discourse with men of business be short and comprehensive.

36. Artificers & persons of low degree ought not to use many ceremonies to lords, or others of high degree but respect and highly honor them, and those of high degree ought to treat them with affability & courtesy, without arrogance.

37. In speaking to men of quality, do not lean nor look them full in the face, nor approach too near them; at least keep a full pace from them.

38. In visiting the sick, do not presently play the physician if you be not knowing therein.

309

RESOLVED

39. In writing or speaking, give to every person his due title according to his degree & the custom of the place.

40. Strive not with your superiors in argument, but always submit your judgment to others with modesty.

41. Undertake not to teach your equal in the art himself professes; it savours of arrogance.

42. Let thy ceremonies in courtesy be proper to the dignity of his place with whom thou converses for it is absurd to act the same with a clown and a prince.

43. Do not express joy before one sick or in pain for that contrary passion will aggravate his misery.

44. When a man does all he can though it succeeds not well, blame not him that did it.

45. Being to advise or reprehend any one, consider whether it ought to be in public or in private; presently, or at some other time in what terms to do it & in reproving show no sign of choler but do it with all sweetness and mildness.

46. Take all admonitions thankfully in what time or place soever given but afterwards not being culpable take a time & place convenient to let him know it that gave them.

47. Mock not nor jest at any thing of importance; break [n]o jest that are sharp biting, and if you deliver anything witty and pleasant, abstain from laughing thereat yourself.

48. Wherein you reprove another, be unblameable yourself; for example is more prevalent than precepts.

49. Use no reproachful language against any one, neither curse nor revile.

50. Be not hasty to believe flying reports to the disparagement of any.

51. Wear not your clothes, foul, ripped or dusty but see they be brushed once every day at least and take heed that you approach not to any uncleanness.

52. In your apparel, be modest and endeavor to accommodate nature, rather than to procure admiration; keep to the fashion of your equals such as are civil and orderly with respect to times and places.

53. Run not in the streets, neither go too slowly nor with mouth open; go not shaking your arms; kick not the earth with your feet, go not upon the toes, nor in a dancing fashion.

54. Play not the peacock, looking every where about you, to see if you be well decked, if your shoes fit well, if your stockings sit neatly, and clothes handsomely.

55. Eat not in the streets, nor in the house, out of season.

APPENDIX A

56. Associate yourself with men of good quality if you esteem your own reputation; for 'is better to be alone than in bad company.

57. In walking up and down in a house, only with one in company if he be greater than yourself, at the first give him the right hand and stop not till he does and be not the first that turns, and when you do turn let it be with your face towards him; if he be a man of great quality, walk not with him cheek by jowl but somewhat behind him, but yet in such a manner that he may easily speak to you.

58. Let your conversation be without malice or envy, for 'is a sign of a tractable and commendable nature: And in all causes of passion, admit reason to govern.

59. Never express anything unbecoming, nor act against the rules moral before your inferiors.

60. Be not immodest in urging your friends to discover a secret.

61. Utter not base and frivolous things amongst grave and learned men, nor very difficult questions or subjects among the ignorant, or things hard to be believed; stuff not your discourse with sentences amongst your betters nor equals.

62. Speak not of doleful things in a time of mirth or at the table; speak not of melancholy things as death and wounds, and if others mention them, change if you can the discourse; tell not your dreams, but to your intimate friend.

63. A man ought not to value himself of his achievements, or rare qualities of wit; much less of his riches, virtue, or kindred.

64. Break not a jest where none take pleasure in mirth; laugh not aloud, nor at all without occasion, deride no man's misfortune, though there seem to be some cause.

65. Speak not injurious words neither in jest nor earnest; scoff at none although they give occasion.

66. Be not froward but friendly and courteous; the first to salute, hear, and answer & be not pensive when it's a time to converse.

67. Detract not from others, neither be excessive in commanding.

68. Go not thither, where you know not, whether you shall be welcome or not. Give not advice without being asked & when desired do it briefly.

311

RESOLVED

69. If two contend together, take not the part of either unconstrained; and be not obstinate in your own opinion; in things indifferent be of the major side.

70. Reprehend not the imperfections of others for that belongs to parents, masters, and superiors.

71. Gaze not on the marks or blemishes of others and ask not how they came. What you may speak in secret to your friend deliver not before others.

72. Speak not in an unknown tongue in company but in your own language and that as those of quality do and not as the vulgar; sublime matters treat seriously.

73. Think before you speak; pronounce not imperfectly nor bring out your words too hastily, but orderly & distinctly.

74. When another speaks, be attentive your self and disturb not the audience; if any hesitate in his words, help him not nor prompt him without desired; interrupt him not, nor answer him till his speech be ended.

75. In the midst of discourse, ask not of what one treateth but if you perceive any stop because of your coming you may well entreat him gently to proceed: If a person of quality comes in while you're conversing, it's handsome to repeat what was said before.

76. While you are talking, point not with your finger at him of whom you discourse nor approach too near him to whom you talk, especially to his face.

77. Treat with men at fit times about business & whisper not in the company of others.

78. Make no comparisons and if any of the company be commended for any brave act of virtue, commend not another for the same.

79. Be not apt to relate news if you know not the truth thereof. In discoursing of things you have heard, name not your author always; a secret discover not.

80. Be not tedious in discourse or in reading unless you find the company pleased therewith.

81. Be not curious to know the affairs of others neither approach those that speak in private.

82. Undertake not what you cannot perform but be careful to keep your promise.

83. When you deliver a matter do it without passion & with discretion, however mean the person be, you do it too.

84. When your superiors talk to any body, hearken not, neither speak nor laugh.

APPENDIX A

85. In company of these of higher quality than yourself, speak not till you are asked a question; then stand upright, put off your hat, & answer in few words.

86. In disputes, be not so desirous to overcome as not to give liberty to each one to deliver his opinion and submit to the judgment of the major part, especially if they are judges of the dispute.

87. Let thy carriage be such as becomes a man grave, settled, and attentive to that which is spoken. Contradict not at every turn what others say.

88. Be not tedious in discourse, make not many digressions, nor repeat often the same manner of discourse.

89. Speak not evil of the absent for it is unjust.

90. Being set at meat, scratch not neither spit, cough, or blow your nose except there's a necessity for it.

91. Make no show of taking great delight in your victuals; feed not with greediness; cut your bread with a knife, lean not on the table, neither find fault with what you eat.

92. Take no salt or cut bread with your knife greasy.

93. Entertaining any one at the table, it is decent to present him with meat; undertake not to help others undesired by the master.

94. If you soak bread in the sauce, let it be no more than what you put in your mouth at a time and blow not your broth at table but stay till cools of itself.

95. Put not your meat to your mouth with your knife in your hand neither spit forth the stones of any fruit pie upon a dish nor cast anything under the table.

96. It's unbecoming to stoop much to one's meat. Keep your fingers clean & when foul, wipe them on a corner of your table napkin.

97. Put not another bit into your mouth till the former be swallowed. Let not your morsels be too big for the jowls.

98. Drink not nor talk with your mouth full; neither gaze about you while you are drinking.

99. Drink not too leisurely nor yet too hastily. Before and after drinking, wipe your lips; breath not then or ever with too great a noise, for it's uncivil.

100. Cleanse not your teeth with the table cloth napkin, fork, or knife; but if others do it, let it be done without a peep to them.

101. Rinse not your mouth in the presence of others.

RESOLVED

102. It is out of use to call upon the company often to eat; nor need you drink to others every time you drink.

103. In the company of your betters, be not longer in eating than they are; lay not your arm but only your hand upon the table.

104. It belongs to the chiefest in company to unfold his napkin and fall to meat first, but he ought then to begin in time & to dispatch with dexterity that the slowest may have time allowed him.

105. Be not angry at the table whatever happens & if you have reason to be so, show it not; put on a cheerful countenance especially if there be strangers, for good humor makes one dish of meat a feast.

106. Set not yourself at the upper of the table; but if it be your due or that the master of the house will have it so, contend not, least you should trouble the company.

107. If others talk at the table, be attentive but talk not with meat in your mouth.

108. When you speak of God or his attributes, let it be seriously & with reverence. Honor & obey our natural parents although they be poor.

109. Let your recreations be manful, not sinful.

110. Labor to keep alive in your breast that little spark of celestial fire called conscience.

APPENDIX B

George Washington's
Partial List of Maxims

1. A slender acquaintance with the world must convince every man that actions, not words, are the true criterion of the attachment of friends.
2. Associate with men of good quality if you esteem your own reputation, for it is better to be alone than in bad company.
3. Be courteous to all, but intimate with few, and let those few be well tried before you give them your confidence.
4. Discipline is the soul of an army. It makes small numbers formidable, procures success to the weak and esteem to all.
5. Experience teaches us that it is much easier to prevent an enemy from posting themselves than it is to dislodge them after they have got possession.
6. Few men have virtue to withstand the highest bidder.
7. True friendship is a plant of slow growth and must undergo and withstand the shocks of adversity before it is entitled to the appellation.
8. Happiness and moral duty are inseparably connected.
9. I hope I shall possess firmness and virtue enough to maintain what I consider the most enviable of all titles, the character of an honest man.
10. It is better to be alone than in bad company.
11. It is better to offer no excuse than a bad one.
12. It is impossible to rightly govern a nation without God and the Bible.
13. It will be found an unjust and unwise jealousy to deprive a man of his natural liberty upon the supposition he may abuse it.
14. Labor to keep alive in your breast that little spark of celestial fire called conscience.
15. Lenience will operate with greater force, in some instances, than rigor. It is therefore my first wish to have all of my conduct distinguished by it.

RESOLVED

16. Let us raise a standard to which the wise and honest can repair; the rest is in the hands of God.

17. Let us with caution indulge the supposition that morality can be maintained without religion. Reason and experience both forbid us to expect that national morality can prevail in exclusion of religious principle.

18. Let your heart feel for the afflictions and distress of everyone, and let your hand give in proportion to your purse.

19. My observation is that whenever one person is found adequate to the discharge of a duty...it is worse executed by two persons, and scarcely done at all if three or more are employed therein.

20. Liberty, when it begins to take root, is a plant of rapid growth.

21. The foolish and wicked practice of profane cursing and swearing is a vice so mean and low that every person of sense and character detests and despises it.

22. To be prepared for war is one of the most effective means of preserving peace.

23. Truth will ultimately prevail where there is pain to bring it to light.

24. We should not look back unless it is to derive useful lessons from past errors, and for the purpose of profiting by dearly bought experience.

25. Worry is the interest paid by those who borrow trouble.

26. Nothing is a greater stranger to my breast, or a sin that my soul more abhors, than that black and detestable one, ingratitude.

27. I shall not be deprived...of a comfort in the worst event, if I retain a consciousness of having acted to the best of my judgment.

28. There is a Destiny which has the control of our actions, not to be resisted by the strongest efforts of Human Nature.

29. It is with pleasure I receive reproof, when reproof is due, because no person can be readier to accuse me than I am to acknowledge an error, when I am guilty of one, nor more desirous of atoning for a crime, when I am sensible of having committed it.

30. I shall make it the most agreeable part of my duty to study merit and reward the brave and deserving.

31. I hold the maxim no less applicable to public than to private affairs that honesty is the best policy.

APPENDIX B

32. To contract new debts is not the way to pay old ones.
33. Three things prompt men to a regular discharge of their duty in time of action: natural bravery, hope of reward, and fear of punishment.
34. Ninety-nine percent of the failures come from people who have the habit of making excuses.
35. The administration of justice is the firmest pillar of government.

APPENDIX C

Ben Franklin's Thirteen Virtues

1. Temperance. Eat not to dullness; drink not to elevation.
2. Silence. Speak not but what may benefit others or yourself; avoid trifling conversation.
3. Order. Let all your things have their places; let each part of your business have its time.
4. Resolution. Resolve to perform what you ought; perform without fail what you resolve.
5. Frugality. Make no expense but to do good to others or yourself; i.e., waste nothing.
6. Industry. Lose no time; be always employ'd in something useful; cut off all unnecessary actions.
7. Sincerity. Use no hurtful deceit; think innocently and justly, and, if you speak, speak accordingly.
8. Justice. Wrong none by doing injuries, or omitting the benefits that are your duty.
9. Moderation. Avoid extremes; forbear resenting injuries so much as you think they deserve.
10. Cleanliness. Tolerate no uncleanliness in body, clothes, or habitation.
11. 11. Tranquility. Be not disturbed at trifles, or at accidents common or unavoidable.
12. Chastity. Rarely use venery but for health or offspring, never to dullness, weakness, or the injury of your own or another's peace or reputation.
13. Humility. Imitate Jesus and Socrates.

APPENDIX D

Jonathan Edwards's Seventy Resolutions

Being sensible that I am unable to do anything without God's help, I do humbly entreat Him by his grace to enable me to keep these resolutions, so far as they are agreeable to His will, for Christ's sake.

1. Resolved, that I will do whatsoever I think to be most to God's glory, and my own good, profit and pleasure, in the whole of my duration, without any consideration of the time, whether now, or never so many myriad's of ages hence. Resolved to do whatever I think to be my duty and most for the good and advantage of mankind in general. Resolved to do this, whatever difficulties I meet with, how many and how great soever.
2. Resolved, to be continually endeavoring to find out some new invention and contrivance to promote the aforementioned things.
3. Resolved, if ever I shall fall and grow dull, so as to neglect to keep any part of these Resolutions, to repent of all I can remember, when I come to myself again.
4. Resolved, never to do any manner of thing, whether in soul or body, less or more, but what tends to the glory of God; nor be, nor suffer it, if I can avoid it.
5. Resolved, never to lose one moment of time; but improve it the most profitable way I possibly can.
6. Resolved, to live with all my might, while I do live.
7. Resolved, never to do anything, which I should be afraid to do, if it were the last hour of my life.
8. Resolved, to act, in all respects, both speaking and doing, as if nobody had been so vile as I, and as if I had committed the same sins, or had the same infirmities or failings as others; and that I will let the knowledge of their failings

321

RESOLVED

promote nothing but shame in myself, and prove only an occasion of my confessing my own sins and misery to God.

9. Resolved, to think much on all occasions of my own dying, and of the common circumstances which attend death.

10. Resolved, when I feel pain, to think of the pains of martyrdom, and of hell.

11. Resolved, when I think of any theorem in divinity to be solved, immediately to do what I can towards solving it, if circumstances don't hinder.

12. Resolved, if I take delight in it as a gratification of pride, or vanity, or on any such account, immediately to throw it by.

13. Resolved, to be endeavoring to find out fit objects of charity and liberality.

14. Resolved, never to do anything out of revenge.

15. Resolved, never to suffer the least motions of anger to irrational beings.

16. Resolved, never to speak evil of anyone, so that it shall tend to his dishonor, more or less, upon no account except for some real good.

17. Resolved, that I will live so as I shall wish I had done when I come to die.

18. Resolved, to live so at all times, as I think is best in my devout frames, and when I have clearest notions of things of the gospel, and another world.

19. Resolved, never to do anything, which I should be afraid to do, if I expected it would not be above an hour, before I should hear the last trump.

20. Resolved, to maintain the strictest temperance in eating and drinking.

21. Resolved, never to do anything, which if I should see in another, I should count a just occasion to despise him for, or to think any way the more meanly of him.

22. Resolved, to endeavor to obtain for myself as much happiness, in the other world, as I possibly can, with all the power; might, vigor, and vehemence, yea violence, I am capable of, or can bring myself to exert, in any way that can be thought of.

23. Resolved, frequently to take some deliberate action, which seems most unlikely to be done, for the glory of God, and trace it back to the original intention, designs and ends of it; and if I find it not to be for God's glory, to repute it as a breach of the 4th Resolution.

APPENDIX D

24. Resolved, whenever I do any conspicuously evil action, to trace it back, till I come to the original cause; and then both carefully endeavor to do so no more, and to fight and pray with all my might against the original of it.

25. Resolved, to examine carefully, and constantly, what that one thing in me is, which causes me in the least to doubt of the love of God; and to direct all my forces against it.

26. Resolved, to cast away such things, as I find do abate my assurance.

27. Resolved, never willfully to omit anything, except the omission be for the glory of God; and frequently to examine my omissions.

28. Resolved, to study the Scriptures so steadily, constantly and frequently, as that I may find, and plainly perceive myself to grow in the knowledge of the same.

29. Resolved, never to count that a prayer, nor to let that pass as a prayer, nor that as a petition of a prayer, which is so made, that I cannot hope that God will answer it; nor that as a confession, which I cannot hope God will accept.

30. Resolved, to strive to my utmost every week to be brought higher in religion, and to a higher exercise of grace, than I was the week before.

31. Resolved, never to say anything at all against anybody, but when it is perfectly agreeable to the highest degree of Christian honor, and of love to mankind, agreeable to the lowest humility, and sense of my own faults and failings, and agreeable to the golden rule; often, when I have said anything against anyone, to bring it to, and try it strictly by the test of this Resolution.

32. Resolved, to be strictly and firmly faithful to my trust, that that in Prov. 20:6, "A faithful man who can find?" may not be partly fulfilled in me.

33. Resolved, always to do what I can towards making, maintaining, establishing and preserving peace, when it can be without over-balancing detriment in other respects. Dec. 26, 1722.

34. Resolved, in narration's never to speak anything but the pure and simple verity.

35. Resolved, whenever I so much question whether I have done my duty, as that my quiet and calm is thereby disturbed, to set it down, and also how the question was resolved. Dec. 18, 1722.

RESOLVED

36. Resolved, never to speak evil of any, except I have some particular good call for it. Dec. 19, 1722.

37. Resolved, to inquire every night, as I am going to bed, wherein I have been negligent, what sin I have committed, and wherein I have denied myself: also at the end of every week, month and year. Dec. 22 and 26, 1722.

38. Resolved, never to speak anything that is ridiculous, sportive, or matter of laughter on the Lord's Day. Sabbath evening, Dec. 23, 1722.

39. Resolved, never to do anything that I so much question the lawfulness of, as that I intend, at the same time, to consider and examine afterwards, whether it be lawful or no; except I as much question the lawfulness of the omission.

40. Resolved, to inquire every night, before I go to bed, whether I have acted in the best way I possibly could, with respect to eating and drinking. Jan. 7, 1723.

41. Resolved, to ask myself at the end of every day, week, month and year, wherein I could possibly in any respect have done better. Jan. 11, 1723.

42. Resolved, frequently to renew the dedication of myself to God, which was made at my baptism; which I solemnly renewed, when I was received into the communion of the church; and which I have solemnly re-made this twelfth day of January, 1723.

43. Resolved, never henceforward, till I die, to act as if I were any way my own, but entirely and altogether God's, agreeable to what is to be found in. Saturday, Jan.12, 1723.

44. Resolved, that no other end but religion, shall have any influence at all on any of my actions; and that no action shall be, in the least circumstance, any otherwise than the religious end will carry it. Jan.12, 1723.

45. Resolved, never to allow any pleasure or grief, joy or sorrow, nor any affection at all, nor any degree of affection, nor any circumstance relating to it, but what helps religion. Jan.12, and 13, 1723.

46. Resolved, never to allow the least measure of any fretting uneasiness at my father or mother. Resolved to suffer no effects of it, so much as in the least alteration of speech, or motion of my eye: and to be especially careful of it, with respect to any of our family.

47. Resolved, to endeavor to my utmost to deny whatever is not most agreeable to a good, and universally sweet and benevolent, quiet, peaceable, contented, easy,

324

APPENDIX D

compassionate, generous, humble, meek, modest, submissive, obliging, diligent and industrious, charitable, even, patient, moderate, forgiving, sincere temper; and to do at all times what such a temper would lead me to. Examine strictly every week, whether I have done so. Sabbath morning. May 5, 1723.

48. Resolved, constantly, with the utmost niceness and diligence, and the strictest scrutiny, to be looking into the state of my soul, that I may know whether I have truly an interest in Christ or no; that when I come to die, I may not have any negligence respecting this to repent of. May 26, 1723.

49. Resolved, that this never shall be, if I can help it.

50. Resolved, I will act so as I think I shall judge would have been best, and most prudent, when I come into the future world. July 5, 1723.

51. Resolved, that I will act so, in every respect, as I think I shall wish I had done, if I should at last be damned. July 8, 1723.

52. I frequently hear persons in old age say how they would live, if they were to live their lives over again: Resolved that I will live just so as I can think I shall wish I had done, supposing I live to old age. July 8, 1723.

53. Resolved, to improve every opportunity, when I am in the best and happiest frame of mind, to cast and venture my soul on the Lord Jesus Christ, to trust and confide in him, and consecrate myself wholly to him; that from this I may have assurance of my safety, knowing that I confide in my Redeemer. July 8, 1723.

54. Whenever I hear anything spoken in conversation of any person, if I think it would be praiseworthy in me, Resolved, to endeavor to imitate it. July 8, 1723.

55. Resolved, to endeavor to my utmost to act as I can think I should do, if I had already seen the happiness of heaven, and hell torments. July 8, 1723.

56. Resolved, never to give over, nor in the least to slacken my fight with my corruptions, however unsuccessful I may be.

57. Resolved, when I fear misfortunes and adversities, to examine whether I have done my duty, and resolve to do it; and let it be just as providence orders it, I will as far as I can, be concerned about nothing but my duty and my sin. June 9, and July 13, 1723.

325

RESOLVED

58. Resolved, not only to refrain from an air of dislike, fretfulness, and anger in conversation, but to exhibit an air of love, cheerfulness and benignity. May 27, and July 13, 1723.

59. Resolved, when I am most conscious of provocations to ill nature and anger, that I will strive most to feel and act good-naturedly; yea, at such times, to manifest good nature, though I think that in other respects it would be disadvantageous, and so as would be imprudent at other times. May 12, July 2, and July 13, 1723.

60. Resolved, whenever my feelings begin to appear in the least out of order, when I am conscious of the least uneasiness within, or the least irregularity without, I will then subject myself to the strictest examination. July 4, and 13, 1723.

61. Resolved, that I will not give way to that listlessness which I find unbends and relaxes my mind from being fully and fixedly set on religion, whatever excuse I may have for it- that what my listlessness inclines me to do, is best to be done, etc. May 21, and July 13, 1723.

62. Resolved, never to do anything but duty; and then according to Eph. 6:6-8, do it willingly and cheerfully as unto the Lord, and not to man; "knowing that whatever good thing any man doth, the same shall he receive of the Lord." June 25 and July 13, 1723.

63. On the supposition, that there never was to be but one individual in the world, at any one time, who was properly a complete Christian, in all respects of a right stamp, having Christianity always shining in its true luster, and appearing excellent and lovely, from whatever part and under whatever character viewed: Resolved, to act just as I would do, if I strove with all my might to be that one, who should live in my time. Jan.14, and July 3, 1723.

64. Resolved, when I find those "groanings which cannot be uttered" (Rom. 8:26), of which the Apostle speaks, and those "breakings of soul for the longing it hath," of which the Psalmist speaks, Psalm 119:20, that I will promote them to the utmost of my power, and that I will not be wear', of earnestly endeavoring to vent my desires, nor of the repetitions of such earnestness. July 23, and August 10, 1723.

65. Resolved, very much to exercise myself in this all my life long, viz. with the greatest openness I am capable of, to declare my ways to God, and lay open my soul to him: all

APPENDIX D

my sins, temptations, difficulties, sorrows, fears, hopes, desires, and every thing, and every circumstance; according to Dr. Manton's 27th Sermon on Psalm 119. July 26, and Aug. 10, 1723.

66. Resolved, that I will endeavor always to keep a benign aspect, and air of acting and speaking in all places, and in all companies, except it should so happen that duty requires otherwise.

67. Resolved, after afflictions, to inquire, what I am the better for them, what good I have got by them, and what I might have got by them.

68. Resolved, to confess frankly to myself all that which I find in myself, either infirmity or sin; and, if it be what concerns religion, also to confess the whole case to God, and implore needed help. July 23, and August 10, 1723.

69. Resolved, always to do that, which I shall wish I had done when I see others do it. Aug. 11, 1723.

70. Let there be something of benevolence, in all that I speak. Aug. 17, 1723.

Bibliography

Introduction

Black, Jim. *When Nations Die*. Tyndale House Publishers, 1995.

Brady, Christopher and Orrin Woodward. *Launching a Leadership Revolution: Mastering the Five Levels of Influence*. New York: Business Plus, 2005.

Brukhiser, Richard. *Founding Father: Rediscovering George Washington*. New York: Free Press, 1997.

Covey, Steven R. *The 7 Habits of Highly Effective People*. New York: Free Press, 2004.

Franklin, Benjamin. *Benjamin Franklin's Autobiography*. New York: EP Dutton & Co., 1913.

Isaacson, Walter. *Benjamin Franklin: An American Life*. Simon Schuster, 2003.

Jones, Martin Lloyd. *Spiritual Depression: Its Causes and Its Cures*. Grand Rapids: Wm. B. Eerdmans Publishing Company, 1965.

Kersten, Katherine. "George Washington's Character." *Star Tribune*. March 6, 1996.

Lee, Major General. *George Washington! A Funeral Oration on His Death*. London: 1800.

Marsden, George M. *Jonathan Edwards: A Life*. New Haven: Yale University Press, 2003.

McGiffert, A. C. Jr. *Jonathan Edwards*. New York: 1932.

RESOLVED

Nichols, Stephen. "The Resolutions of Jonathan Edwards." *Table Talk Magazine*, 2009.

Ortega y Gasset, José. *The Revolt of the Masses*. New York: W. W. Norton & Company, Inc., 1960.

Roepke, Wilhelm. *Human Economy*. ISI Books, 1998.

Senge, Peter. *The Fifth Discipline*. New York: Doubleday Currency, 1990.

Smith, Richard Norton. *Patriarch: George Washington and the New American Nation*. New York: Houghton Mifflin Company, 1993.

Stewart, Randall. American Literature and Christian Doctrine. Louisiana: Louisiana Press, 1958.

Chapter 1

Allen, Woody. http://thinkexist.com. 2011.

Collins, Jim. *Good to Great*. New York: Harper Business, 2001.

Covey, Steven R. *First Things First*. New York: Free Press, 1996.

Elliot, Jay and William L. Simon. *The Steve Jobs Way*. New York: Harper, 2001.

Emmerson, Ralph Waldo. Essays. 1841.

Gladwell, Malcom. *Outliers*. New York: Little, Brown and Company, 2008.

Gray, E. N. *The Common Denominator of Success*. E-Book, 1940.

Munroe, Myles. Power of Vision. Kensington, PA: Whitaker House, 2003.

BIBLIOGRAPHY

Nietzsche, Friedrich. *Thus Spoke Zarathustra: A Book for All and None*. Germany: Ernst Schmeitzner, 1883.

Perkhurst, Charles. http://httpthinkexist.com. 2011. Pink, Daniel H. Drive. New York: Riverhead Books, 2009. Russell, Bertrand. "A Free Man's Worship." 1903.

Senge, Peter. *The Fifth Discipline*. New York: Doubleday Currency, 1990.

Smith, Hyrum W. *10 Natural Laws of Successful Time and Life Management*. New York: Warner Books, 1994.

Warren, Rick. The Purpose Driven Life. Grand Rapids: Zondervan, 2002.

Williamson, Marianne. "Our Deepest Fear." A Return to Love. New York: Harper Perennial, 1993.

Wyatt, Ian. "Top 5 Priorities: The Story of Ivy Lee and Bethlehem Steel." January 24, 2001. http://www.marksanborn.com.

John Wooden

Carty, Jay. *Coach Wooden's Pyramid of Success*. New York: Gospel Light Publishers, 2005.

Wooden, John and Don Yaeger. *A Game Plan for Life: The Power of Mentoring*. New York: Bloomsbury USA, 2009.

Wooden, John and Steve Jamison. *Wooden*. New York: McGraw-Hill, 1999.

Wooden, John and Steve Jamison. *Wooden on Leadership*. New York: McGraw-Hill, 2005.

Chapter 2

Bastiat, Frédéric. *The Law*. Kessinger Publishing, 2004.

Canfield, Jack. *The Success Principles*. New York: Harper Collins, 2005.

Colson, Chuck. "The Wages of Secularism." *Christianity Today*. June 10, 2002.

Connolly, Cyril. "C.S. Lewis in the Unquiet Grave," 1944. Csorba, Les. Trust. Nashville, Tennessee: Thomas Nelson,
Inc., 2006.

Covey, Stephen M. R. The Speed of Trust. New York: Free Press, 2006.

Kramnick, Isaac, ed. *The Portable Edmund Burke*. Penguin Book, 1999.

Lee, Gus. *Courage*. San Francisco: Jossey-Bass Publishing, 2006.

Lewis, C. S. *Mere Christianity*. San Francisco: Harper Publishing, 2001.

Luther, Martin. *Biblical Studies Ministries International*. http://www.bsmi.org.

Niemoller, Martin. "Speech to the Confessing Church in Frankfurt." January 6, 1946.

Plato. Georgia's Project. Gutenberg.

Sanborn, Mark. "Failure of Leadership." November 9, 2009. http://www.marksanborn.com.

Scott, Walter. "Marmion." 1808. http://www.online-literature.com.

"Time Theft." Mission Outreach. January 1986.

Wooden, John and Steve Jamison. Wooden. New York: McGraw-Hill, 1999.

BIBLIOGRAPHY

Ludwig von Mises

Heilbroner, Robert. The World after Communism. Dissent, 1990.

Hitler, Adolf. http://thinkexist.com.

Holsmann, Jorg. *Last Knight of Liberalism*. Auburn, Alabama: Ludwig von Mises Institute, 2007.

Keynes, John Maynard. http://thinkexist.com. Lenin, V. I. http://thinkexist.com.
Mises, Ludwig von. *Human Action*. Auburn, Alabama: Ludwig von Mises Institute, 2007.

Rothbard, Murray Newton. *Biography of Ludwig von Mises*. Auburn, Alabama: Ludwig von Mises Institute, 2007.

Virgil. http://thinkexist.com

Chapter 3

Canfield, Jack. *Success Principles*. New York: Harper Collins, 2005.

Ford, Henry II. http://www.quotationsbook.com. "

Reframe Your Thinking to Change Your Attitude." 2008. http://www.creators.com.

Swindoll, Charles. http://thinkexist.com.

Ziglar, Zig. *See You at the Top*. Pelican Publishing, 1982.

Chapter 4

Bristol, Claude. The Magic of Believing. New York: Pocket Books, 1991.

Bonaparte, Napoleon. http://thinkexist.com.

333

RESOLVED

Brooke, Richard Bliss. Mach II with Your Hair on Fire: The Art of Vision and Self Motivation. Couer d' Aleno, Idaho: High Performance People LLC, 2000.

Calonius, Erik. *Ten Steps Ahead*. New York: Penguin, 2011. Canfield, Jack. Success Principles. New York: Harper Collins, 2005.

Einstein, Albert. http://thinkexist.com.

Maltz, Maxwell. *Pshycho-Cybernetics*. New York: Pocket Books, 1964.

Ponscente, Vince. Ant and the Elephant. Mechanicsburg, Pennsylvannia: Executive Books, 2004.

Thoreau, Henry David. http://thinkexist.com.

Wilson, Timothy. *Strangers to Ourselves*. Boston: Belknap Press, 2004.

Chapter 5

Colvin, Geoff. *Talent Is Overrated: What Really Separates World-Class Performers from Everybody Else*. New York: Portfolio, 2008.

Gladwell, Malcom. *Outliers*. New York: Little, Brown and Company, 2008.

Grudin, Robert. *The Grace of Great Things: Creativity and Innovation*. Mariner Bros., 1991.

Lincoln, Abraham. http://thinkexist.com.

Link, Henry. *The Rediscovery of Man. MacMillon Co.*, 1939. Roche, George Charles. *A World without Heroes*. Hillsdale College Press, 1989.

Smith, Will. "Secrets to Success." YouTube. Accessed June 8, 2009. http://youtube.com.

BIBLIOGRAPHY

Stoltz, Paul G. *Adversity Quotient*. New York: John Wiley & Sons Inc., 1997.

Holtz, Lou. *Wins, Losses, and Lessons*. New York: Harper Collins, 2006.

Chapter 6

Anderson, Hans Christian. *The Emperor's New Clothes*. 1837.

Collins, Jim. *Good to Great*. New York: Harper Business, 2000.

Dell, Michael. *Direct from Dell*. New York: Warner Books, 1999.

Gates, Bill. *Business @ the Speed of Thought*. New York: Warner Books, 1999.

Holtz, Lou. *Wins, Losses, and Lessons*. New York: Harper Collins, 2006.

Walton, Sam and John Huey. *Sam Walton: Made in America*. New York: Double Day, 1992.

Chapter 7

http://www.christianhistory.net

"Fable of the Pots." http://www.aesopsfables.org. Hareyan, Armen. "American's Circle of Friends Sinking."

EMax Health. June 23, 2006. http://www.emax-health.com.

"Isolation in America." Editorial. *Christianity Today*. November 14, 2006. http://www.christianitytoday.com.

RESOLVED

Putnam, Robert D. *Bowling Alone: The Collapse and Revival of American Community*. New York: Simon & Schuster, 2000.

Smith, Fred. *You and Your Network*. Mechanicsburg, Pennsylvania: Executive Books, 1984.

Tolkien, J. R. R. *The Return of the King: Being the Third Part of the Lord of the Rings*. Boston: Houghton Mifflin, 2001.

Chapter 8

Marchex Sales Inc. Money101.com—Money. http://money101.com.

Word Press. Own the Dollar: Don't Let the Dollar Own You. 2012. http://ownthedollar.com.

Chapter 9

Brady, Christopher and Orrin Woodward. *Launching a Leadership Revolution: Mastering the Five Levels of Influence*. New York: Business Plus, 2005.

Collins, Jim. *Good to Great*. New York: Harper Business, 2001.

Covey, Steven R. The 7 Habits of Highly Effective People. New York: Free Press, 2004.

Emerson, Ralph Waldo. http://thinkexist.com.

Gerber, Michael E. *The E Myth Revisited*. New York: Harper Audio, 1995.

Johnson, Spencer. *Who Moved My Cheese?: An Amazing Way to Deal with Change in Your Work and in Your Life*. New York: Putnam, 1998.

BIBLIOGRAPHY

Schein, Edgar and Bill Breen. *The Future of Management.* Boston: Harvard Business Press, 2007.

Walton, Sam and John Huey. *Sam Walton: Made in America.* New York: Double Day, 1992.

Chapter 10

Covey, Steven R. *The 7 Habits of Highly Effective People.* New York: Free Press, 2004.

Lee, Gus and Diane Elliot-Lee. *Courage.* San Francisco: Jossey-Bass, 2006.

Patterson, Kerry, Joseph Grenny, and Al Switzler. *Crucial Conversations.* New York: McGraw-Hill, 2012.

Tolkien, J. R. R. *The Return of the King: Being the Third Part of the Lord of the Rings.* Boston: Houghton Mifflin, 2001.

Chapter 11

"Chaos Theory." Crystalinks Home Page. http://www.crystalinks.com/chaos.html.

Gabriel, Linda. "The Power of Trim Tabs—How Small Changes Create Big Results." *Thought Medicine.* July 2010. http://www.thoughtmedicine.com.

Gerber, Michael E. The E Myth. Cambridge, Massachusetts: Ballinger Publishing Company, 1986.

Meadows, Donella H. and Diana Wright. *Thinking in Systems: A Primer.* White River Junction VT: Chelsea Green Pub., 2008. Print.

Senge, Peter. *The Fifth Discipline.* New York: Doubleday Currency, 1990.

RESOLVED

Einstein, Albert. http://thinkexist.com.

Kroc, Ray and Robert Anderson. *Grinding It Out: The Making of McDonald's*. New York: St. Martin's Press, 1977.

Love, John F. *McDonald's: Behind the Arches*. New York: Bantam, 1995.

Tedlow, Richard S. *Giants of Enterprise*. New York: Harper Collins, 2001.

Chapter 12

Bradberry, Travis and Jean Greaves. *The Emotional Intelligence Quickbook: Everything You Need to Know*. San Diego CA: Talentsmart, 2003.

Brady, Chris. Rascal: *Making a Difference by Becoming an Original Character*. Flint, Michigan: Obstaclés Press, Inc., 2010.

Grudin, Robert. *Grace of Great Things: Creativity and Innovation*. Mariner Bros., 1991.

Locke, John. http://thinkexist.com.

Robbins, Tony. *Notes from a Friend*. Fireside, 1995.

Weisenberger, Bernard. *Dream Maker: William Durant Founder of General Motors*. Little, Brown and Co., 1979.

Chapter 13

Bastiat, Frédéric. *The Law*. Irvington-on-Hudson, NY: Foundation for Economic Education, 1950.

Lewis, C. S. *The Abolition of Man*. New York: Macmillan, 1947.

BIBLIOGRAPHY

Hazlitt, Henry. *Economics in One Lesson*. New York: Arlington House, 1979.

Nock, Albert Jay. *Memoirs of a Superfluous Man*. Chicago: Regnery, 1964.

Nock, Albert Jay. *Our Enemy, the State: Albert Jay Nock's Classic Critique Distinguishing "Government" from "the State."* Delavan WI: Hallberg Pub., 1983.

McElroy, Wendy. "Nock on Education." http://www.wendymcelroy. com.

Schaffer, Francis. *How Should We Then Live?* Wheaton IL: Crossway Books, 2005.

Spengler, Oswald, Helmut Werner, Arthur Helps, and Charles Francis Atkinson. *The Decline of the West*. New York: Vintage, 2006.

"Sturgeon's Law." http://www.tvtropes.org.

Toynbee, Arnold and D. C. Somervell. *A Study of History*. New York: Oxford UP, 1947.

Yeats, W. B. "Second Coming." 1920.

Rothbard, Murray Newton. *A History of Money and Banking in the United States: The Colonial Era to World War II*. Auburn AL: Ludwig von Mises Institute, 2002

Shafer, Susan and Emma Lazarus. *Emma Lazarus's The New Colossus: A Play Adaptation*. Pelham, NY: Benchmark Education, 2007.
"the State." Delavan WI: Hallberg Pub., 1983.

McElroy, Wendy. "Nock on Education." http://www.wendymcelroy. com.

Schaffer, Francis. *How Should We Then Live?* Wheaton IL: Crossway Books, 2005.

RESOLVED

Spengler, Oswald, Helmut Werner, Arthur Helps, and Charles Francis Atkinson. *The Decline of the West.* New York: Vintage, 2006.

"Sturgeon's Law." http://www.tvtropes.org.

Toynbee, Arnold and D. C. Somervell. *A Study of History.* New York: Oxford UP, 1947.

Yeats, W. B. "Second Coming." 1920.

Colonial New England Fiat Money

Rothbard, Murray Newton. *A History of Money and Banking in the United States: The Colonial Era to World War II.* Auburn AL: Ludwig von Mises Institute, 2002

Shafer, Susan and Emma Lazarus. *Emma Lazarus's The New Colossus: A Play Adaptation.* Pelham, NY: Benchmark Education, 2007.

OTHER BOOKS BY ORRIN WOODWARD

Launching a Leadership Revolution by Chris Brady and Orrin Woodward
Get the book that started the revolution! Chris Brady and Orrin Woodward's smash-hit best-seller will not only clear up many myths about leadership, but will convince you that the principles of leadership apply to anyone and everyone. All of us will be called upon to lead at some (or many) point(s) in life. The question isn't whether or not you are a leader, but rather, will you be ready when called? Historical examples illustrate key concepts, while the wit and charm of Brady and Woodward's writing style will keep you glued to each page.

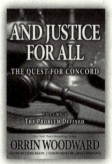

And Justice for All by Orrin Woodward
Orrin Woodward combines staggering scholarship and boundless creativity to distill the lessons of two and a half millennia into a concise picture. This book will present the reader with a clear comprehension of the root of the trouble, and then lead to the historical underpinnings that, once understood, provide the final resolution of the quest. Why should peace and harmony among the citizens of the earth be so elusive? Why when it is accomplished, does it almost immediately begin to erode and swing toward either chaos on one side or tyranny on the other? Orrin answers these questions and more!

The Financial Matrix by Orrin Woodward
New York Times bestselling author Orrin Woodward exposes the Financial Matrix that imprisons you in perpetual debt and reveals the principles and habits that will free you for good. *The Financial Matrix* is the best, most effective system elites have employed to control the masses. Because it is difficult to detect, the Financial Matrix easily seduces people into willingly enslaving themselves with debt. But Orrin Woodward discovered its existence and managed to free himself. Now his book brings you that same awareness and gives you the tools and principles to break free and create a life of abundance.

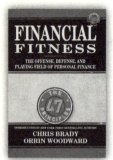

***Financial Fitness* by Chris Brady and Orrin Woodward**
Even if you are deep in debt and cannot seem to envision a better financial future, you can achieve financial fitness and have fun doing it with the help of the *Financial Fitness* book! Just as with becoming physically or mentally fit, becoming financially fit requires two things: knowing what to do and taking the necessary action to do it. Regardless of your current financial situation, you can learn to prosper, conserve, and multiply the fruits of your labor through a basic understanding of the principles behind the Offense, Defense, and Playing Field of personal finance. And the Financial Fitness book brings all of these fundamentals together in one convenient location so you can quickly and easily become the master of your money and the kind of person who can prosper in any economy!

***Beyond Financial Fitness* by Chris Brady and Orrin Woodward**
Drawn from many of the greatest minds in the history of personal finance, *Beyond Financial Fitness* teaches you to gain mastery over your money once and for all through ***A Comprehensive Financial Plan*** that will show you how to earn, save, spend, borrow and invest. ***An Investment Policy***, that teaches how to spell out your approach to investing and how to turn your efforts into assets. ***And, An Asset Allocation Plan*** to show you how much money to keep in different investment categories and how to understand the risks of assets relative to each other.

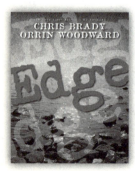

***Edge* by Chris Brady and Orrin Woodward**
Get the Edge on insight, inspiration, and plenty of practical advice by studying the experience of those who have been there and done that. There is no age limit on success. The *Edge* book delivers life-changing information to give you a head start on accomplishing your dreams. It's time to get started on building your dream life! A full-color coffee table book that is sure to spark conversation and thoughts from anyone who picks it up!

LeaderShift by Orrin Woodward and Oliver DeMille
A most provocative business parable for our troubled times, *LeaderShift* is the story of how David Mersher, the successful CEO of IndyTech, sets out to discover why the United States is losing its leadership edge and what he can do to turn things around and make America truly great again. In the process, they learn how the Five Laws of Decline are eroding the nation's economy. When Mersher and his team get help from a surprising source, the result is stunning and unexpected-and it's one that concerned Americans will certainly reflect upon for decades to come. The next *LeaderShift* is almost here.

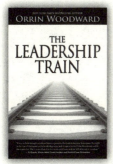

The Leadership Train by Orrin Woodward
This captivating narrative details one man's complete turnaround after struggling for years with finding fulfillment in his career. He soon embarks on a journey that helps him find his true purpose. This is a dream builder's dream come true! Learn how to build a successful network marketing business from one of the greatest networkers in history, and help others to do the same. Discover how to handle pyramid and other objections and wipe out any doubts, untruths, and false beliefs that prospective members and customers, and possibly even you yourself, might have. The leadership train is going places fast, and you don't want to miss out!

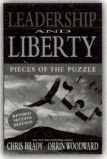

Leadership & Liberty: Pieces of the Puzzle by Chris Brady and Orrin Woodward
This book is designed to build upon Launching a Leadership Revolution by not only reviewing timeless leadership principles, but by focusing them upon leadership as applied by the concepts of liberty and freedom, and specifically to winning back much of what has been lost in our lands. Our intent is that this book will not only inform and educate, but equip leaders both new and experienced alike, to make an increasing difference in the fight for the first principles of freedom. As Thomas Jefferson wrote, "If a nation expects to be ignorant and free...it expects what never was and will never be."